Ninety Years of
HORSE and HOUND

HORSE AND HOUND.

A JOURNAL OF SPORT AND AGRICULTURE.

"I freely confess that the best of my fun,
I owe it to Horse and Hound."—WHYTE-MELVILLE.

VOL. I.—No. 1. SATURDAY, MARCH 29, 1884. REGISTERED FOR TRANSMISSION ABROAD. TWOPENCE.

This Paper contains Messrs. TATTERSALL'S MONDAY CATALOGUE in FULL.

SEVEN HUNDRED SOVEREIGNS ADDED MONEY GIVEN TO THIS MEETING.

THE LEEDS AND WEST RIDING HUNT AND STEEPLE-CHASE MEETING will take place over the New Course at LEEDS, on SATURDAY and MONDAY, April 12 and 14, 1884, under the Grand National Hunt Rules.

FIRST DAY.

1. The TEMPLE SELLING STEEPLE-CHASE PLATE of 40 sovs; four year olds 11st 5lb, five 12st 3lb, six and aged 12st 7lb; the winner to be sold for 100 sovs; if for 50 sovs, allowed 7lb; entrance 3 sovs; two miles and a half.

To close and name on Tuesday, April 8th.

2. The UNITED HUNT FLAT RACE PLATE of 40 sovs, for duly qualified hunters; four year olds 11st 6lb, five 11st 12lb, six and aged 12st; entrance 3 sovs; two miles.

To close and name on Tuesday, April 1st.

3. The LEEDS GRAND NATIONAL HANDICAP STEEPLE-CHASE of 150 sovs, added to a sweepstakes of 10 sovs each for starters, 5 sovs for non-starters; winners of a handicap steeplechase after the declaration of the weights to carry 7lb, twice or of any race value 200 sovs 10lb extra; entrance 3 sovs; about two miles and a half.

To close and name on Tuesday, April 1st.

4. The BRAMHAM PARK HUNTERS' STEEPLECHASE PLATE, a handsome Tea and Coffee Service value 50 sovs, for *bona-fide* hunters that have never won a race of any description the property of Farmers, Merchants, or Tradesmen residing within ten miles of Leeds; about two miles and a quarter.

To close and name on Tuesday, April 8th.

5. The RED COAT TALLY HO STEEPLECHASE PLATE, of 40 sovs, for *bona-fide* hunters that have been regularly hunted with any established pack of Foxhounds; about three miles; entrance 3 sovs; about three miles.

To close and name on Tuesday, April 8th.

6. The SELLING HURDLE PLATE, of 40 sovs. Four year olds to carry 1st, five 11st 10lb, six and aged 12st; the winner to be sold by auction for 100 sovs, if entered to be sold for 50 sovs allowed 7lb; maidens at starting allowed 4lb in addition; entrance 3 sovs; two miles over eight flights of hurdles.

To close and name on Tuesday, April 8th.

SECOND DAY.

1. The HAREWOOD HUNTERS' FLAT RACE SELLING PLATE of 50 sovs, for duly qualified hunters; four year olds 12st, five 12st 5lb, six and aged 12st 7lb; entrance 3 sovs; two miles.

To close and name on Tuesday, April 8th.

2. The LEEDS LICENSED VICTUALLERS' HUNTERS' STEEPLE-CHASE PLATE of 50 sovs, for *bona fide* hunters; four year olds 10 st 3lb, five 11st 8lb, six and aged 12st 3lb; entrance 3 sovs; about two miles and a quarter.

To close and name on Tuesday, April 8th.

3. FIRST GRAND HANDICAP STEEPLE CHASE of 100 sovs added, a sweepstakes of 10 sovs each for starters, 5 sovs for non-starters; winners of a handicap steeple-chase after the declaration of the weights to carry 7lb, twice or of any race value 200 sovs 10lb extra; entrance 3 sovs; about two miles and a-half.

To close and name on Tuesday, April 1st.

4. The TEMPLE HANDICAP HURDLE PLATE of 40 sovs; the winner of any hurdle race after the publication of the weights, (   ) to carry 6lb; twice 9lb, thrice or once of 100 sovs, 12lb extra; entrance 3 sovs; two miles over eight flights of hurdles.

To close and name on Tuesday, April 8th, and the weights to be published on Thursday before running.

5. A MAIDEN HUNTERS' STEEPLE-CHASE PLATE of 40 sovs, for horses that have never won a steeple-chase, hurdle race, or hunters' flat race, value 20 sovs; about three miles.

To close and name on Monday, April 7th.

6. A SELLING HANDICAP STEEPLE-CHASE PLATE of 40 sovs; a winner of any steeple-chase or hurdle race after the publication of the weights (   ) to carry 9lb extra; the winner to be sold by auction for 50 sovs; entrance 3 sovs; about two miles and a quarter.

To close and name on Thursday, April 8th, and the weights to be published Thursday before running.

STEWARDS.

Rt. Hon. Viscount LASCELLES.	T. H. D. BAYLY, Esq., M.F.H.
Rt. Hon. Vis. CASTLEREAGH, M.P.	H. D. BROCKLEHURST, Esq., M.F.H.
Hon. E. WILLOUGHBY.	Sir George WOMBWELL,
Wm. PARKS, Esq.	T. LIVSEY, Esq.
	S. BROADBENT, Esq.

OFFICIALS.

Judge, Handicapper, and Clerk of the Scales: Richard JOHNSON, York.	Course Keeper: Mr Richd. CLAYTON.
Starter: Mr. Geo. WADDINGTON, Harrogate.	Auctioneers: Messrs. HEPPER & SON, Leeds.
Clerks of the Course: Mr. SAM ODDY, Leeds; and Mr. John PARSON, Leeds.	Secretary and Stakeholder: Mr. G. BENT, 11, Market-street, Leeds.

Entries received by Mr. R. Mills, 28, York-place, Leeds; Mr George Waddington, Harrowgate; and Richard Johnson, Esq., York.

The new course at Leeds is easy of access, being distant from the stations about 1½ miles. The steeplechase course is almost entirely over grass land, and the greater part of the fences are natural.

FOUR OAKS PARK (EASTER), April 14th and 15th.

FIRST DAY—(to Close April 1st.)

The following close and name on Tuesday next, April 1st, to Mr. John Sheldon, Temple Chambers, 50, New-street, Birmingham; Messrs. Weatherby, Old Burlington-street, or Messrs. Pratt & Co, 9, George-street, Hanover-square, London.

The JUVENILE PLATE of 100 guineas, for two year olds; colts 9st, fillies and geldings 8st 11lb; the winner to be sold by auction for 100 sovs, if entered to be sold for 50 sovs allowed 7lb; entrance 3 guineas; 5 fur., straight.

The FOUR OAKS SELLING WELTER PLATE of 100 guineas; three year olds 10st 12lb, four 12st 5lb, five and upwards 12st 7lb; mares and geldings allowed 3lb; the winner to be sold by auction for 100 sovs; no restriction as to riders, but if ridden by a member of the Four Oaks Park Club allowed 5lb; entrance 3 guineas; one mile.

SECOND DAY—(to Close April 3rd.)

The following close and name on Thursday next, April 3rd, to Mr. John Sheldon, Temple Chambers, 50, New-street, Birmingham; Messrs. Weatherby, Old Burlington-street, or to Messrs. Pratt & Co., 9, George-street, Hanover square, London.

The OAKLEY HUNTERS' STEEPLE-CHASE PLATE of 40 sovs; four year olds 10st 3lb, five 11st 8lb, six and aged 12st 3lb; the winner of any steeple-chase or hurdle race to carry 6lb, twice 10lb, three times or more 14lb extra; horses not having won in 1883 or 1884 only half the penalties; maiden five year olds and upwards at starting allowed 10lb; entrance 2 guineas; two miles and a half.

The MIDDLETON HUNTERS' HURDLE PLATE of 50 sovs; four year olds 11st 7lb, five 12st 3lb, six and aged 12st 7lb; horses that have not won in 1883 or 1884 allowed 7lb; the winner to be sold by auction for 100 sovs, if entered to be sold for 50 sovs allowed 10lb in addition; entrance 3 guineas; two miles, over eight hurdles.

Mr. J. SHELDON, Clerk of the Course.

THE WETHERBY ANNUAL STEEPLE-CHASES will be held as usual on EASTER MONDAY and TUESDAY, April 14th and 15th, 1884, under the Grand National Rules.

BLANSHARD and SERGEANT, Secs., Wetherby.

THE THIRD HUSSARS' STEEPLE-CHASES, &c., will take place at KEMPTON PARK On MONDAY, APRIL 21st, 1884.

Under the Grand National Hunt Rules and the usual regulations and conditions of the Kempton Park Meetings.

The following stakes close and name to Mr. Richard Bell, Clerk of the Course, 3, Agar-street, Charing-cross, London, W.C.; Messrs. Weatherby, 6, Old Burlington-street, London, W.; or Messrs. Pratt and Co., 9, George-street, Hanover-square, London, W., or Newmarket, on Tuesday, April 8th, 1884:—

The UPPER TEN STEEPLE-CHASE of 100 sovs, for maiden hunters at the time of entry the property of members of the Kempton Park and Sandown Park Clubs, masters of any established pack of foxhounds, officers on full or half pay of the Army and Navy, or present members of the Universities of Oxford and Cambridge, and to be ridden by the same; to carry 12st 7lb; any winner after date of entry once to carry 7lb, twice, 10lb extra; entrance 3 guineas; about four miles.

A SELLING HUNTERS' FLAT RACE of 100 sovs, for qualified hunters, to be entered and ridden by members of the Kempton Park and Sandown Park Clubs, masters of any established pack of foxhounds, officers on full or half pay of the Army and Navy, or present members of the Universities of Oxford and Cambridge; four year olds to carry 13st, five 13st 7lb, six and aged 13st 10lb; the winner to be sold for 100 sovs, if for 50 sovs allowed 10lb; entrance 3 guineas; two miles.

The OPEN HANDICAP HURDLE RACE of 100 sovs, added to a Sweepstakes of 5 sovs each for starters; a winner of 100 sovs after the publication of the weights to carry 7lb extra; entrance 3 guineas, the only liability for non-starters; two miles, over eight flights of hurdles.

Three horses, the property of different owners, to start for these races, or only half the added money will be given.

The following races close and name to Major Napier, Third Hussars, Kensington Barracks, only, on or before Tuesday, April 8th, 1884:—

The REGIMENTAL CHALLENGE CUP, value 100 sovs, with 40 sovs added; entrance 2 sovs, to the Fund; for hunters the property of officers serving, or having served, in the regiment; 12st each; previous winners of this cup or of any steeple-chase to carry 7lb, of this cup twice, twice of 20 sovs, or once of 40 sovs, 12lb extra, the second to save entrance fee; the cup to be won three times by the same officer before becoming his property; about three miles.

The SUBALTERNS' CHALLENGE CUP, value 50 sovs, with 40 sovs added; entrance 2 sovs, to the Fund; for hunters the property of, and to be ridden by, subalterns in the regiment; four year olds to carry 11st, five 12st, six and aged 12st 7lb; any winner 7lb extra; horses that have never started allowed 7lb; the second to save entrance fee; the cup to be won three times by the same officer before becoming his property; about two miles and a half.

The THIRD HUSSARS' STARKEY CHALLENGE CUP, value 200 sovs, with 40 sovs added; entrance 2 sovs, to the Fund; for hunters the property of officers serving in the regiment; to be ridden by officers who are serving, or have served, in the regiment; four year olds to carry 11st 7lb; five 11st 12lb, six and aged 12st 7lb; any winner of a steeple chase to carry 7lb, of 50 sovs 10lb extra; the second to save entrance fee; the cup to be won three times by the same officer before becoming his property; two miles and a half.

Stewards for the Third Hussars' Races.
Colonel VINCENT.
Lieutenant-Colonel WALKER.
Major JERVOISE.
Captain ALEXANDER.
JOHN SCOTT, Esq.

Hon. Secretary and Stakeholder—Major NAPIER.

Stewards for the Kempton Park Races.
His Grace the Duke of HAMILTON.
His Grace the Duke of MONTROSE.
Lord FITZHARDINGE, M.F.H.
Lord ALINGTON.
Lord MARCUS BERESFORD.
The Hon. RUPERT CARINGTON, M.P.
Sir F. JOHNSTONE, Bart.
Sir W. THROCKMORTON, Bart.
Captain MACHELL.
Captain D. BAYLEY.
Captain D. LANE.
LEOPOLD DE ROTHSCHILD, Esq.
T. V. MORGAN, Esq.

Handicappers—Messrs. WEATHERBY.
Hon. Starter—Major DIXON.
Judge and Clerk of the Scales—Mr. T. LAWLEY.
Clerk of the Course—Mr. RICHARD BELL.
Stakeholder—Mr. SEYMOUR PORTMAN.

HARPENDEN, 1884, will take place on FRIDAY, the 23rd of May. Under the Rules of Racing.

The GREAT HERTFORDSHIRE HANDICAP of 15 sovs each, 10 ft, with 200 added; the second horse to receive 30 sovs out of the stakes; entrance 3 guineas each, to the fund, which will be the only liability if forfeit be declared on a day to be named when the weights appear; the winner (selling races excepted) of any race after the weights appear (   ) to carry 5lb, of two races, or one value 500 sovs 10lb extra; about one mile and a half, on the New Course.

To close and name to Messrs. Weatherby, Messrs. Pratt and Co., or the Clerks of the Course, by Tuesday next, April 1st.

MR. SAMUEL BIGNOLD, VETERINARY SURGEON, M.R.C.V.S.L., attends TATTERSALL'S EVERY SATURDAY and MONDAY to examine horses, and to assist gentlemen in the selection of them. Good loose boxes and Infirmary for horses at residence, LILLIE BRIDGE, WEST BROMPTON. Straw yard and loose boxes for summering horses at Friars-place, East Acton.

HORSES EXAMINED as to SOUNDNESS. GENTLEMEN Professionally assisted in the SELECTION and PURCHASE of HORSES. Tattersall's and other Sales attended by WILLIAM SEWELL, Veterinary Surgeon, M.R.C.V.S., 53, Elizabeth Street, Eaton-square, London. Five minutes from Tattersall's.

IMPORTANT SALES OF PURE-BRED CATTLE.

SHORTHORNS.

TUESDAY, April 8th.—Thirty-first Annual Sale of Young Bulls, from the herd belonging to W. T. Talbot-Crosbie, Esq., Ardfert Abbey, Tralee, co. Kerry.

WEDNESDAY, April 9th.—Seventeen Young Bulls at Mallow Junction, the property of Lord Lismore, Mr. H. Smith, and Mr. H. R. Poe.

WEDNESDAY, April 23rd.—Sale of about Fifty head from the herds of Lord Moreton, Miss Barnett, Mr. H. D. de Vitre, and Mr. S. Hughes, at Langston Arms, adjoining Chipping Norton Junction Station, Oxon. Also about a score of the Tortworth White Pigs.

THURSDAY, April 24th.—Sale of young Bulls and Heifers from the herd of Sir John Swinburne, Bart., and other breeders, at Dringhouses, York, restrictions permitting.

FRIDAY, May 2nd.—About Fifty head from the head belonging to H. Sharpley, Esq., at Limber Magna, Brocklesby, Lincolnshire.

THURSDAY, May 8th.—The herd, including the Grand Duchesses, belonging to R. E. Oliver, Esq., at Sholebroke Lodge, Towcester.

FRIDAY, May 9th.—About 40 head from the herd the property of R. Loder, Esq., Whittlebury, Towcester.

TUESDAY, May 13th.—About Forty head from the herd belonging to Geo. Fox, Esq., at Elmhurst Hall, Lichfield.

THURSDAY, May 15th.—Mr. J. H. Blundell's entire herd at Woodside, Luton, Beds.

TUESDAY, May 20th.—The Hon. C. W. Fitzwilliams's herd at Alwalton, Peterborough.

WEDNESDAY, May 21st.—Mr. Chalk's herd at Linton, Cambridge.

THURSDAY, June 5th.—The entire herd belonging to Sir F. C. Smythe, Bart., and the bulk of Mr. A. E. W. Darby's herd, at Acton Burnell, Shrewsbury.

JERSEYS.

TUESDAY, April 29th.—Mr. F. A. Hordern's herd, at Sheering Hall, Harlow, Essex.

SATURDAY, May 24th.—About Thirty head from the first-class stocks belonging to Hugh C. Smith, Esq., of Roehampton, and E. A. Hambro, Esq., at Hayes Place, Beckenham, Kent.

THURSDAY, June 19.—The entire herd belonging to F. Willan, Esq., at Thornhill Park, Bitterne, Hants.

TUESDAY, July 1.—About Thirty head from the first-class herd belonging to Geo. Simpson, Esq., at Wray Park, Reigate.

Catalogues with pedigrees will be issued in due course, and may be had of JOHN THORNTON, 7, Princes Street, Hanover Square, London, W.

FOUR DOORS FROM MESSRS. TATTERSALL'S.

THE WEST-END DEPOT FOR SPECIALITIES FOR HORSES, CARRIAGES, HARNESS, &c., 24 and 26, BROMPTON ROAD, ALBERT GATE, LONDON, S.W.

The Nobility, Gentry, and County Families supplied with all requisites for Stable use.

Carriages, Horses, Harness, Bicycles, and Tricycles Sold and Bought on Commission.

The Proprietors direct attention to the REGISTRY DEPARTMENT for High-Class Men Servants for the House or Stable Wanted or Requiring Employment, also for the Sale or Purchase of Horses, Carriages, and Dogs. The fees for this Department are as follows, viz:—

	s.	d.
Entry of Servant Wanted	5	0
,, ,, Requiring Employment	2	0
,, of Horses, Carriages, &c., for Sale	5	0
,, of Dog ,,	2	6

Applications for forms and all communications to be addressed to the Proprietors of THE ALBERT GATE MART AND REGISTRY, 24 & 26, BROMPTON ROAD, ALBERT GATE, LONDON, S.W.

"HORSE AND HOUND" can be purchased at the above establishment every day, Sundays included.

THE NEW
PRINCE OF WALES'
RIDING SCHOOL,
SOUTH KENSINGTON.
PRIVATE ENTRANCE — HOLLYWOOD-ROAD,
REDCLIFFE-SQUARE, S.W.

THE handsomest and most commodious in LONDON. The ride is perfection, and fittings and arrangements for bar and hurdle jumping on the most approved principles.

SPECIAL attention to the instruction and comfort of children and beginners in riding.

Quiet and thoroughly-trained ponies, hacks, and hunters.

Mr. AXTENS, for several years principal instructor at Mr. F. ALLEN'S (not Mr. Haines's) Riding Establishment, has been engaged as Riding Master, and his thorough practical experience will ensure a proper management of the School and perfect teaching of the Art of Riding to Pupils.

Lessons given on the Road as well as in the School.

Classes Daily, and Private Lessons by appointment.

Proprietor, Mr. J. A. PREECE.

Branch establishments, Victoria-grove, Queen's-gate; Craven-road, Westbourne-terrace, and Alexandra mews, Westbourne-park. Communication from each place by private telephone.

TONANS,
Trained on the
SPECIALLY PREPARED FOOD
FOR
RACEHORSES.
Apply, by letter, to the Inventor and Sole Manufacturer,
C. W. GOODE,
BLACKETT MILL,
BOW, E.

BUGGY HARNESS,
Made on the American principle by
T. U. CLARKE,
Near TATTERSALL'S,
RUGBY.
Established 120 Years.

Australian Saddles as used in the Bush, Hunting and Race Saddles, English Harness, and every requisite for the Hunting Field, Stable, Road, or Farm.

THE MAXWELL CATTLE COMPANY.

ISSUE of £200,000 EIGHT PER CENT. STERLING FIRST MORTGAGE BONDS.

TRUSTEES FOR THE BONDHOLDERS.

MANAGING TRUSTEE—JOHN GUTHRIE SMITH, Esq. (Sheriff of Aberdeen, Kincardine, and Banff), Chairman of the Prairie Cattle Company (Limited), Edinburgh.

His Grace the Duke of Manchester, K.P., Chairman of the Land Corporation of Canada (Limited)

The Right Hon. the Earl of Rosslyn, Dysart House, Dysart, N.B.

Wm. B. Strong, Esq., President Atchison, Topeka, and Santa Fé Railroad.

Wm. Dowd, Esq., President Hannibal and St. Joseph Railroad, and President of the Bank of North America, New York.

The deed of mortgage requires that there shall always be three trustees resident in England.

London offices—25, Abchurch Lane, E.C.

Subscriptions at par for the balance of the above Bonds remaining unissued are being received as below, interest to run from date of payment.

The security for these Bonds is the cattle purchased with the net proceeds of same, and in addition a lease of about a million and a half acres of the finest grazing land in the United States at a peppercorn rent, which lease alone is valued at a sum considerably in excess of the total Bond issue.

A statement by the trustees to the bondholders as to the present position of the trust, prospectuses, and full particulars can be obtained on application—

In London: To Messrs. Smith, Payne, and Smiths, Bankers, 1, Lombard-street, E.C.; or To the Company's London Agents, Messrs. Hume, Webster, Hoare & Co., 25, Abchurch-lane, E.C.

In Scotland—To the Commercial Bank of Scotland, Edinburgh, and Branches. Messrs. Torrie, Brodie, and Maclagan, 53, George-street, Edinburgh.

Any of whom will Receive Subscriptions.

HUNT SERVANTS' BENEFIT SOCIETY. Office: 40, BROMPTON-ROAD, LONDON, S.W.

PATRON.
H.R.H. the Prince of WALES.
PRESIDENT.
Duke of BUCCLEUCH.
VICE-PRESIDENTS.

Duke of BEAUFORT,	The MASTER of the BUCKHOUNDS,
Duke of RUTLAND,	The Marquis of WATERFORD.
Duke of RICHMOND and GORDON,	

EXECUTIVE COMMITTEE.

Earl of RADNOR,	W. MORTIMER, Esq.,
Hon. ROBT. GRIMSTON,	THOMAS PAIN, Esq.,
Hon. FRANCIS SCOTT,	Mr. FRANK GOODALL,
ROBERT ARKWRIGHT, Esq.,	Mr. FRANK GILLARD,
	Mr. FRANK BEERS.

TRUSTEES.
Earl of MACCLESFIELD, Sir W. W. WYNN, Bart., M.P.
GEORGE LANE-FOX, Esq.
HONORARY AUDITOR.
W. N. HEYSHAM, Esq.
HONORARY SECRETARY.
Lieut.-Col. J. ANSTRUTHER THOMSON.
AUDITOR.
ALEXANDER WILSON, Esq.
SECRETARY.
JOSIAH CARTLEDGE, Esq.

The Society now comprises about 1,970 Honorary and 396 Benefit Members.

The objects of the Society are to provide to Huntsmen and Whippers-in of a fox or stag-hunting establishment, being Benefit Members—

1st.—A weekly allowance of fifteen shillings in case of sickness or accident.

2nd.—An annuity of £39, after the age of 60 or 65 years.

3rd.—A provision for Widows and Children.

Payment of a donation of £5 or more, or an annual Subscription of £1 and upwards, for the purpose of increasing the payments to Benefit Members, constitutes an Honorary Member; but smaller Donations are thankfully received.

An Annual Subscription according to scale, to participate in any or all of the three provisions before stated, constitutes a Benefit Member.

Ladies and Gentlemen disposed to become Honorary Members are requested to send their names, addresses, donations, and subscriptions to Josiah Cartledge, Esq., the Secretary, 40, Brompton-road, London, S.W.

The PAXTON STABLES, 34, Brompton-road, and COMMISSION STABLES, 66, Brompton-road, both close to Tattersall's.

C. S. WARD & SONS, Johmasters and Dealers, have always on view Match Pairs of Carriage, Phaeton, and Brougham Horses, well trained Teams for Sale or Hire. Horses sold on Commission. Lessons in all kinds of Driving, as usual. Horses Broken to Harness. Ladies and Gentlemen taught Riding; also Horses Trained for Riding.

LLOYD'S PLACE, BROMPTON ROAD.
J. FOWLER'S
LIVERY AND COMMISSION STABLES.

GENTLEMEN having Horses for disposal will find a ready Sale for them at this establishment, at a charge of 5 per cent. commission.

Several HARNESS and RIDING HORSES, with good action, now on Sale.

Horses broken to ride and drive.

HORSE, CARRIAGE, CATTLE } INSURANCE.

THE LONDON AND PROVINCIAL HORSE & CARRIAGE INSURANCE CO., LIMITED, and THE HORSE INSURANCE COMPANY, LIMITED.
Chief Office: 17, QUEEN VICTORIA ST., LONDON, E.C.
A. WATERS, Secretary.
The oldest Office in the United Kingdom for this class of Insurance.
AGENTS WANTED.

BICYCLE AND TRICYCLE SALE ROOM COMPANY,
55 and 56, CHANCERY LANE, LONDON.

THE "SUTTON" TRICYCLE.
Price £25.
All makes of machines in stock.

The best medium for the sale or exchange of machines in London.

Ninety Years of
HORSE and HOUND

Compiled by Walter O. Case
Foreword by Colonel Sir Michael Ansell CBE DSO

Country Life Books

Distributed for Country Life Books by
The Hamlyn Publishing Group Limited
London · New York · Sydney · Toronto
Astronaut House, Feltham, Middlesex, England

First published 1977
ISBN 0 600 36570 0

Phototypeset in England by
Tradespools Limited, Frome
Printed in England by
Cox & Wyman Limited, Fakenham

FOREWORD
By Colonel Sir Michael Ansell CBE DSO

On March 29th, 1884, the Hon. Wyndham Berkeley Portman founded a weekly journal, *Horse and Hound*. It then cost 2d. It is now approaching its centenary. This continuity has happened for two reasons: our love of the horse and the hound, and also because the editors have focussed wholly on these interests.

During the past ninety years our love of the horse and hound has not diminished. On the contrary, it has grown.

Berkeley Portman appointed his son, Arthur Berkeley Portman as editor of *Horse and Hound* in 1890. Arthur was a great authority on race horse breeding. Nevertheless he made his journal cover every horse sport including hunting. Throughout the world, *Horse and Hound* became the authority on racing, breeding, polo, hunting and hackney. In more recent years, Horse Shows and Show Jumping have been followed by Eventing, Driving and Dressage.

Tragically Arthur Berkeley Portman and his wife were killed in September 1940 during an air raid. It was a question then if *Horse and Hound* could survive. For who had the knowledge and enthusiasm to ensure its success? But such a man emerged from the management when he returned from serving overseas. He was Mr Walter Case who, having worked for ten years under the previous editor, had learned much from his friend Arthur. Walter, too, was determined that this unique journal should not deviate from its original focus. For thirty years, under his leadership, *Horse and Hound* stimulated interest in the horse and particularly the many new equine sports which were emerging.

It is almost incredible that since 1884 there have been only three editors: Portman, Walter Case and now Michael Clayton.

This anthology will bring back many happy memories to all who are fond of the horse. At the same time it will interest the younger generation who are keen to know how these sports developed over the last century. The reader will enjoy coming across many people in these pages whom he will remember because they have distinguished themselves, including perhaps the greatest of all – Sir Winston Churchill. There is, after all, no greater stimulant to leadership than association with horses and hounds.

We owe much to Walter Case who with Country Life Books has given us this fascinating collection of events and memories.

> Hey for boot and horse, lad!
> Around the world away!
> Young blood will have its course, lad!
> And every dog his day!

MIKE ANSELL

PREFACE

Horse and Hound was first published on March 29, 1884, being founded by the Hon. Wyndham Berkeley Portman, a younger brother of the first Viscount Portman. The object was to provide the public with a reliable weekly journal at a popular price (2d.) that, "by reason of its sober presentation of fact, and attention to bloodstock breeding, was different to the majority of sporting periodicals on sale at the time." In September 1890 Arthur Fitzhardinge Berkeley Portman, born at Bashley Lodge, Leamington, on August 22, 1861, a son of Wyndham Berkeley Portman, took over the editorship of the paper under the *nom de plume* of "Audax", and in due course became recognised as the leading authority on Turf matters and one of the finest judges of bloodstock in the country. He was soon on intimate terms with everybody worth knowing in two generations on the Turf, and one newspaper correspondent later wrote that in his time he was the only racing journalist whose views were sought by Royalty. The late King George V and Arthur Portman, who had a phenomenal memory for Thoroughbred pedigrees and racing history, were firm friends.

In his day Mr Portman, who had seen every Derby for more than sixty years, was also an outstanding shot, and spent many happy days in the company of most of the finest marksmen in Great Britain. He came of a family long celebrated by their connection with racing, his great-grandfather on his mother's side, Thomas Thornhill, of Riddlesworth Hall, Norfolk, having won the Derby of 1818 with Sam, and that of 1820 with Sailor, as well as other historic races. Mr Portman himself occasionally entered the ranks of owners, but he was more successful when acting as a judge and historian of other peoples' victories.

In many ways he belonged to a bygone age, and *The Times* described him as one of the ablest racing journalists that there has ever been. He was a great traveller and never happier than when setting out with his wife, Mary Augusta Leslie, for a winter cruise to the distant parts of the Empire, as it was in those days, perhaps to South Africa, on a visit to his great friend Sir Abe Bailey, another racing celebrity.

Mr Portman was "an English Gentleman" in the best sense of the words, for this was the standard which he always set himself. About a year after the outbreak of war, on September 17, 1940, in fact, when the bombing of this country had been going on for some time, Mr Portman and his wife, with all but one of their seven household staff, were killed together when their home at 29 Montagu Square, London W1, suffered a direct hit. The death at the age of 79 of "The Guv'nor", as the few members of the staff affectionately knew him, was a terrible blow for the paper as it left a gap that could never be filled. In those difficult days similar tragedies were occurring all over London, and indeed the whole country, so it was understandable that the late Viscount Portman and myself were the only two to attend the funeral. But all sections of the sporting world were represented among the large number of well known people in all walks of life who attended the memorial service at St Mark's, North Audley Street, W1, a few weeks later, and tributes to Arthur Portman as an English sporting gentleman, and particularly for his extensive knowledge of racing, appeared in the Press throughout the world.

The last article which he wrote was the account of his fifty years as Editor, and his notes on the Ripon meeting, which appeared at the time in the paper's Turf and Stud column. It was almost as if he had a premonition of the danger ahead, and the disaster occurred before he had time to read the final proof. One of the reasons for his staying in London after war had started was his devotion to the interests of this paper, and his determination not to run away, as he termed it, from the responsibilities of his position.

Five years before the war Mr Portman had turned the business into a small limited company, dividing the majority of the shares between himself and his wife and the rest to a few senior members of his staff. He being several years older than his wife, he no doubt anticipated his decease would probably be prior to Mrs Portman's, that his shares would pass to her in due course, and that as soon as convenient she would review the whole position. They had no children. Apart from the terms expressed in his will and its codicils, it was clearly evident that Mr Portman's intentions were to ensure the continuity of the paper and to see, as far as he could, that the staff should be looked after. To provide for the possibility that she might die first, Mrs Portman left her shares back to her husband. The position was complicated by the fact that they probably died together, so the Court was asked to decide the destination of all the shares they both possessed. In the event they passed to the administrators of Mrs Portman's estate on behalf of a number of beneficiaries, most of whom were ladies.

In these trying times my remaining co-director and myself (I had already been appointed secretary of the company), with only two other staff members, had a few more trials to contend with in order to keep *Horse and Hound* going. Our somewhat Dickensian offices, which some older readers may remember, in Duke Street, Adelphi, were also severely damaged by bombing, with the loss of many of our reference books and records. And on another occasion, a few weeks later, our printers in Fetter Lane, EC4, where several hundred pounds' worth of paper, which was severely rationed, were stored, together with standing type, blocks and proofs, were completely destroyed in another heavy week-end raid. But in such circumstances there are always to be found people kind enough to help out others who are in difficulties. At a few hours' notice we managed to obtain other offices in Norfolk Street, Strand. And I can still recall the efforts on the Monday morning, after the loss of our printers, to find another house who could bring out the next week's issue without a break. By a superhuman effort on the part of some real workers, including the management and staff of St Clements Press, behind Kingsway, *Horse and Hound* came out that week, and we had the satisfaction of knowing that not a single issue had been either lost or even delayed.

We then had some more bad news in the sudden death of Arthur Portman's family solicitor, who, knowing his wishes, had been a great friend to us by watching our interests, as far as he was able to do so, in the legal matters being conducted, although the law had to take its course.

To comply with legal requirements, the next thing was to try to sell *Horse and Hound*. Anyway, my co-director, for

Her Majesty the Queen
at Ascot in 1961.

Her Majesty the Queen at Ascot in 1961.

health reasons, felt compelled to retire, and I was due to go into the Services. At that time no one could have guessed which way the war was likely to go, so there were comparatively few likely buyers for a sporting magazine, however famous. However, John Dunbar, editorial director of Odhams Press, who was interested in horses, although not particularly keen on hunting, was an enthusiastic admirer of *Horse and Hound*—he had generously offered temporarily to accommodate us at the time our offices were damaged. He induced his board to buy the Portman shares, and although I knew that Arthur Portman would have turned in his grave to know his paper was falling into the hands of one of the big publishing houses, contrary to his frequently expressed wishes, I had no possible alternative but to accept the offer.

I had joined *Horse and Hound* in 1933, when I expressed my admiration for the paper, but suggested it seriously lacked national advertising in its columns, and a publicity folder I designed and produced was most successful. Later I was asked to join the staff. Now, in the official position of company secretary, shareholder, director and editor—there was no other senior staff member left—my last task before joining the services was to hand over *Horse and Hound* into the safe keeping of Ben Clements, editor of *The Sporting Life* (also owned by Odhams), and share their offices, on the understanding that if and when I returned I should take over again.

After a spell with the Royal Signals in India, Ceylon and Singapore I was only too glad to get back to the world of horses and sport. On my return to the office I found Phyllis Hinton on the staff. She was previously owner of the Somerset Riding Stables on Wimbledon Common and was now our very able show reporter over the *nom de plume* of "Curlew". A few years later she left me to take over the editorship of *Riding*. The general shortage of quality horses was fairly evident for some time. In the early years of the war thousands of people, finding it impossible to keep their horses for a variety of reasons, gave them away or, in many cases, had them put down. But with the end of hostilities it was not long before the various sports began to revive. Racing, hunting, showing, show-jumping and polo all gradually attracted public interest again.

In the case of polo, of course, Lord Cowdray was one of those principally responsible for bringing the game back on a high level by opening his grounds for it at Cowdray Park, Midhurst, while another who did much to popularise polo at the other end of the scale was Arthur Lucas, at Woolmers Park in Hertfordshire.

A comparatively new post-war development was the formation of Hunt Supporters Clubs, formed from the country foot followers and farming friends of the Hunts. The initial object was to introduce some control over the motorcar followers and try to prevent them unintentionally spoiling sport. I recall many years ago being invited to attend the annual meeting of the Secretaries of Foxhounds

H.R.H. the Duke of Edinburgh playing for Polo Cottage in a Preliminary Round of the County Cup at Roehampton in 1953.

Association at the Cavalry Club with Mr B. L. Kearly, (founder and chairman of the Whaddon Chasers) who in an interesting talk explained the purpose of the clubs. But it was evident that at that time the Hunt Secretaries were not particularly enthusiastic about them. The point is, of course, that one cannot prevent the motorcar followers from attending the meets, and so, providing their activities out hunting can be controlled, why not enlist their support? Many Hunts have found that the genuine enthusiasm for sport on the part of the club members has led in many cases to some very helpful fundraising efforts on behalf of the Hunts.

Eventing is another post-war activity that has developed on a tremendous scale since the 1948 Olympic Games Three-day

Event at Aldershot. For the following year the Duke of Beaufort originated the Three-day Event at Badminton, and a modified version of this now takes place all over the country in the form of one-day, two-day and three-day horse trials, under the blanket name of Combined Training.

Among other things I was to find was that whereas *Horse and Hound* throughout its long history had never lost an issue, it apparently needed a miners' strike to stop its publication for several weeks.

The management of the publishing group had no headaches or problems with *Horse and Hound*, and we had few difficulties with them, apart from a bad scare in the 1960s when there was a move, eventually scotched, to sell the magazine to a rival group. Indeed, since Odhams had bought the magazine in 1943, it had continued to prove a remarkable financial success every year, and I must admit that there was practically no interference from above. On the contrary, as far as I know, all the directors appreciated the success of the paper.

In particular Mr H. L. Gibson, chairman for five years until he retired in 1968, was a keen hunting enthusiast, being a regular follower of the Old Berkeley Beagles. When he retired it was reported that "the journal he reads with the utmost pleasure is *Horse and Hound*, which I am sure he will uphold with his dying breath."

One of the principal features of *Horse and Hound* from its first issue was the insertion in full of Tattersall's Catalogue of their Monday sales at Albert Gate, Hyde Park, which was of great interest and value to both vendors and purchasers of horses. In the early days the regular contents also included reports of the main race meetings, breeding notes, and factual accounts of hunting and of a few other sports such as football, cricket, coursing, rowing and shooting, etc. Besides these, theatre reviews and comment on agricultural topics found their way into the columns. The first issue, incidentally, contained a report and detailed results of the Lincoln Spring Meeting and of the Grand National of 1,000 guineas, won by Mr H. F. Boyd's six-year-old Voluptuary carrying 10st 5lb—a flat racer with the extraordinary qualification of having no previous steeplechasing experience. The year 1884 also saw reported the famous dead-heat Derby in which Mr J.

Prince Charles playing for Stowell Park against San Flamingo in the Queen's Cup at Smith's Lawn, Windsor.

Hammond's St Gatien and Harvester, belonging to Sir John Willoughby, divided the stakes. Not for 56 years when The Colonel and Cadland were bracketed together in 1828, had there been such a result.

During the first year of the paper's existence, it is interesting to read the editor's tribute to the sporting characteristics of the present Duke of Beaufort's forebears. Referring to the annual meeting of the Hunt Servants Benefit Society, held as usual, in Tattersall's Subscription Room at Albert Gate, *Horse and Hound* reported that it was "under the presidency of the Duke of Beaufort who has been unanimously selected to fill the seat vacated by the death of the Duke of Buccleuch. Under no circumstance could the mantle have descended upon better shoulders, for Badminton has for generations been known as the stronghold of the chase, and no more enthusiastic fox-hunter can be found than the noble president and his son, the Marquess of Worcester."

If the editorial contents of *Horse and Hound* comprising 16 pages in the early years were mainly confined to racing, breeding and hunting, the editor's "Town and Country Gossip" page, in very brief snippets, roamed over a far wider range of subjects. These included politics, the eternal troubles in Ireland, Society marriages arranged, notorious police court cases, obituaries and, in fact, comment on practically any subject under the sun which appealed to the writer. The style of expression in the Victorian era and about the turn of the century may be thought fascinating and rather quaint in this modern age.

Point-to-point racing was, of course, well established by the early years of the century, and it is no exaggeration to claim that it was largely due to the publicity given by *Horse and Hound* to Hunt racing over the years that the sport became so popular with town and country folk. Horse shows, too, were becoming popular in the early 1900s, and a fixture that was intended to eclipse all others throughout the world was the International Horse Show first held at Olympia, London, in June 1907, to which *Horse and Hound* afforded considerable space, and to which, in later years, special issues were always devoted. It was, indeed, an international show in the full sense, with English, American and Canadian directors on the board, and ten other members representing the continent, as well as innumerable foreign competitors. Chairman of the show, and the moving spirit behind it all, was Lord Lonsdale, with the other English directors comprising Sir Gilbert Greenall, Bt, Arthur Evans, R. G. Heaton, John Kerr, H. H. Konig, Walter Lloyd and Walter Winans. The show was an overwhelming success—far greater even than the management had hoped for. It was a most lavishly produced show, and it was estimated that during the six days nearly 140,000 people visited it, while on the "champion's day some 30,000 were admitted, and during the week the takings were over £37,000". There were 124 classes, including 12 for Hackneys, 13 for show hunters, some of which were also required to jump, and 13 for jumpers. One class for jumpers, in which the late Tommy Glencross came third, attracted 75 entries, and 14 divided the prize money of over £390. There were numerous cups and trophies on offer, but it is interesting to reflect that even in those faraway days top prize money for most of the classes was about £30 or £40— figures which nearly 70 years later comparatively few shows have been able to increase. For all that, horse show fixtures have increased enormously in number in recent years, and

Princess Anne on H.M. the Queen's horse, Goodwill, making her way back from the dressage area after competing in the 1972 Goodwood Horse Trials accompanied by Mrs Alison Oliver on one of Princess's other event horses, Columbus.

there is a constant clamour for previews and reports in *Horse and Hound*.

There have always been enthusiastic followers of field sports—I do not use the meaningless and emotive term "blood sports"—and others who are violently opposed to them, while still others hold mixed views, preferring to support only certain of these sports. For example, some foxhunters may not care for shooting, coursing or, say, staghunting, but nearly 90 years ago the editor of *Horse and Hound* clearly emphasised that it was a weakness in the defence of field sports to divide one's interests and support, and frequently urged his readers to stand together to protect *all* field sports rather than support any one in particular, on the principle that "united we stand", etc.

In 1929 the R.S.P.C.A. organised the presentation of a Bill in the House of Commons demanding the abolition of staghunting, after considerable propaganda to whip up support for making it illegal. That effort failed, but it was a danger signal to farseeing sportsmen, who prophesied greater and possibly more skilled attacks, not only upon staghunting, but upon all forms of hunting and field sports in the future.

The following year the British Field Sports Society was formed, not only to defend all field sports from uninformed attacks, but to promote their interests wherever possible. Thus it was that, besides hunting, all the associations representing shooting and fishing, field trials, gamekeepers, wildfowlers, falconry and gun-dog interests readily came under the umbrella of the B.F.S.S. whose energetic President from the start has been the Duke of Beaufort. *Horse and Hound* has supported the society on every possible occasion, and in recent years, as a result of the *Horse and Hound* Ball, raised several thousand pounds for it.

The threat to field sports again raised its head late in the 1940s when the abolitionists presented a Bill demanding the stopping of hunting and also of coursing. This was serious and presaged the suppression of all field sports. On the evening of February 25, 1949, the day the Bill came up in the House and was soundly defeated, our *Horse and Hound* Ball in the West End of London was invaded by members of the "Piccadilly Hunt" who had ridden up to London from Gloucestershire to protest against the Bill. Everyone, of course, was in the mood for celebration, and, needless to say, we welcomed our friends, although it was evident a few had already been celebrating this great victory—and why not?

In the 1920s and 1930s, with the gradual disappearance of the cavalry, riding schools, some run by ex-cavalry instructors, sprang up, and many became well known and popular for the high standard of their tuition. Many people will still recall names like Capt. Jack Hance (Malvern Equitation School), Major Harry Faudel-Phillips (Temple House, Waltham Cross), Capt. Jack Webber (Great Missenden, Bucks), Oliver Dixon (Reading), Sam Marsh (Scamperdale, Redhill), Horace and Sybil Smith (Cadogan School, Belgrave Square, and Holyport, Berks), George Brine (Kenilworth, Great Bookham, Surrey), Douglas Mould (Bramleys, Old Southgate), Mrs Joan Nelson (Epsom), Horace Callaby (Kings Lynn), Tony Collings (Porlock Vale), and Capt. S. J. Laurence (Clapham Park, Balham); and there were many others who opened schools all over the country to cater for the increasing enthusiasm for riding. This reflected itself in much larger fields out hunting, and in the formation of a number of now well established horse societies. Regular reports in the columns of *Horse and Hound* kept its readers abreast of all their developing activities.

Amongst these societies and apart from the many breed societies was the British Show Jumping Association, formed in 1921 to improve the standard of jumping by one or two leading figures such as Colonels "Taffy" Walwyn and V. D. S. Williams (then Majors). Elementary rules were drawn up, and several riders began to make a name for themselves in this hitherto mildly interesting form of competition. They included Fred Foster, Tommy Glencross, who had won at Olympia in 1907, Frank Alison, Phil Blackmore, Sam Marsh, etc., but it was not until after the end of the second world war that the sport and its controlling authority really began to forge ahead. This followed the return of Col. Mike Ansell and Col. Nat Kindersley, who, while prisoners of war had between them planned vast changes in the post-war world of show jumping, such as designing new fences and courses, and introducing the speed element.

The year after the formation of the British Show Jumping Association, 1922, saw the start of the National Horse Association of Great Britain whose President, the late Sir Walter Gilbey, Bt, remained in office until 1928. Besides being a good judge of most breeds of horse, he was a stickler for correctness, and, after publicly criticising some riders for their untidy appearance, judged the dress of riding club members in Hyde Park's Rotten Row—the first show of its kind held there in 1932.

The Pony Club, aimed at helping young people under 17 years (and Associate members between 17 and 21) to gain correct riding instruction, was founded in 1929. Another of its objects is to encourage members to enjoy sport connected with ponies and horses, such as polo and eventing.

The British Show Hack and Cob Association came into being at a meeting of a few owners and breeders of hacks and cobs held in the offices of *Horse and Hound* in 1938, later with Sir Archibald Weigall, Bt, as President.

All this public interest in the horse and popular riding, which led to the formation of these societies, grew again after the second world war. It is possible that when hostilities ended people started to look for some form of relaxation as a relief, and found that recreational riding and the horse in a spectator sport provided the answer.

The British Horse Society dates from 1947 and was the

result of an amalgamation of the National Horse Association and the Institute of the Horse and Pony Club. It is the national federation for all horses and ponies in Great Britain with the exception of the bodies controlling racing. One must not forget the British Driving Society, affiliated to the B.H.S. since it was founded in 1957 to assist everyone interested in driving.

The Ponies of Britain Club came into being in 1952. Its founder, chairman, organising secretary and moving spirit is Mrs Glenda Spooner who started it with the help of the late Miss Gladys Yule. It is a great pony welfare society and also exists to encourage the breeding of quality ponies. Its invaluable pony trekking inspection scheme was suggested by *Horse and Hound*. Three of the oldest societies, excluding breed societies, however, are the Coaching Club (founded 1871), the Hunters' Improvement and National Light Horse Breeding Society (1885) and the National Pony Society (1893). The first-named was formed to provide an overflow driving club to the much older Four-in-Hand Club, which was limited in membership, and to meet the growing enthusiasm for coaching. On June 2, 1894, a record number of 39 coaches paraded in Hyde Park.

One of the aims of the H.I.S. is to stimulate and promote the breeding of hunters and other horses used for riding and driving. With its dedicated committees who operate the premium stallion and brood mare schemes, no other society can claim to have a better record of carrying out its objects so consistently over the years. This is evident from the long list every year of the winning point-to-point horses, show jumpers and general show horses, all bred via the H.I.S. schemes.

Objects of the N.P.S. are to encourage the breeding of riding and polo ponies, and to foster the breeds of native Mountain and Moorland ponies.

Horse and Hound can claim not only to have assisted these and other societies and the people who run them by regularly reporting their activities, but in many cases to have helped their ventures with advance publicity in support of their efforts.

In addition to this the paper sponsors a large variety of events and competitions with prize money, many cups and trophies and programme advertising. But even all this publicity, together with television coverage, so valuable to those events lucky enough to have it, is really insignificant compared with the indirect contribution to horse and pony interests made by the Queen, Prince Philip and other members of the Royal Family. We are fortunate indeed that the Monarch and practically all her family take such a keen personal and active interest in the horse and pony in some form or other.

In December 1973 I retired and passed the editorship of *Horse and Hound* into the capable hands of Michael Clayton. I had had 40 years on the staff, including 30 years as editor. In that time I did a job I loved, received great kindness and help from people in many walks of life, and made countless good friends. Who could ask for more?

WALTER O. CASE

ALL ROADS TO EPSOM

THE 1884 Derby will long be remembered as a dead-heat race. Such an occurrence has not taken place for fifty-six years, when The Colonel and Cadland were bracketed together, Cadland beating The Colonel at the second try, but this year other counsels have prevailed, and the stakes were divided. In The Colonel and Cadland's year no railway tickets were available, the *road* being the only way of getting to Epsom, and the scenes there enacted were far more exciting than now, although at the present time much fun and amusement are to be had both in going to the downs and when there. Wednesday last was dull in comparison to many Derby Days during recent years, and no doubt much of this is owing to the dulness of trade, the fact that the Grand Old Man is in office, and the Prince of Wales absent from England. A journey by that well-arranged line, the London, Brighton, and South Coast Railway, from Victoria, is pleasant and easy, and on landing at Epsom Downs Station on Wednesday, a quiet walk of a few minutes takes one to the Grand Stand, but before reaching that ugly and uncomfortable building, much laughter is afforded by the constant application for coppers from young ladies without shoes or stockings, who go through the performance of turning a "Catherine wheel," which until lately was only practised by the other sex. The Stand reached, after battling with "A card of the races, sir," or "Clean your boots, sir," one gives up one's ticket to be nipped, and after a deal of up and down stairs we reach that *commodious* saloon stall box named on our ticket by a deal of pushing and beg-pardoning, and we are located in a very small sort of pen, 4ft by 6ft, with little red curtains on each side to protect you from the gaze of your neighbour whilst eating your small mustard and cress sandwich and imbibing your "dry."

But the course takes your attention, where all sorts of horrible people assemble to pass away time by witnessing two ugly fellows pretending to "box," so as to get a crowd round them, for their "pals" to empty the pockets of the "gapers."

The most amusing scene that I witnessed was an old gentleman of bucolic appearance, who had arrived at the good age of some threescore and five, being filched of his money by urchins. The old chap had been telling his squire that it was his first appearance at a Derby, and fearing he might be robbed he had carried the only sov he possessed in his mouth. The young'ns heard this, and soon fell a-crying, and falling down on the ground screamed out they had lost all their money. The sympathy of the bystanders was soon shown by an appeal to the boys to know how they had lost all their cash, when they declared for a lark they had turned head-over-heels and had dropped their coppers, but Charley had a "quid" in his pocket, which had tumbled out, and that old villain had picked it up and put it into his mouth. No sooner said than the old countryman was collared, and he had to disgorge the sov for the benefit of the youthful tumblers. Poor Hodge swore he was robbed, but being advised he had better cut it before the "beaks" put in an appearance he handed the sov to the boys and was off.

Then, soldiers with clasps and medals were there, looking on with delight upon England's great festival, enjoying the crush and the crowd. Old veterans who had fought the black niggers in Egypt were seen having a merry-go-round, just for a penny; but what amused me the most was a well-known City knight, booted and spurred, riding as usual his good old mare amongst the traps and the drags as if he was the only one privileged to do such a piece of horsemanship. He had pulled up close to the drag of a certain regiment, his old mare's tail close to the boot of the drag, and was looking on at the doings of the crowd, when a young officer quietly slipped off the coach on to the back of the mare behind the worthy knight, who for once was not on the *watch*, the mare began swerving, the young soldier felt going, so, clinging to the booted knight, they both tumbled off together, much to the delight of the onlookers. Sir John was not to be done, so, with good-nature, he stood up and threw down his gauntlet and challenged the soldier, who very properly apologised, and the knight was soon landed on the drag, and, after several glasses of excellent Geisler, made a speech to the crowd upon the pluck and hospitality of the British soldier.

The Derby dog was absent to-day, the first time for many

a year, but there stood the undaunted inspector, whose white hairs (or rather airs) were reverenced by all. What a day for old Greyhairs and his quad; what a shame that a statue is not erected in his honour, and perhaps when he has departed a Liberal Government will cut off his head, then his body, his horse's head and tail, and transport him to Epsom Downs, where the little boys will be enabled to say, "Bill, this 'ere chap who looks so well and so 'ealthy owes his good looks to the Epsom air and not to the Epsom salts." But the bell is ringing, and the course is being cleared, which, marvellous to say, takes but ten or fifteen minutes; and where the prize-fighters, the flag-bearers, the standard-bearers of Charley Jones and Bill Travers, the betting men, fly to is marvellous, only to appear directly the race is over. Why, let us ask, should those bundles of papers be allowed to be thrown all over the course, not only to the annoyance of the people, but to the jeopardy of the horses who are coming out to do battle for the Blue Riband of the Turf? An order from the authorities to stop this disgusting waste of literature would soon have effect, and I trust this hint will not be useless. Out come the steeds, blue and silver, pink and white, yellow and white, red, white, and blue, and every colour conceivable. They walk down in front of me (the Prince being absent), and then do me the favour of just cantering by. I make my remarks, and tell the sweet lady who has just had a nice glass of fiz that I think the mare is a fine mover, but the great horse of the day, to my mind, is the Dutchman, who should, from his excellent action, be certainly the hero of the day. The lady smiles, thinks I ought to know, and when asked by the youth which horse she would like to back, says, "The Dutchman, for six pairs of gloves." The race it is run, but before it is finished I see the grand horse is like to be awkwardly placed, and before the excitement and the finish is over I depart to the crowd—no welsher, but considered a fool.

What a race! How Dawson must chuckle. Lord Falmouth must improve in health at the thought that Harvester has proved such a good horse, and old Mat—that king of the trainers—how pleased he must feel when he remembers his words at Newmarket, just before the sale—"I have trained the horses to be sold just as I would if Lord Falmouth had

COACHING.

TIME TABLE.

DORKING, BOX HILL, AND LONDON.—The "Perseverance," four-horse coach (Mr. W. Sheather, proprietor,) leaves Hatchett's Hotel, Piccadilly, every day (Sundays excepted) at 11.15 a.m., *viâ* Clapham 11.45 a.m., Tooting 12, *Merton, King's Head, 12.10 p.m., Ewell, Spring Hotel, 12.48 p.m., *Epsom, Marquis of Granby, 1.0 p.m., Leatherhead, Swan Hotel, 1.28 p.m., Box Hill 1.50 p.m., arriving at Dorking, White Horse Hotel, at 2 p.m.; returning at 3.15 p.m., *Epsom 4.15 p.m., *Merton 5.5 p.m. arriving in Piccadilly at 6 p.m.

EASTBOURNE AND BRIGHTON.—"The Express," a fast and well-appointed four-horse coach (Mr. Beckett, proprietor), leaves the Queen's Hotel, Eastbourne, every day (Sundays excepted) at 11 a.m., *viâ* *Polegate 11.35 a.m., *Berwick, 12.10 p.m., *Lewes (White Hart Hotel) 12.50 p.m., arriving at the Grand Hotel, Brighton, at 1.40 p.m.; returning at 3.45 p.m., *Lewes 4.30 p.m., *Berwick 5.20 p.m., *Polegate 5.55 p.m., arriving at Eastbourne (The Queen's Hotel) at 6.30 p.m.

GUILDFORD AND LONDON.—"The New Times," Mr. Walter Shoolbred, proprietor, leaves the White Horse Cellars every day, Sundays excepted, at 11 a.m., *viâ* *Putney Vale 11.50 a.m., Kingston 12.8 p.m., *Esher 12.32 p.m., Cobham 12.55 p.m., *Ripley 1.20 p.m., arriving at the Angel Hotel, Guildford, at 2 p.m.; returning at 4 p.m., *Ripley 4.32 p.m., Cobham 5 p.m., *Esher 5.20 p.m., Putney Vale 6.6 p.m., arriving in Piccadilly at 7 p.m.

LEAMINGTON AND STRATFORD.—The "Shakespeare," a well-appointed four-horse coach, leaves the Regent Hotel, Leamington, on Mondays, Tuesdays, Fridays, and Saturdays, at 10.30, returning from the Red House, Stratford, at 4 p.m.

LEDBURY AND GLOUCESTER.—The mail coach leaves the Feathers Hotel, Ledbury, every morning at 8, arriving at the Greyhound Hotel, Gloucester, at 10.15 a.m.; returning at 3.25 p.m.

ST. ALBANS.—"The Defiance," a well-appointed four-horse coach (Mr. E Fownes proprietor), leaves the White Horse Cellars every morning (Sundays excepted) at 10.45 a.m., *viâ* *Hendon 11.30 a m., Edgware 11.45 a.m., *Stanmore 12.10 p.m., *Watford 12.55 p.m., arriving at St. Albans, (George Hotel), at 1.45 p.m.; returning at 3.15 p.m., *Watford 4.14 p.m., *Stanmore 4.45 p.m., Edgware 5.15 p.m., *Hendon 5.25 p.m., arriving in Piccadilly at 6.15 p.m.

VIRGINIA WATER.—Oatlands Park and London. "The Old Times," a fast and well-appointed four-horse coach, Mr. J. W. Selby, proprietor, leaves Hatchett's Hotel, Piccadilly, every morning (Sundays excepted) at 10.45 a.m., *viâ* *East Sheen, Bull Hotel, 11.30 a.m., Richmond, Greyhound, 11.45 a.m., Teddington 12 noon, *Hampton Court, King's Arms, 12.15 p.m., Walton 12.40 p.m., *Oatlands Park Hotel 12.50 p.m., *Chertsey, Crown, 1.20 p.m., arriving at the Wheatsheaf, Virginia Water, at 1.45 p.m.; returning at 3.30 p.m., *Chertsey 3.58 p.m., Oatlands Park Hotel 4.25 p.m., Walton 4.35 p.m., *Hampton Court 5.5 p.m., Teddington 5.15 p.m., Richmond 5.30 p.m., *East Sheen 5.45 p.m., arriving a Hatchett's Hotel, Piccadilly, at 6.30 p.m.

*Change horses.

been going to race them himself." "St. Gatien is a good horse," says the owner: "I put down the dust, and meant him." No doubt he did; and I have no doubt Harvester meant it too, although done up in swaddling clothes. Ye touts, ye are done this time, by Jove! Just before the race I heard the greatest authority on handicaps say to a friend of mine, "I will give you a tip—Harvester." Well, it is all over now; I may be put down as a BUSYBODY, but a greater one than I am showed on Friday.

31 May 1884

TOWN AND COUNTRY GOSSIP

Last week I complained at having to pay four guineas for a bedroom at Doncaster for three nights, but, thank goodness I have found a greater martyr in one who paid eight guineas for a bedroom and sitting-room for the four days at Goodwood. Backers and layers complain alike of bad times, but who can be surprised when we see what they pay for accommodation. Newmarket is fortunately within reach of London and hundreds of visitors therefore return each night.

29 September 1884

DEATH OF FRED ARCHER

THE one absorbing topic in Turf circles this week has been the melancholy death of Fred Archer, and never have I noted more signs of genuine grief than when it transpired at Albert Gate on Monday afternoon that he had passed away by his own hand whilst under the influence of delirium. So much has been written on the subject that I will not fill our pages with a lengthened account of his career, but briefly express my own sorrow for the death of the brightest ornament of his profession and one who made many real friends by his undeviating truthfulness, his modesty under adulation which might have turned weaker heads, and his gentlemanly bearing in every relation of life.

As a jockey I never saw his superior, and I have seen James Robinson, Sam Chifney, Frank Butler, Sam Rogers, Alfred Day, Custance, Tom French, Tom Aldcroft, and the immortal George Fordham show their brilliant skill in the pigskin. Many of these may have shown as grand horsemanship in special instances, but as an all-round jockey Fred Archer has had no equal, in my opinion. One main secret of his success was his undeviating attention to business, always seeing that his weight was right, his horse properly saddled, and that he reached the post in good time. The starters will miss him, as he set a bright example of submission to those in authority, never attempting to take advantage until the flag was dropped; yet so skilful was he, and so keenly did he watch the starter's movements, that he knew when to go, and

won scores of races by his judgment at the starting-post. In the actual race, too, how different was his riding to that of the many headless horsemen that call themselves jockeys, and I pause to think how many races I have seen him snatch out of the fire, and drop a tear of unfeigned sorrow to think I shall never see his brilliant horsemanship again.

Born at Cheltenham in 1857, when eleven years old he won a steeple-chase at Bangor on a noted pony, Maid of Kent, and two years later on, in 1870, he won a Nursery at Chesterfield on Athol Daisy. In 1872 he won the Cesarewitch on Salvanos for poor Joe Radcliffe, who has since joined the great majority, and from the moment that, in 1874, he won the Two Thousand Guineas for Lord Falmouth on Atlantic his name has been a household word, as he won that race four times, the One Thousand twice, and he can claim five Derbies, four Oaks, and the St. Leger six times, and I learn from a contemporary that he has had in England 8084 mounts, and ridden 2748 winners, whilst he has won the City and Suburban five times, the Great Metropolitan once, Woodcote Stakes six times, Lincolnshire Handicap once, Northamptonshire Stakes once, Cesarewitch twice, Clearwell Stakes eight times, Middle Park Plate thrice, Dewhurst Plate five times, Ascot Stakes once, Prince of Wales's Stakes (Ascot) three times, Royal Hunt Cup twice, Alexandra Plate twice, Great

Ebor Handicap twice, Great Yorkshire Stakes once, North-umberland Plate once, Stewards' (Goodwood) twice, Great Yorkshire Handicap once, Champagne Stakes seven times, Portland Plate twice, Doncaster Cup once, Liverpool Autumn Cup thrice, and Manchester Cup once.

Whilst dwelling on poor Fred's career, it is not too much to say that his success in life is in no small degree owing to the kindness of Lord Falmouth and his good friend and relative, Mr. Matthew Dawson. Singularly enough, his first great success in the classic races was in the ever-popular magpie jacket of Lord Falmouth, and it was the last he wore to victory, when he won on Blanchland the last race of the Houghton Friday. Would to heavens that, like the jockeys of old, he had wound up the year on that Houghton afternoon, as the cold, treacherous air of the Southdowns no doubt aggravated what would only too probably have proved a fatal illness. What hope there may have been was cut short, alas! by a fit of frenzy that has caused deep grief amongst racing men of every grade; for, from the first gentleman in the land to the mildest punter at the street corner, his name was respected as the emblem of manliness and integrity.

I fear that poor Fred Archer only adds another to the list of those whose lives have been shortened by excessive wasting —at least, I can call to mind that Tom French, another of the best type of *horsemen*, wrecked his brilliant career by excessive wasting to ride in France. Men, however wealthy, will run extraordinary risks to gratify their ambition in winning races, and Archer pinched himself cruelly to ride St. Mirin for the Cambridgeshire, as he fully thought he could win on him; whilst last week one of the richest commoners in England faced the starter in a silk jacket, minus his shirt, to save half a pound, when riding at a country meeting, in spite of the advice of his friends, who begged him to put on a thick flannel and declare the extra weight.

I do not on this account desire a higher scale of weights, as there is no necessity for those who cannot get down to a certain standard to sport silk, and there are plenty of lads anxious to ride intermediate weights. Now that there is "No Best" left in the riding world, owners need require no one to make special exertions on their account, and the almost super-human excellence of one bright star will not confound the

A horsedrawn tram operating in London around 1888.

most careful calculations of handicappers; although I would not have it understood that I consider that many of the existing jockeys do not ride quite up to the average of the present or past years.

AUDAX   13 November 1886

TOWN AND COUNTRY GOSSIP

A New Year has begun, and will, I trust, prove a highly successful one to all readers of this journal, and the world at large. May it also be less fatal to the titled class of this country than did 1891 when four dukes, eighteen earls, six barons, and twenty-nine baronets were taken by the Great Destroyer. Also, may we hear less of strikes than has been the case last season, when, amongst others, were the very serious Scotch Railway, the "Bus", and the Carron and Hermitage Wharves strikes.

2 January 1892

FOX-HUNTING IN WILTS AND GLOUCESTERSHIRE.

SIR,—We have had some good sport with the V.W.H. and the Duke of Beaufort's Hounds, sometimes in a snowstorm, then in a hurricane, or in pouring rain. There is nearly always scent, and hounds can run in any weather.

It was a wild, rough day on Friday, Feb. 2, when the V.W.H. (Earl Bathurst's) Hounds met at Eastcourt House, but there was a good scent, and hounds ran fast. The first fox was found in Flintridge, but he was a twisting bad brute, and gave us little sport. Stonehill Wood held a brace; unfortunately we chopped the vixen, but got away on good terms with her mate, and raced after him to Braydon Pond Plantations, flash through the covers, and out by the Pond Farm, ran the vale, pointing for Swatnage, but turn to the right and cross the Malmesbury road to Bullock's Horn. The pace, fast before, is faster still, and every fence seems bigger than the last, as we ran past Cloatley to Eastcourt. The company is getting very select, and there are empty saddles in all directions when hounds get their heads up near Morley. They eventually own a line to the shrubbery by Eastcourt House, but can take it no farther. This run was over a splendid line of country every inch of it grass—no railways, canals, or barb wire, but the fences wanted jumping. Found another good fox at Hankerton Purley, and got away on good terms with him over Dog-trap lane to Perry Keen's Gorse, and hounds are soon on the Great Western Railway, and only just missed being run into by a train; but they are soon away to Minety Moor, cross Swillbrook, pointing for Somerford Kaynes, run on to Ashton, and have a long check, but own the line at the Brick-kiln, and take it on to Clayhill, through the cover and away to South Cerney. The first part of this was over a grass country, and fast; the end over deep plough, and slow. There were any quantity of falls. Mr. James Joicey came a cropper over some wire netting in the middle of a field.

But of all good days the best was Monday, with the Duke of Beaufort's. The meet was Shipton Moyne, and a fox, found in Shipton Wood, went away by the mill to Merchant's Farm. crossed the Foss to the Bell Farm, through Hide Brake, and over the brook to Brokenbro', then recrossed the Foss by the Brick-kiln, leaving Shipton Moyne on the left, run over the Park Farm to Eastcourt House, through the Thorn Covert, and away pointing for Starveal, with three foxes in front of us. As we ride down a lane, we can see a brace on the right-

The Marquess of Abergavenny, K.G., O.B.E., J.P., MFH, President of The British Horse Society 1970–71.

hand side, but hounds are running on our left, and never leave the line; with Elmstree half a mile to our left, we run by Beverstone and Chavenage, have two lines at the Hermit Cave, but don't think we changed, as the leading hounds never got their heads up; but run on through Upton Grove, over Lowfield Farm, through Titcomb's Gorse to Tetbury Common, over Tetbury Warren, and on to Culkerton, cross the railway at Culkerton Station, and on to Trull, run through the Trull Covers, and are at fault for the first time after running fast for an hour and 8 minutes. There are only ten men with hounds, but one of them is Lord Worcester, and it does not take him long to hit off the line, and as hounds hunt slowly through Blackrock and Hazelton the stragglers come up, and at Tarlton Downs the field would be more than fifty. We are soon in Hailey Wood, cross the railway, and run through the Cirencester Woods, near the Ten Rides, and out towards Pimbury Park, turn to the left to Sapperton, back to Hailey Wood, run round the wood, and out away towards Tarlton Downs, as if the old varmint meant making tracks for home. I should have liked to have seen the end of it, but it looked as if the whole thing had to be done over again, and hounds had been running nearly three hours, the first hour so fast that many a good nag stood still, and the last two hours in pouring rain—the farthest point was about ten miles as the crow flies. I could count the field on my fingers, but the Master and huntsman were going strong and well when I had to say goodbye.

W.W.   10 February 1894

AGRICULTURAL GOSSIP.

THE great advantages of the late bounteous fall of rain have been temporarily reduced by a cold north wind and lack of sunshine. But although the benefits of the rainfall are not yet as striking as they would have been if the genial weather that preceded it had also followed it, still the parched earth has been well moistened, and all fear of another failure of the hay crop, like that of last year, has subsided. It would have been strange, indeed, if April had gone out without its usual contribution of cold weather, and instead of grumbling at a temporary arrest of rapid vegetation we have every reason to be thankful that there has not been any severe frost during the month so far. This is, however, not all that there is to be said by way of congratulation. The oldest farmer can hardly recall a season so satisfactory as the present one has been, from its commencement to the last week of April.

It began with a splendid period for fallowing the land after harvest, and was followed in due course by equally propitious times for sowing the winter crops, for bringing them forward with full vigour, for the sowing of the spring corn and planting potatoes, and lastly for the sowing of mangolds, the preparation of the land for other root crops, for starting grass and clover in growing well for a hay crop, and for flushing a fairly early growth of feed. As a legacy of last year's drought, there is in many places a gappy plant of clover; but every other farm crop at present above ground is looking well for the time of year, while the land was never in better condition for crops yet to be put in. Hops again are coming on well, and the promise in the fruit plantations and market gardens is magnificent. To what extent the hopes based on their fair appearances will be realised no one can tell, but the season can scarcely fail to result in a bounteous harvest.

The extraordinary imports of hay rendered necessary by the shortness of our last crop have continued up to the present time, and may be expected to be kept up until our new crop is ready for sale. During the three months ended with March, we received 99,844 tons, as compared with 30,090 tons, imported in the corresponding period of 1893. The United States sent more than half the total, and Russia more than one-fifth. Eighteen countries contributed to the supply, including such distant lands as Canada, Chili, Asiatic Turkey, and New Zealand.

It seems hardly worth while to pass an Act of Parliament to empower the Board of Agriculture to prosecute under the Merchandise Marks Act, as far as the sale of imported meat as British is concerned, without strengthening the law in this connection. If every seller of imported meat were required to display a notice stating that such meat was sold on the premises, consumers would be put on the alert, and there would be some chance of convicting butchers who sell meat under a misrepresentation. If Mr. Gardner would make his promised Bill cover the latter arrangement it might do some

good, and there is no reason to suppose that there would be
any difficulty in passing it.

In consequence of the improved prospects for feed, store
cattle and sheep have increased in value, and there is every
reason to expect much better prices than those which prevailed last year, when they were ruinously low. At a sale held
in Sussex the other day, the prices of sheep were reported to
have advanced 4s. to 5s. a head. Sheep and lambs will
probably sell better than bullocks because of their comparative scarcity.

As regards wheat, the ten purchasing countries of the world are now reckoned to be taking a million quarters of wheat and flour weekly. If the United Kingdom were only receiving a tenth of this amount, the situation would be full of encouragement; unfortunately, out of the million, at least 400,000qrs. are consigned to this country. Belgium and Holland are taking about 200,000qrs. between them, France and Spain another 100,000qrs., and Italy and Greece again 100,000qrs. This leaves about 200,000qrs. weekly to meet the demands of Germany, China, and tropical America, the latter including all countries south of Mexico until we reach the Uruguayan frontier of Brazil. The proportion of flour to wheat now being taken by the United Kingdom is rather less than that of some recent years, about 85,000qrs. against 315,000qrs., as compared with 120,000qrs. against 280,000qrs. or thereabouts. It is, however, no great while since the imports of wheat in the form of flour were only about a tithe of the whole, instead of a full fourth, or even a third, as in 1893.

It is asserted that 90cents. per bushel, or 30s. per quarter, is the lowest price at which the American farmer can sell wheat, and pay a profit on farming. If this be true, the situation in the United States is becoming grave. It is true that by 30s. per quarter is meant 30s. paid at Mark Lane, and by the payment of profit is meant some cash gain after the farmer and his family have been fed, lodged, and clothed. But the price of average American wheat at Mark Lane is now 26s. per quarter, so it would seem that our Transatlantic cousins are no longer able to outsell us in the matter of cereals. This may mean a bad future for American agriculture, but, at all events, it ought to encourage the waning hopes of the British farmer.

Lord Churchill's Cornbury estate, Oxfordshire, is in the market. This fine sporting and residential domain was once the Royal hunting ground of Henry II., when the wild boar was hunted in the celebrated Wychwood Forest, then extending to nearly 7000 acres, which adjoins the park. The house stands in a finely-timbered park of about 500 acres, containing three magnificent avenues.

28 April 1894

OUR Post Office is always developing something new and useful, and at Grantham a cycle post has just been started to serve a group of villages covering a circuit of several miles. A mounted postman leaves the Grantham head post office daily at 12.30 p.m. taking letters and parcels for delivery in Little Ponton, Great Ponton, Rochford, Colsterworth, Stainby, Senstern, Buckminster, and Skillington. The bicycle is specially constructed for postal purposes, and is enamelled in "pillar-box red" and is already much appreciated by the inhabitants of the district.

28 October 1899

Few people know nowadays how the Army and Navy Club, generally called "The Rag" got this sobriquet. In its early days it went so badly, financially and otherwise, that it got talked about as "the rag and famish club." Thus was devised the far from flattering name which the place is almost invariably called at the present time.

2 September 1905

On Wednesday our beloved King unlocked with a golden key the gates across Kingsway, which forthwith became open to the public, one of the finest thoroughfares in the world, made on the site of what used to be about the worst and most dangerous slums in London.

21 October 1905

THE FIRST INTERNATIONAL HORSE SHOW.

THE Paddock on Derby Day was, in its multiplicity of languages, not exactly a preliminary canter, but rather a rehearsal of the various languages heard at the great world-wide horse show which opened yesterday at Olympia. Nothing in the history of horse shows has been so comprehensive—nothing before has included such a large number of well-filled classes. All nations have sent the best of their kind, and the Olympia Company has spared neither trouble nor expenses in their reception. The arrangements were most elaborate, the prizes princely, and the decorations highly artistic, hence a large and fashionable attendance, which included a goodly proportion of ladies. Olympia is a splendid building for the purpose, and its preparation must have been a matter of considerable anxiety—the cost being reckoned in thousands. In the 124 classes the 600 horses supplied 2000 entries. In each class the first-prize horse was placed near the elaborate floral decorations of the principal arena, this position giving a splendid view from the commodious grand stands and also the Press galleries.

The tanned flooring of the ring suited the feet and legs of the highly valuable exhibits, and it gave such good foothold that the hackney classes, with which the exhibition opened, could fearlessly show their best paces. Taken as a whole, the hackneys looked far better on the coat than they ever do at Islington in March, the chief reason being that at this time of the year the silky summer coat has fully grown. In other respects the condition of the horses generally bespoke the watchful management of experts, and it may safely be said that in the matured classes the winners are incapable of further improvement.

A coach-horn is not only a sporting instrument: but, blown by an expert in the ring, it is an excellent method of calling forward the successive classes. The judges of ten classes of hackneys in hand were: Mr. Edward Cooke, representing England; Mr. Clarence Moore, America; and Mr. Anton Jurgens, Holland, and their various awards were well received generally. Neither the hackneys in the arena, nor the plain working horses which, exactly at noon on Friday, carted in on trucks the artificial fences seemed in the least disturbed at the programme of music by the Earl of Lonsdale's private band, nor by the band of the Grenadier Guards, which played later in the day.

Soon after twelve o'clock the jumping commenced, and the foreign horses certainly made a startling show over the timbers, and the bank, and also the artificial brook. The bay mare Blink Bonny (named after the winner of the Derby of fifty years back), the property of Mr. Glencross, of Frome, Somerset, flew the fences like a steeple chaser, and others were clever, but not many so brilliant. One horse swerved at a timber fence, and charged the ornamental hedge which bounds the arena, but there was no mishap. In Class 108, the total of the judging prizes was £395, the first prize being £120.

34

A grocer's van.

Mr. Walter Winans's Bilboquet, a smart bay, made a good show, he having the advantage of M. Leclerc in the saddle, this gentleman being, by some, considered one of the best horsemen in France. Mr. Johnson, of Melton Mowbray, was represented by a black gelding named Darkie, which brought down the house by his fine jumping, but many of the imported jumpers will be hard to beat.

It should be understood that the show is promoted by a limited liability company, with a capital of £20,000, and it is an open secret that Mr. Walter Winans took the whole of the remaining shares at one sweep.

At the luncheon, to which the Press were welcomed, the Earl of Lonsdale, chairman of directors, referred to improvements in horse-breeding which must result from such an important international exhibition; and others considered that the amity of nations must necessarily be promoted and increased by such comprehensive and far-reaching arrangements. Mr. Euren, secretary of Hackney Horse Society, was the instigator and promoter, and many of his financial supporters do not think primarily of profit, though there will probably be a good dividend. There are three shows for each of the days, the paying public, at the end of each entertainment, making room for other paying visitors.

8 June 1907

THE NATIONAL HORSE SUPPLY.

In the House of Lords on Monday the Earl of Donoughmore called attention to the recent report of the Royal Commission on Horse Breeding and to the question of the provision of horses for military purposes, and moved for papers. What he wanted to know was whether the Government intended to take definite action in the near future. The position of affairs was becoming much more serious. Two breeding seasons had been lost, and he hoped they were not going to lose a third. At present to mobilise all our troops we required 173,000 horses, 59,000 for cavalry, with a reserve of 10 per cent., at once. The wastage of war would probably need rehorsing in six months. The resources of the United Kingdom were 1,500,000 horses, but only 150,000 were fit for cavalry use. Therefore, there were in this country 30,000 fewer horses than would be required during the first year of a war. The birth-rate among horses was also decreasing. There were 10,000 fewer foals in 1906 than in 1905, so that we were becoming more and more dependent on the foreigner. He was horrified to hear that the number of horses in Canada and Australia was decreasing. On the other hand, the export of horses showed an increase, and buyers came to buy our best. In almost every direction there was found an increased difficulty in getting horses. Obviously something must be done, and there must be activity on the part of the Government—extension of organisation. It was only Government action that could help them to deal properly with the foreign competition that we were suffering from.

Lord Ribblesdale held that, although there were reservations, we were at present face to face with a combination of various circumstances which, if it became normal, would be exceedingly hazardous. The present Minister for War was the only Minister who had given direct attention to this difficulty, but the man they had to convince was the Chancellor of the Exchequer, who very properly had a jealous care of his key from the taxpayers' point of view.

Lord Lovat asked what was the number of horses in the United Kingdom.

Earl Carrington: 2,087,000.

Lord Lovat said the bulk of these were used for agricultural purposes. The question was to discover the number of horses suitable for military purposes, and he suggested that there should be a census of all horses in the country, not only respecting number, but class and suitability, and that there should be an annual report on the subject.

Earl Carrington, in reply, said it was proposed to arrange for the registration of a large number of suitable stallions and mares, and the subsequent registration of such of their offspring as might be approved by the military authorities. No breeding animal would be accepted unless it had been passed by a veterinary surgeon as sound for breeding purposes. All registered animals would thus be officially certified to be sound. The ultimate goal would be to secure the breeding annually in the United Kingdom of 15,000 foals of the various classes of horses required. There was a general agreement that great encouragement to breeding would be given if horses were purchased for the Army at three years old instead of at five years old, and he was glad to say that the Army Council had expressed their willingness to make arrangements for the inspection of the produce of registered breeding animals at three years old and to purchase their annual supplies of remounts from the young stock approved as suitable.

They would also report the remainder of the young stock suitable to the Board of Agriculture for registration by them. He was sanguine that such a register of young horses would be a long step in the direction of bringing sellers and purchasers of young horses into direct relationship. That was only a brief outline of the scheme, but their intention was that it should be carried out by the departments directly concerned, with the assistance and advice of a consultative committee composed of leading representatives of the industry, and, if funds allowed, there would [be] engrafted on to it special local schemes, and possibly the establishment of prizes for registered stock at local shows. The possible requirements of the Regular Army must be first kept in view, but should the stimulus given to the breeding of light horses be so great as to meet those requirements, there would be no great difficulty in extending the system of registration so as to allow the County Associations to take advantage of it in connection with the supply of horses for the Territorial Army.

It would be improper for him to deal with the question of the cost of these proposals at this stage, as the matter was under the consideration of the Chancellor of the Exchequer, and until he had reviewed it in connection with the calls of all sorts which were daily being made upon the Exchequer it was not possible to say how financial considerations would admit of its adoption. He was at liberty to state, however, that Mr. Lloyd-George was giving to their proposals his most careful consideration, and he was confident that his right hon. friend would meet their views to the utmost of his ability. The scheme would depend for its success on the support that might be given it by horse owners.

11 July 1908

Capt. G. H. S. Webber, O.B.E., Secretary-General of The British Show Jumping Association from 1945 to 1971, Chairman of The British Show Jumping Association 1972–73.

TOWN AND COUNTRY GOSSIP

THE dangers of London street traffic are becoming so serious that, if it goes on people will hardly dare to venture about the roads, and perhaps this, together with bad times, is the cause of some fifty thousand houses now being let in the Metropolis. One most monstrous thing is the manner in which many drivers, those controlling the "taxis" being especially bad, ignore the rules of the road by passing other carriages on the left instead of the right; and bicyclists, too, are very bad offenders in this respect, and really, the police ought to stop and punish this in the promptest and most severe manner that the law allows.

20 June 1908

In view of certain legislative tendencies it is interesting to note that Mr. H. G. Wells, in an interview recently expressed the opinion that the agricultural labourer has a very fair time of it, although he admits his astonishment on discovering the fact. "I have been a good deal in Essex lately" he said, "and many of the families there hardly make a pound a week when all earnings are added together. But rent is cheap, and they have big gardens, and they keep a pig, and they seem well enough off."

13 June 1912

The most remarkable cavalry charge in history, by the way, was that of General Pichegru's Horse in 1795 over the ice of the Zuyder Zee against the Dutch fleet, which was captured! This is most probably the only instance on record of cavalry capturing a fleet. Kellerman's charge at Marengo was another remarkable feat. This was the occasion when Desaix remarked to Napoleon, "It is only four o'clock, and although we have lost the battle there is time to win another one." Kellerman had 400 mounted sabres which dashed out from behind a vineyard at the critical moment on the flank of the Hungarian infantry and turned defeat into victory. Amongst famous charges that of the Light Brigade in the Crimea, will of course, always occupy a foremost place.

19 February 1917

Sir Charles Frederick, Master of the Pytchley Hounds, in proposing the health of the Prince of Wales at a dinner in connection with the Hunt on Tuesday, said, according to the "Morning Post":– "When the Prince came down to hunt in the Pytchley country I asked Captain Drummond, one of the most experienced of our followers, to pilot His Royal Highness. Later I heard that the Prince had had a fall over a stile into the road. So I said to Captain Drummond: 'You've

done a nice thing,' and Captain Drummond replied: 'I
started off to pilot the Prince round, but before we had gone
very far he was piloting me.'" The Master added that the
Prince had asked him to tell the members of the Hunt that
he had immensely enjoyed his days with the Pytchley, and
hoped to hunt with them again next season.

20 March 1920

At Olympia on Saturday a new association was formed called
the Association of Show Jumpers. The object of the new
organisation is to advance the interests of those connected
with jumping at shows, and to place the pursuit upon a
regularised basis. The registration and identification of
jumpers, as well as the standardisation of obstacles, are among
the ends in view. Major C. T. Walwyn is prominently associated with the movement, and Lord Lonsdale has consented
to be president of the organisation, while Colonel V. D. S.
Williams, previously secretary of the Aldershot Command
Show, will carry out the secretarial duties. A strong executive
committee has been formed, including British Army officers
and professional show jumpers, and there is every prospect
that show jumping will largely benefit as a result of the
movement.

26 March 1926

ROYAL DAY WITH THE BELVOIR

To Folkingham belongs the distinction of being the first
Lincolnshire hunting fixture of the Belvoir graced by the
presence of royalty, the occasion being Friday, the 7th inst.,
when H.R.H. the Duke of York, staying with the Master,
Major T. Bouch, at Woolsthorpe, enjoyed two good runs
across a fine hunting country. Many years ago the late King
Edward, when Prince of Wales, also rode in a good hunt from
Folkingham Big Gorse, and there were some left, and riding
with us to-day, who treasure the memory of that occasion.
Folkingham is a little old-world coaching town, most pic-
turesquely placed on the hillside through which passes the
famous London and Lincoln main road. The wide street,
forming a great hollow square of red-brick houses on three

The London–Oxford
mail coach
photographed in May
1890.

sides, is an admirable staging ground for a meet of hounds, and became an established fixture when Sir Gilbert and Lady Greenall ruled over the destinies of the Belvoir. For generations Folkingham was a cherished possession of the Heathcote family, purchased by the first Sir Gilbert Heathcote, of the Durdans, Epsom, just before he won the Derby with Amato, the bells in the fine church tower which crowns the hilltop ringing out a merry peal to honour that occasion.

A good riding field assembled, noticeable for the number and excellence of the young hunters bred and made in the district, which offers the opportunity to thoroughly learn their business when crossing a country that stands no trifling with. The assembly of sightseers is always a congratulation at this fixture, the fine roads and the convenience of the old coaching inns favouring those on wheels who delight to view the stirring scenes of the chase, their interest and good-will being a valuable asset for the welfare of fox-hunting. The hounds arrived in the motor-van from Belvoir, twenty-five miles distant, in charge of Nimrod Capell, the kennel-huntsman and first whipper-in, who, with an admiring crowd around the $15\frac{1}{2}$ couples of graceful ladies, was busy recruiting puppy-walkers. Major Bouch arrived with the

Duke of York, and a nice-sized field included Mrs. Bouch, sen., Lady Helen Brocklehurst, Lord Ivor Churchill, Sir George Whichcote (Field-Master) and others. The Duke, who was mounted by the Master, was riding Wood-pigeon, a big brown horse that Major Whyte-Melville might have described as "the clipper that stands in the stall at the top". Well, Wood-pigeon deserves the title, for he has the best-laid shoulder you could desire for a hunter, and was purchased this season at Colonel R. Clayton-Swan's sale of hunters for 1025 guineas.

Hounds moved away to Folkingham Little Gorse, and without delay Nimrod Capell's cap notified the well-known bob-brushed fox away from the west side of covert, with a point for the line of country that at once delights the eye of the riding man. Major Bouch quickly had the pack laid on, and after hunting steadily across the parched fallows, they swung left-handed to the line of grass along the brookside, and raced away as only Belvoir bitches can. Crossing the brook half a mile from the town, they sped on up the grass slope for the windmill, and the field scattered right and left, riding in hot haste to find a possible crossing. Some big blackthorn fences gave the leading division plenty to do to keep with hounds, who crossed the Bourne and Sleaford main road, going away across the undulating line of grass to Laughton Oaks. Here the hunted one was evidently headed, for he turned left-handed and travelled the line of plough country by Laughton Manor, going on upwind nearly to Sempringham. Scent was not so serving on the plough, and, gaining distance, he beat his pursuers after completing a big ring, in a hunt lasting fifty minutes. Folkingham Big Gorse did not respond to the call, but Heathcote's Covert next supplied a fox, roused in the belt of young firs in the valley, planted by the late Mr. "Tom" Heathcote. A nice hunt of forty-five minutes resulted through the beautiful woodlands of Keisby, Aslackby, and Irnham, where sanctuary was found.

H.R.H. the Duke of York expressed pleasure with the day's sport, and his torn scarlet coat testified to an encounter with the Folkingham blackthorn fences during the first twenty minutes, which was far and away the best.

WHIPSTER.   15 April 1922

PRINCES' DAY WITH THE COTTESMORE.

A gig.

A heaven-born morning of spring rather than winter, glinting sunshine, and silvery vapour, Leicestershire smiled in fascinating mood to welcome the Cottesmore on Saturday last. The fixture was at the house at Somerby of Mr. "Sam" Hames, one who has shown two if not three generations the shortest way to hounds. An exceptionally large following included the Prince of Wales and the Duke of York to greet the Master, Mr. J. W. Baird, who hunted hounds himself for a week in the absence of his huntsman. Welsh, however, to-day was back again in the saddle after his accident. There is inspiration in numbers, and it was the largest and smartest hunting assembly of fair ladies and scarlet we have seen for several seasons, the best of youth and horses that England can show, and many gallant elders who have ridden all their time with the Cottesmore. There were moments to view the whole following as they rode in the wake of hounds across the great green rollers of Leicestershire, an army with the delight of battle in their hearts, man and horse—as perfect a riding

43

fixture of four hundred or more imaginable. But Leicestershire is the country of many a song and story, and we call to mind the graceful lines of one riding on this occasion, a gallant ex-Master, whose pen gained inspiration when hunting the Belvoir over these classic acres:—

"Here sleeps the vale with its morning mist
Spread like a guardian angel's pinions;
Out of it soar the hills dawn-kissed,
Apparelled in garments of amethyst,
Into ætherial domains.
And over the hills there are hills again,
Hills and a valley, hills and a plain;
And wherever you go, or wherever you are,
The delectable land lies ever so far.
Over the hills, where it always lay—
Over the hills and far away!"

The Belvoir and Quorn fixtures were wide of Melton, so all Leicestershire on this day rode with the Cottesmore, glad to be in the saddle and on the grass, in fair weather and surroundings, after the drenchings of dreary November, when twelve soakings were registered in thirteen days' consecutive hunting. Leicestershire huntsmen are to the manner born. The tall figure of Welsh with his hounds flitted hither and thither, never in a hurry, but always with them, unconscious of the following crowd, or sightseers ahead. To start with a hesitating fox paid the penalty in Hames's Gorse, and unsuccessful raids were made on Peake's Cover and the Punch Bowl, but the Dalby Hall Plantations provided a pilot which ran across to the Wheathills. It was a pretty hunt at times, and there was scent on the grass, a fast burst away over the Pickwell and Little Dalby road ending with a kill by Leesthorpe. In this well-foxed area hounds were on the move and never off the grass all the afternoon, although scent was in favour of the pursued.

The two Princes at the conclusion of the day's sport returned to Craven Lodge, Melton Mowbray, and were present at the dance that night attended by many prominent hunting people.

WHIPSTER   11 December 1926

FROM THE PYTCHLEY COUNTRY.

THERE was a regular old-fashioned Pytchley crowd out at Oxenden on Saturday, the occasion being the meet after Mrs. Ismay's most successful ball on Friday, at which the whole world attended and refreshed exceedingly well. However, when the Masters elected to go to Waterloo Gorse by way of the slippery Cresta Run on the Harborough road a general sob of dismay arose as the field for the first time realised the effect of "the night before" and all that their vanishing spirits meant. It was pleasant, very, to see in our midst once more Mrs. Borwick and her daughter, who had torn themselves away from the delights of the Middleton, and to notice that the daughter had inherited the seat of her mother and of her grandfather, "Bay" Middleton. It was like old times, too, to see Hubbersty of the Quorn, one of the best men who ever rode to hounds with that famous pack, but who was for some time incapacitated by illness; and we love hearing that that marvellous old gentleman Sam Hames still rides all day and every day on anything and everything, in the front rank. Everybody seemed to be at Oxenden, although what the owner of Papillon was doing on his feet, instead of witching the world with good and finished horsemanship, I cannot imagine.

Hounds found at once in Waterloo, and ran up a raging wind with a rare cry for one field, when their fox turned down-wind and, running a left-hand ring, returned to the covert. Again he essayed to leave, and this time headed for the railway, where he met, not a man but men, and many of them, and once more returned to the covert. Do I not know it all, and the brave deeds that were done as I stood still on the hill above the gorse—almost as good a vantage point as Robin a Tipeoe in Leicestershire!

They came with the rush of the southern surf
  On the bar of the storm-girt bay;
And like muffled drums on the sounding turf
  Their hoof-strokes echo away.

For a third time the fox broke away and presently ran to

ground near Braybrook, with the champagne-drinkers now beginning to wonder whether the world was not upside down. Finding again in Loatland Wood, hounds ran like mad, parallel to the lane, to ground at the Midland Railway. About a dozen took part in the mad pursuit over the fences close to the lane. Hounds found again in the gorse near Sunderland Wood, and after passing through Rabbit Hill put their fox to ground close to Harrington. As usual, Blue Covert proved a sure find, and hounds ran hard to Scotland Wood and back, once more to ground; and so home.

Monday saw the Pytchley at Great Billing on, actually, a fine morning for a change—but what a season! Report goes that Captain Venn has resigned the secretaryship, and it is, as everybody knows, a difficult and rather thankless task.

A former Master of the Pytchley, who probably knows more of the history of the Hunt than any living man, writes to remind me that Charles Isaac was the hero of the "Galloping Whip" poem, and not John Isaac. Charles is still alive, and, as everybody knows, was promoted from first whipper-in with the Pytchley to being Mr. Fernie's huntsman. For many years he showed great sport with Fernie's, and was indeed *fidus Achates* to his Master and Mrs. Fernie. John, who joined the great majority a year or so ago, became huntsman to the Pytchley under that great and knowledgeable Master Willie Wroughton, than whom very few men ever worked harder for their country. He knew more about the Pytchley coverts and how to look after them than any man in recent years, and to this day sees as much sport as anybody when hounds really run.

It's a long way to Tipperary—at least so the song said, and a good song too, during the war; but in these days everything is forgotten at once. I should, however, be wanting in my duty, especially to the so-called fair sex, if I did not remind them of an episode reported quite lately in the papers, of how a lady—name unknown, of course—*very nearly* kicked a certain Gentleman (big "G" in gentleman, please, Mr. Editor) out hunting. That lady cannot have been very young or have ever been at school, as otherwise she would easily have kicked any gentleman, even above his head; but of course that would not be done—*could* not be done—in public, in what we may call full dress. But when, shall we say

46

Tattersall's old sales yard in Knightsbridge, London. For many years horse auctions were held each Monday.

properly attired, young ladies can easily kick over a man's head. If however, she just fails and has a shoe on, it is apt to hurt the young man's forehead, but I am assured that in the Pytchley country no foreheads are bruised in that way. The ladies know their business far too well.

It is unfortunately common property now that the Joint-Masters have resigned the Mastership of the Fernie. We hear various names mentioned as their successors, but imagine nothing is yet settled, although there seems a chance of an amateur, well known in the Midlands, carrying the horn; or possibly of another American invasion and, of course, victory. There can be, alas! no return to the old days when "the two ladies" led the Hunt, and it was ever "encore une victoire," as Eugene de Beauharnais wrote to Napoleon, Carlins Spinney gave us a Marengo, Walton Holt an Austerlitz, and Glooston the Bridge of Lodi. Cavalry charges worthy of the Old Guard took place then out hunting, and the devil indeed took the hindmost. Arthur Thatcher, flinging away his horn (!!!) and waving us on with his hand (do I dream, do I dream?), even as Murat threw down his sword to lead with a riding whip the cavalry at Jena. George Brudenell, who has reminded me of all this, was at the zenith of his form, with that fine horseman Harry Mills bearing the burden and heat of the hunt when the humour took him; and when the Man with the Black Cap and old Tom Hobbs went sailing along like pigeons, and Arthur Thatcher could catch blue-rocks, as indeed he can to-day when the band plays. And may he do it again and again is the wish of all of us.

And still of a night, when the moonlight is stealing
    Across the dark ride of the woodland, they say
The shade of old Thatcher is seen, ever feeling
    The reins as he handles the shade of the grey.

And over the open still lashing and driving,
    The phantom-shaped pack ever gallantly fly:
Each hound in his place, and the leaders contriving
    To keep up the pace, for the scent is breast high.

And still in the hunt—there are those who maintain it—
    Unseen in the daylight he rides by your side,
And when you have got a good start, and retain it,
    He moves you to gallop and stirs you to ride.

CORONET.   28 January 1928

VARIOUS QUESTIONS ANSWERED.

SIR,—The habit of rolling when fording a stream or crossing muddy land like plough is quite natural to any horse when at liberty, and the wonder to me is that more do not do it when under saddle.

If any of your correspondents do not feel equal to it himself, let him put someone else up armed with an ashplant, and when the horse gives the signal of what he is about to do let him drop him "a domino," as they say, on his near-side ear—not on the poll (too dangerous), nor yet the off-side ear, by missing which you might hit his eye.

Two or three good plugs in the ribs with the spurs should send him forward and put such thoughts out of his head. A few lessons like this should cure him. The stick should be carried over the shoulder like a drawn sword.

A large black sow belonging to a neighbouring farmer was turned loose to do some acorning in a fox-covert of mine. She farrowed a litter of pigs in a dry ditch outside the covert, and a fox was seen to come out and snap them up just after they were born and carry them away to a distance, and some of the earlier ones were found bitten and half-buried.

There is no cure for a kicker, but if you do find yourself in a crowded gateway (which you "didn't ought") "niggle" at her mouth and make her feel as uncomfortable and self-conscious as possible till you get free.

If she should kick, and you can bring your crop down on her near-side ear at the "psychological moment," do so. She may connect cause with effect. But do not (as some do) take her out of the crowd and then give her a hiding. She won't know what it is for. As she is only four she may grow out of it. I would much sooner hope for this in a mare than a gelding.

If it is certain, after dosing for them, that worms are not the cause of a dog's skin irritation, drop all bread and biscuit in the diet and feed raw meat alone.

It is very difficult, once a grey is badly stained, to get it out. Try a little ammonia in the water and some powdered blue. When nearly dry rub in some whitening and brush off in the morning. To prevent staining, the best bed is peat-moss or sawdust, with no straw, but it must be laid very thick—8in at least. At night an extra rug can be put on back to front, the chest part buckled above the hocks.

As to the tongue over the bit, if you want to tie the tongue down don't use a strap or tape. Both of them cause much pain and discomfort. I have seen a tongue so swollen at the end of a day that it was a matter of difficulty to get the strap off. Take a big skein of thick Berlin wool and cut it through. Draw the tongue forward and put the wool over the tongue. Divide one side into two, and put the whole of the other side between; draw quite tight and tie together under the jaw. This will not hurt the tongue or the horse in the least, but it is not a method I care for myself. Another dodge is to ride him in a plain jointed snaffle. Thread a piece of thick indiarubber elastic through the joint, take both ends upwards, and fasten to the front of the noseband, tight enough so that when the reins are slack the mouth-piece is pulled up and lies against the horse's palate.

Another plan is to have a snaffle bridle fitted with the extra head-piece required for two snaffles, but with buckles on but no reins. Hang a small bridoon loose in his mouth, fairly high up in the corners; if this has no effect add another one, and yet another, and go on until his mouth is full. This is nearly always effective. One horse I know was cured by fastening the whole of a big carriage sponge to the bit.

F. H. UNWIN   8 February 1935

"HORSE & HOUND" LUNCHEON.

THE *Horse and Hound* Luncheon was held on June 24 1935, at the Park Lane Hotel, Piccadilly and was generally regarded as a most successful and enjoyable affair. It was a get together of over 360 readers and supporters of *Horse and Hound* and included many well-known and distinguished sportsmen.

SIR FREDERICK HOBDAY, F.R.C.V.S., C.M.G., F.R.S.E., Principal and Dean of the Royal Veterinary College, was in the chair.

The speakers included Sir Walter Gilbey who thanked *Horse and Hound* for what the paper had done to encourage children's riding, and the breeding of good quality horses and ponies; Mr. John Corfield, "Stubbins", a popular and regular contributor, Commander A. B. Campbell, a member of the B.B.C. Brains Trust, and Mr. A. F. B. Portman. Also Professor Sir Frederick Hobday, who said:

"Sir, I feel honoured in having been asked to preside at this luncheon. It is a very great occasion, and one which I appreciate much more highly than I can express. Your paper, sir, is over fifty years old, and is appreciated in every sporting establishment in Britain. It is equally popular in the saddle-room as it is in the master's study. Your quality seems to be that you particularly encourage the younger generation not only to ride but also to look after their horses and ponies properly. The attention which you give to the Pony Clubs is full evidence of that. What strikes me more than anything else in your columns is the amazing knowledge of 'Audax' in the pedigrees and life-history of practically every well-known racehorse. To me it seems a terribly hard task to fill those 'Turf and Stud Gossip' columns week after week, and as a brother journalist I raise my hat to you. The only things I will not follow are your tips!

"Of the extent of your courtesy and generosity I know full well, for it was your paper which collected £5000 for my old College through your columns at a time when we were in despair. With walls propped up, roofs leaking, and everything old and tumbling down, we had almost given up the

E. TAUTZ & SONS,

BREECHES MAKERS,

MILITARY TAILORS

and OUTFITTERS.

Hunting, Riding, Racing, Polo, and Shooting Breeches in all materials.

Buckskins, Hunting and Military.

ORIGINAL Makers of the KNICKERBOCKER BREECHES, designed to wear for SHOOTING or RIDING, with BOOTS, LEGGINGS, or STOCKINGS.

Beware of IMITATIONS of above.

Special Materials for Breeches and Suits for INDIA, the COLONIES, or for FOREIGN SERVICE. LEGGINGS and GAITERS of all kinds. SPATS, RIDING TROUSERS, CAVALRY OVERALLS and PANTALOONS. Speciality in PINKS, RIDING SUITS, COVERT COATS, DRIVING COATS, HUNTING WAISTCOATS, HUNTING and RIDING DRAWERS, KNEE-CAPS, RIDING or DRIVING APRONS, and RUGS.

THOROUGHLY WATERPROOF BLACK or OXFORD MELTON FOR HUNTING COATS.

RACING COLOURS.

Breeches Trees, Hunting Cases, Knives, Riding, Driving, or Military Gloves, Riding Belts.

E. TAUTZ & SONS' Bleaching Powder for cleaning LEATHERS, and Fluid for restoring PINK COATS.

NOTICE.

LADIES' DEPARTMENT for HABITS and BREECHES of SPECIAL CUT.

Ladies' Measurer and Fitter kept.

Patterns and Instructions for SELF-MEASUREMENT forwarded on application.

485, Oxford Street, London, W.

84 Rue du Faubourg, St. Honore, Paris.

N.B.—No Other Address.

struggle; but with the help of your Fund and the propaganda which it engendered we took the new lease of life which has led to the production of entirely new laboratories, loose boxes, and hospital equipment such as we are not ashamed to show to foreigners, as well as British visitors.

I feel quite sure that this luncheon is the predecessor of many successful gatherings." (Hear, hear.) After Mr. Portman had expressed thanks to Sir Frederick for presiding the proceedings terminated.

28 June 1935

A REMARKABLE STAGHUNT.

SIR,—I read in last week's issue an account of a memorable day with the Devon and Somerset Staghounds. What do you think of the following account of another memorable day, with a vengeance? It is headed "A remarkable run with the King's Buckhounds in August, 1681." The reigning monarch then would have been Charles II., and I presume the Duke of York his brother:—

"A stag was roused at Swinley rails, in Windsor Forest, which, bending his course northwards over Broad Commons through Bray Woods, crossed the River Thames at Maidenhead and through the County of Bucks, between High Wycombe and Beaconsfield. Passing by the towns of Amersham and Chesham he made over the hills toward Berkhampstead, in Herts. Then, turning eastward to Redburn and Hatfield, he crossed the river (Lea) a little below Hoddesdon and entered the County of Essex. Was afterwards driven to Epping, High Ongar Park, Kelvedon Common, Pilgrim's Hatch, Brentwood, and Thorndon Park, near Lord Petre's house, where he fell gloriously, after running a course of seventy miles and upwards. The Duke of York rode the whole chase and, with five persons more, was in at the death."

I make the point from near Maidenhead, where the stag crossed the Thames, to Thorndon Park, where he was killed, a good forty-five miles, and, by measuring on the map the actual length of the run, as described, I cannot make it less than ninety-five miles as hounds ran—truly a "remarkable"

performance, which took place 254 years ago, and what a nice trot back to Windsor they must have had after killing their stag, for as the crow flies it is forty miles. Doubtless they lay out at Thorndon Park or somewhere handy for that night.

The Duke of York and his five companions who were in at the death must have been well mounted, and their horses in wonderful condition to have got through a nice little hunt of ninety-five miles! They must have well understood all about "condition," both in horses and hounds, in those days to have survived a hunt of that distance and duration. Doubtless hounds were not very fast, and allowing that they travelled on an average six miles an hour all through it would have been a hunt of some 16 hours! Yours, &c.,

P.   9 August 1935

ORIGIN OF SCARLET AND GREEN.
BY LADY APSLEY

SIR,—I read once that "deerhound packs as the senior branch stuck to red coats." Surely the fact is that with ancient staghounds the correct wear was green. Most of our hunting customs came from France. The Norman barons imported ideas of "benerie" or hunting as a sport as distinct from hunting as a food-catching or vermin-slaying operation. Throughout the Middle Ages green was the correct colour

53

of venerie for the greenwood. Staghunting took place in the summer, and green was worn by all true *veneurs* hunting the hart, as grey was the colour for wild-boar hunting in winter. Red was added about the time of that ardent hunter Francis I. of France; old writers describe the gay cavalcades setting out with ladies dressed in red and green.

Red has ever been the colour for Royal livery; French servants out hunting, *valets-de-chiens*, &c., would wear Royal livery. In France staghunting was strictly limited to the King only, and anyone who wanted to hunt deer hunted with the King—if of suitable rank.

French ideas as the *dernier cri* were imported into England at various times; the French ambassadors laughed heartily at Queen Elizabeth's ideas of staghunting—pot shots with a cross-bow or "arblast" at park deer, coursed by a magnificent breed of strong swift hounds who were trained to seize a wounded hart or buck by the ear and hold it until someone came up to slit its throat.

French hunting customs were in use in Scotland and introduced to England by James I., who imported French *veneurs* from the Court of Henri IV. and Louis XIII. "to teach his English huntsmen to hunt a stag after the French fashion." Hence came much of our hound language and horn music.

In the early days of staghunting in England every gentleman was an accomplished *veneur*, and only gentlemen rode to hounds—the others ran on foot. But relatively soon, red deer, owing to their depredations in the open fields, were banished to out-back hills, Exmoor, the Welsh marches, remaining slips of Royal Forests, &c., while fallow deer were confined to paled parks.

"Lincoln green" was ever the colour connected with forest country. English forests dated back to at least the time of Canute, and were not thick woods but the unenclosed, well-marked area of the King's private hunting preserves—right to hunt there was a great privilege. The Stuarts, at wits' end for money, perforce sold many of these forest rights. Falconry was the golf and tennis of Tudor and Stuart days. King Charles's falconers were dressed in red.

When foxhunting evolved in the late seventeenth century it continued many of the customs of venerie and the Royal

Mr Dorian Williams, MFH, Chairman of The British Horse Society 1975.

staghunting of France, including green coats in the hunting field. Hunting the hare for a long time was the premier sport of the eighteenth-century squires, green being naturally adopted as the "field sport" colour, as, unlike the fox, the hare had ever been a "beast of venerie."

As professional Hunt staffs came gradually into use, like other private servants of the time they wore their employers' livery. The accounts of an Elizabethan steward at Berkeley Castle refer to the green cloth and the bales of "orange tawny" bought for the Hunt staff of the day—employed, by the way, in any sport from buckhunting to hawking for larks!

The Duke of Beaufort's livery is blue and buff; blue being said to have been adopted in the days of Jacobite sympathisers, as yellow was later by Whig noblemen. The Duke's Hunt staff wear green by right of their status as staghunters of the old days: likewise the Heythrop, which formerly belonged to Dukes of Beaufort living at the old Heythrop House!

The Hunt servants of the Royal Buckhounds of course wore Royal livery, like other Royal servants, the Master being privileged to wear the green plush coat. The staff of the New Forest Buckhounds wear green, and many Hunt uniforms are witness to former staghunting or harrier connections by green collars on their red coats, such as the New Forest Foxhounds or the Tedworth.

Followers of hounds in the eighteenth century mostly wore their ordinary clothes out hunting—plush coats of various colours. Red as a uniform for foxhunting commenced in the middle of Mr. Hugo Meynell's long Mastership, and by 1820 was definitely established as the foxhunter's colour. The reason is said to have been that as hunting is technically a Royal sport it was natural that red should be adopted. But why white breeches? I think that the return of Wellington's young heroes was responsible. Ex-officers in those days continued to wear their uniform in the hunting-field as elsewhere. The Duke made it the fashion for all his officers to hunt, and the splash of scarlet and white had as great a success in the hunting-field as no doubt it had in the drawing-rooms of the day. Gradually, every man with any pretensions to fashion out hunting wore a red coat and white "leathers," only certain provincials who had never come in contact with the young bloods in Leicestershire with Squire Osbaldeston or Assheton-Smith continued to wear old-time livery, "flat hats," bottle-green coats, and fancy collars and waistcoats with "drab cord" breeches.

The wearing of velvet caps out hunting was initiated by George III. (see Lord Ribblesdale's "The Queen's Hounds"). Previous to this the velvet cap was the hall mark of the private mounted servant—postilions, out-riders, jockeys, &c.; coach-men, grooms on second horses, &c., wearing hats with crowns like their masters. I believe Squire Osbaldeston was the first M.F.H. hunting hounds himself to wear a velvet cap—many professional huntsmen and amateurs wore "flat hats" then and for some years.

25 October 1935

THE MYSTERIES OF SCENT.
BY COLONEL A. V. T. WAKELY, D.S.O., M.C.

ON February 28th last a pamphlet by Flight Lieutenant Veryard, R.A.F., dealing with some investigations on scent in India was reviewed in these columns. In the following issue of "Horse and Hound" Mr. H. M. Budgett drew attention to several points in which the results obtained in India were at variance with his theories as expounded in his book "Hunting by Scent." This is not surprising.

No scientist will disagree with the statement that if two people make experiments under widely different conditions, such as those existing in England on the one hand and in India on the other, they are hardly likely to arrive at identical results. It is sufficient to give two simple examples of how varying circumstances can affect results.

Mr. Budgett describes very clearly in his book how he measures the temperature of the ground. He does it by inserting the bulb of the thermometer just underneath the soil. In meteorological records as used by Mr. Veryard in India, temperature at the ground is recorded by a thermo-meter lying just above the surface. There may be a considerable difference between the two readings.

Mr. Budgett maintains that scent is at its best when the

ground temperature, as measured by his method, is greater than that of the air—i.e., when the ground is warmer than the air. But his opinion is not at variance with Mr. Veryard's contention that scent is best when the air above the ground is stable. Both conditions can, and frequently do, exist at the same instant. Again, in India, due to the effect of the hot sun, there can be a difference of as much as 30° F. between the temperature near the surface of the ground and the temperature at a height of a couple of yards. In India such a condition can, and frequently does, destroy any chance of good scent, but it cannot occur in England owing to our different climate.

Since the review of Mr. Veryard's booklet was published some further investigations have been made in this country. Notes of the scent on about 300 hunting days were very kindly supplied by Mr. Budgett from his hunting diary, and they have been compared with meteorological records. In nearly every case it was found that there was a meteorological explanation for good or bad scent. It was also found that the results were illustrated and confirmed by statements in Mr. Budgett's book and by practically similar statements in Mr. Veryard's pamphlet. This does not look as if their theories were in opposition.

Mr. Budgett has shown us in his book how scent is produced. Each time the fox puts a pad on the ground he deposits some scent-oil. This evaporates and forms scent-vapour, which is a gas. It is this gas that hounds smell.

You cannot see the scent-oil deposited by a fox. You have to use a microscope. The particles of scent-vapour are smaller still. They are like the air, quite invisible. In nature small things like these are very rapidly destroyed by the powerful forces that act upon them. The minute particles of scent-vapour would have a bad time in a gale strong enough to blow your hat off or uproot trees. They would not have much chance of existence in a sun fierce enough to burn up the grass like it does in India.

In the theories of scent which have been so admirably explained by Mr. Budgett and Mr. Veryard, the most important stage is the change from scent-oil to scent-vapour, or the vaporisation of the oil. The latter, having been deposited by the fox, must evaporate either slowly or rapidly or not at all. If it hardly evaporates at all, as occurs when the ground is very cold, there will be very little scent indeed. Hounds cannot smell the oil—it is the vapour from the oil that they smell.

If the scent-oil evaporates fairly slowly the remaining oil forms a sort of reservoir for scent-vapour giving off only so much at a time. This is the best condition for a lasting scent, because there is a continuous supply of vapour until all the scent oil is exhausted. It is like a lighted cigarette end thrown on the ground and giving off smoke until it is burnt out or goes out.

The scent-vapour, when produced by evaporation, can only do two things. It can go downwards into the ground, or upwards into the air. Mr. Budgett has shown that it can be inhaled into the ground, and we can see our cigarette smoke going upwards. When the scent vapour ascends like that it can be received by the hounds' nostrils, provided that it is not washed away by rain nor blown away by wind before the hounds reach it. If the meteorological conditions are such that scent-vapour is being given off slowly and is not being inhaled into the ground nor blown nor washed away, we shall get a continuous supply of vapour for the hounds for a limited time until all the fox's scent-oil is used up.

Thus, the quality of the scent which hounds get depends, in the first instance, upon the amount of scent-oil deposited by the fox and the rate of its evaporation. As soon as scent-vapour is produced, other forces at once act upon it, such as temperature, humidity, wind, and rain. It is the play of these forces which makes scent good, fair, catchy, or bad. The above, in non-technical language, is the theory of scent as propounded by our scientists.

It is of interest to give the general results of the investigations into scenting conditions on 300 hunting days, to which reference has already been made. In the table below the results are shown as percentages of the total days studied:—

	Days.
Good scent	15 per cent.
Fair scent	45 ,, ,,
Bad scent	40 ,, ,,

Causes of bad scent:—

	Of total days.
Cold weather and ground colder than the air	13 per cent.
High wind or gales	11 ,, ,,
Heavy rain	5 ,, ,,
Dry Air	4 ,, ,,
Hot Sun	2 ,, ,,
No meteorological cause found	5 ,, ,,
	40 ,, ,,

From this rather imperfect survey we can see the kind of forces that act upon the scent-oil and scent-vapour causing scent to be bad. They are cold weather, cold ground, gales, heavy rain, hot sun, and dry air. When these predominate scent is bad. The favourable factors are moisture, light rain, settled weather, and light warm breezes. When these are in the ascendency scent is good.

When the favourable and unfavourable factors are about equal scent is likely to be moderate. When the bad factors are slightly stronger than the good, scent will be indifferent or catchy. Other comparisons can easily be made.

It may be noted also that the balance between these forces can change during the day, and we all know that there can be bad scent in the morning and good in the afternoon, and vice versa. The worst part of this investigation is the discovery that our wretched climate is responsible for 120 really bad days' hunting out of 300—i.e., 40 per cent. The bad weather is a real enemy of foxhunting, nearly as bad as any of the "five f.s"—frost, fog, floods, foot-and-mouth, and funerals. The first three of these are particularly obnoxious forms of bad weather, because they stop us hunting altogether.

3 July 1936

The late Mr Lionel Edwards.

BREEDING FOR STRENGTH AND QUALITY.

Sir,—Whilst I am in general agreement with the prejudice against the modern Hackney, it is quite true that the roadster, also called a Hackney until about 1870, was a type that furnished many valuable mares for hunter-breeding in Yorkshire. I remember these roadsters well. Many of them were 15 hands 2in to 15 hands 3in, compact, active, and good hunters, as well as ideal hacks. They were in some degree responsible for the outstanding reputation of Yorkshire hunters in the last century. They bore no resemblance to the modern Hackney. As there were no stud books in those days, except the General Stud Book, few of their pedigrees are recorded, yet they were bred with the same skill with which Yorkshire hunters and carriage-horses were produced, and in much the same way.

Yorkshire's former pre-eminence in those directions was due to—first, that the owners of racing sires placed the very best Thoroughbred stallions at the service of the farmers and breeders, including the winners of the classic races, at nominal fees; and, second, that in Yorkshire and adjacent districts there was an even older fixed type than the Thoroughbred—namely, the Cleveland Bay. By a long and careful mixture of these two breeds the very beautiful Yorkshire Coach Horse was evolved as a third fixed type. Both the pure Cleveland and the Yorkshire Coaching breed provided hundreds of mares that were the best for mating with the Thoroughbred for getting high-class hunters up to weight.

The roadsters were often got by or out of Yorkshire Coaching stock, and that gave them their free, fast, and light action as well as stamina. These roadsters or "gentlemen's hacks" were judged at shows by their manners and comfort in all paces, and had to be up to a certain amount of weight.

In the years immediately preceding the publication of the Hackney Stud Book there were two other classes of Hackneys beside these roadsters—Norfolk cobs or trotters; and a high-actioned Hackney, largely Norfolk in origin. Both these were driven as well as ridden by farmers and breeders. Some very good hunters were bred from the mares of the latter, and I have had a good and clever hunter (not fast) by a Norfolk cob out of a blood hunter mare. Both sorts had great wear-and-tear qualities, and as everyone knows, had racing blood in their veins. We had a very fast "Shepherd F. Knapp" Hackney, a terrible puller, and in one desperate attempt to get him to "settle down" he was allowed to go sixty miles in about four hours on the hard high road; but he pulled as hard at the end as at the start; and about settled the driver. He had legs and feet like iron, and his legs never filled. I mention this as evidence of courage and stamina in the Hackney.

The Holderness clean-legged cart breed has died out, as the similar one in the North Riding and Durham and the Northumberland Vardy did long ago. Of course, these were superior sources of strength to the coarse, hairy-heeled, heavy draught breeds of to-day.

My father, who represented the West of Durham County from 1865 to 1903, travelled Norfolk cob stallions to improve the breed, and the late Sir Jonathan Backhouse, Bt., also travelled some excellent pony stallions in the dales with more quality than the Norfolk cobs, but all these stallions were great improvers.

At the present time the general idea in England is that the only way to get weight-carrying power is to use modern coarse heavy draught blood directly or indirectly on the female side, which are the worst possible strains for their purpose. They have allowed all the old sources of strength which could be tapped without loss of activity, courage, stamina, and quality to die out, such as the roadster, the Yorkshire Coach horse, and the clean-legged active cart breeds. They have allowed the most valuable of all, the Cleveland Bay, by long-continued neglect, to dwindle in numbers.

ALFRED E. PEASE   19 February 1937

MORE FROM THE BORDER.

"Then hey for boot and spur, lad, and round the world away,
For youth must have its fling, lad, and every dog his day."

IN response to many letters, I have written to my friend Ivor Humbug, the famous whipper-in to the Scruff and Sniffem, about writing his reminiscences, but have as yet had no reply. Personally, I do not think it is a good idea. "A little leaven leaveneth the whole lump" is a truth to be remembered by those of us who attempt to interest and amuse our fortunate fellow beings by writing in this paper and elsewhere. "A *little* leaven" I said—or perhaps Leonard, our barman, would express my meaning more clearly with his famous refusal to have just one more. "Too much pudden would choke a dog," says he, and I feel sure that we would very soon have a surfeit of Ivor Humbug and his life-story.

Apart from that, we are in trouble about it. The post-man arrived with a most suspicious registered envelope; and it is not money that comes in registered envelopes, my dear—not these days (its cruel hard, Mr. Editor, when one hides in the kennel to dodge the bum-bailiff, and in the loft to evade the policeman, and then the postman brings them and you have to sign for them). But this was neither a writ nor a summons, but merely this letter:—

"Sir,—I take this opportunity of writing to express in very strong terms the disapproval and resentment that I feel over the letter you published from a certain Ivor Humbug. I take it as a direct insult to myself and to my Hunt staff, and demand

an apology in next week's publication, or my solicitors will write to you. I also wish to ascertain how you came to hear of this occurrence, as the owner of the circus was heavily compensated to retain his discretion in the matter. In any case, the animal was a camel and not, as you erroneously state, a dromedary.—Yours faithfully—".

I cannot give you his signature, as it is a household word, and needless to say a letter of explanation was sent at once. It just shows how careful one must be. It is only this necessary solicitude that deters me, too, from entering the ranks of the "reminiscencers" I somehow think I could tell a tale or two.

Yes, I am quite sure I could tell a tale or two! I could tell you tales of Mardale Green and dear old Joe Bowman, and "Brait Wilson", to whom perhaps I will ever be in debt for his unfailing kindness and help to me, when, as a very little boy, I used to follow him as best I could over the fell tops and mountains of that country that must ever be home to me and to him. There are tales that I could tell of all that dear land from Sedbergh to the Solway sea, and one day, if I am spared, so I will.

I was thinking the other day about these amazing feats of endurance and skill that these sportsmen apparently so effortlessly perform, and my mind turned to a very curious wager that two of my friends indulged in when we were all, as I tried to say above, "Pattendale lads". Money being scarce, needless to say the stakes were small, but the contest was entered into none the less keenly for that. These two friends of mine gambled that one would ascend five mountains in a week (the last being Scawfell) before his comrade accomplished the same feat, and the debt would be discharged before closing time on the Saturday evening at the Dungeon Ghyll Hotel.

But not only had they to ascend Saddleback, Helvellyn, Skiddaw, Crossfell, and Scawfell in the seven days; they also had to persuade a member of the opposite sex to climb with them, and a different one upon each occasion, and to kiss her upon reaching the summit; and she had, so to speak, to reciprocate—no struggling and no pecking on the cheek; the genuine thing, if you understand me. Although this would have been a very difficult task for many people to undertake, my two friends had very little difficulty, although one of them had to make three ascents of Helvellyn before he could satisfy the conditions of the wager on the summit. And then at last there were a party of sandwich-eaters right on the very cairn itself—and my friend was modest. I am afraid he was no gentleman, either, for he could not wait for his companion to potter and falter back along Striking Edge, but rushed head-long down into Grisdale by himself, and made what haste he could to get to Scawfell before his rival.

There are several ways of ascending Scawfell, but it is a long climb in any case, and great difficulty (this being miles out of my friends' stumping ground) was experienced in

64

getting the right sort of companions for the ascent. It was Saturday afternoon before the attempt was made, and I remember climbing—or rather I remember *my friend* telling me how he was laughing to himself when he reached the cross where the track runs down to Styhead, with no sign of his rival, and he going at his ease with the most delightful companion imaginable. On they went, both enjoying themselves immensely, when suddenly above them descended apparently an avalanche, and to my friends' dismay down the mountain in great leaps and bounds, amidst a shower of small stones came his rival, whilst holding him firmly by the hand, her face wreathed in smiles, was a tremendous fourteen-stone female, with a countenance like the map of Ireland, only rather less picturesque.

Mrs Pat Keochlin Smythe.

"I win, I think," shouted the rival, pausing in his descent. "And you deserve to," said my particular friend, surveying the other half of the winning team. "But I think I will finish the course," said he, "in case there is an objection." There was no objection. What curious things one does (or one's friends do) when one (or one's friends) is young.

Last Wednesday week we met at Little Stretton, and Mr. and Mrs. Simonds welcomed us most hospitably. The pup they walked last year, and the best bitch we have, very wisely stayed behind at the farm instead of going with us to draw Rayleth. It was a very bad-scenting day, and we had a lot of hunting, but could not catch a fox.

Next morning the "Stratford Express" was on the road soon after six, and we were at the Welcome Monument as the clock struck ten. "There are seven foxes in my four-acre covert," said our secretary. He was wrong—there were at least ten. Never was there such a capital little fox-covert anywhere. Hounds hunted well, in spite of innumerable halloes and wild cries, eventually going away and killing a fox in the fields above the covert. A hunted fox had gone on to Clifton Gorse, and hounds raced this one around the covert and caught him, too. And so home.

Next morning it was so foggy that we deliberated a great deal before we eventually went to beagle at the Cider House Pool, where Tom Botwood was indignantly awaiting us. Moving off we found a hare at once, but hounds slipped us in the mist, and we found them miles away by the Newtown

66

road at fault. On the following morning, after a very wet night, we found a fox below Spring Hill, but could do very little with him in the bracken. "I do not believe you," said I to "Salopian", "when you write that a pack you were with last week hunted well in the impenetrable and unending bracken". "So they did," he said, "and yours will when there's a scent". At half-past two we found again on Graig Hill, and hounds found their noses, so to speak, at 5 o'clock. Frank went home on his four year old, and we managed to stop hounds soon after, still running hard through bracken 4 ft. high.

On Monday was our opening meet, by invitation of the Warwickshire, at the Dun Cow, and we had a fair day, killing a fox in the afternoon from Red Hill. "Couldn't he get over the wire, Maister?" said Ted, our honorary terrier-man, arriving almost exhausted in company with "Gunga Din", whose halloa had put us right. And so home, and, instead of to bed, to write this; and now it is half-past twelve.

DALESMAN   5 November 1937

BRIGHTON BEAGLES' MEMORABLE FOXHUNT

SIR,—In reply to "Beagler," I was one of the only two persons who saw this hunt right through; the other was Johnson, the professional huntsman to the pack. I was whipping-in to him.

This fine hunt took place on December 26th, 1922, after hounds had met at the kennels (then at West Blachington). We had one or two good hunts in the morning. Then, as the last hare we hunted ran into a patch of kale close to the kennels, a fox went away on the other side. Hounds picked up the line at once, and nothing could stop them. They went on through the Hove allotment gardens, swinging left-handed round the kennels and going down Toads Hole.

Johnson and I stopped at the kennels to get a bold old hound called Nobleman. When we got back to the road hounds were nearly at the Dyke road, about a mile and a half away. Fortunately at that moment a car came along, and we (including Nobleman) got in, and were driven to the Dyke road. By this time hounds had crossed Water Hall Valley and were going up Water Hall Brow. They checked here for a short time (the only check of the hunt), and we caught them up. They soon put themselves right, going on over Sweet Hill and by North Heath Barn to West Hill.

Having a good knowledge of the run of foxes in the South-down country, I guessed our fox would swing round for Pond Brow, so persuaded Johnson to cut across in this direction, while I went on with hounds. They ran on to Cow Down and Newtimber Hill, where they made the unexpected (and longed for) turn and came down by Saddlescombe, over the road, and up the hill just south of Pond Brow. Johnson picked them up here and went on well (he was a dead game runner), and several of our field joined in also. Hounds went away over the hill, down by the Dyke Hotel, and killed our fox outside a teahouse—a dog-fox about five or six years old, and weighing about 15lb.

The point was about $3\frac{3}{4}$ miles, and $7\frac{1}{4}$ miles as hounds ran; time, 86min. To the best of my recollection and from my hunting notes this is a true account.

FRED. F. WOOD. 11 March 1938

CONTINENTAL AND ENGLISH RIDING.

SIR,—The various arguments which have appeared in your "Letter Box" concerning Continental and English riding have interested me greatly. In the following comments I will endeavour to explain why differences of opinion exist upon this subject, and try to find their origins. In my opinion the existing differences are due to the historical evolution of riding in the various countries. It is interesting to go far back and study the development of riding, in order to find out the dominating factors which have influenced the various nations to ride in the way they do.

The first of these nations to be discussed are the ancient Greeks. The use of the saddle and stirrup was unknown to them. They rode, as other nations and tribes of those days, on just a rug, but their horsemanship, even so, attained a very high standard. The books of Xenophon (the great cavalry leader of 400 B.C.) are still interesting and worthy of inclusion

Mrs Butcher driving
Mr W. S. Cunard's
Orchards Sensation,
winner of the
Appointments Class at
the International Horse
Show at Olympia in
1908.

in any horseman's library. The reliefs of the Parthenon, to be seen in the British Museum, also provide a very obvious example of the advanced stage of ancient Greek horsemanship.

The Romans did nothing to further the art of riding, and their cavalry was composed chiefly of German and Gaelic horsemen. It is only towards the end of the Western Roman Empire that we first hear of the saddle. Its actual origin is unknown, but it probably came from one of the many nomadic tribes then in Europe. The stirrup was an invention of the Huns. They knocked three pieces of wood together in the form of a triangle, hung one of these on each side of their horse and put their feet into them—hence the stirrup!

Among the ancient Germans there were many mounted tribes such as the Goths, Vandals and Alans. These, however, all perished in North Africa or in the South of Europe, leaving no records of their riding.

The style of riding in the Middle Ages was characterised by the knights, but this age of great romance with its mounted tournaments and displays, contrary to belief, is insignificant where horsemanship is concerned. The knights in their cumbersome suits of armour adopted a rigid and ungainly attitude in the saddle which necessitated their using cruel and severe bits to manage their rather heavy horses. From our point of view not at all an impressive era!

It was only at the height of the Renaissance (the second

half of the sixteenth century), when all art was influenced and revolutionised, that a fundamental change in riding was brought about. While the ancient Romans were unproductive in their riding, their descendants, the Italians, were the people who many years later rejuvenated the classic Greek school of horsemanship.

The following Baroque period, with its pomp and splendour, did not fail to influence the riding of its day. The teaching of the Italians had by then spread to and influenced all European countries. France owed its dominant position in the horse world during the reign of the first three Bourbon kings to Antoine de la Baume Pluvinel, who for nine years studied the low and high schools with the famous Italian Pignatelli.

At the same time England, by breeding the Thoroughbred horse, brought all riding one step further. This achievement was probably the most important happening in the history of the horse and horse-riding.

The eighteenth century continued to improve on the teachings of the old Riding Masters by stressing the importance of greater liberty and suppleness of the trained horse. The severe bits disappeared, and the saying that the less you put in a horse's mouth the better he will go and feel, was generally adopted. Although the fashions of the time demanded elaborate and ostentatious displays of horsemanship, the military riding of this period was content to aim at producing an obedient, enduring, and quick steed, and the Army regulations did not demand any further training.

On the Continent civil riding was undoubtedly influenced by the Army, therefore Continental horsemanship became more standardised. At this point I would like to mention that the education of an army riding instructor on the Continent in pre-War days took five to six years; hunting and race-riding were compulsory.

The Continental countries have always had the same aims as England, namely, the producing of a quick and obedient cross-country horse, but the Continent demands that the same animal be also a well-trained "riding horse," and the reasons for this I will give later.

One must never forget that the foremost happening in the history of the horse is, as previously mentioned, the breeding

Miss Joan Hunloke on Rennet, winner of the class for children's riding pony (rider not over 15), in an early International Horse Show.

of the Thoroughbred horse in England. Without the Thoroughbred we would have no well-bred horses with achievements which have amazed the world. Even in the days of the Romans, the English wild horses were much valued for their speed and endurance, but nobody troubled greatly about their breeding.

During the reign of Henry VII. laws were made to regulate horse-breeding in this country. Henry VIII. followed this good example by instituting stud farms and importing horses from Turkey, Spain, Naples, and Friesland. He also had two pupils of Pignatelli, the great Italian horseman, to improve the standard of riding in this country. Queen Elizabeth, who was similarly enthusiastic, endeavoured to maintain the standard, but it was not until later that Oriental stallions were imported. The progeny of these stallions were a success, and their trials for speed proved satisfactory. The gentlemen of the country eventually developed a taste for matching the speeds of their hunters and riding horses, and these trials, together with the Englishman's love of gambling, were the origin of horse-racing. The first English racing rules were drawn up as a result of the growing popularity of this new form of sport. At this point we must note that, whilst on the Continent "school riding" was at its peak, in England the sport of racing had taken root and was beginning to flourish.

71

Before I discuss further the riding history of England, it is surprising to note that it was not until the end of the nineteenth century that the American (jockey) racing seat was generally adopted.

Civilian riders in England receive their instruction from varied sources. For example, the father may teach the son or the old groom the children of the family, often on the "next-best" horse. This method has much to commend it, as it ensures that the beginner acquires "horse sense," which is the most important quality to be aimed at in a horseman.

Another reason for the standardised horsemanship on the Continent is that there one is forced to make a useful riding horse of every sound animal, irrespective of the trouble it might be, but this can only be achieved by specific knowledge and not by the use of martingales and severe bits. In England people can afford to discard a spoiled or difficult horse.

It would take too long to explain how and when the Continent adopted the many English riding customs and sports. Hunting, racing, and polo, with all their written and unwritten rules, have been taken over without exception. On the other hand, the centuries-old experiences of the great riding masters, who built up their art in a scientific manner, were completely ignored by the English riding world. This is not criticism, but a statement of facts, which helps me to point out the essential reasons for differences between the English and Continental style. The Italians, for instance, although originally the regenerators of dressage, now do not use it in their training. The Italian or "natural school," in my opinion, does not ensure enough obedience.

From the fact that dressage tests and best-trained horse competitions and also hack classes have become popular, it is obvious that a well-trained horse is appreciated in England.

The practical horseman needs foremost a supple and free-going horse when is absolutely obedient to the aids. It is only then that the ultimate effect can be effortless for both horse and rider. The horse should show level, smooth, and easily balanced paces, carrying his rider on a supple and springy back.

On the Continent this is termed the "low school," and the opinion is that the following advantages result from it:—

(i) Obedience—the rider on such a horse is able to get

Decorations in the early years of the International Horse Show at Olympia, London.

anywhere alone in "cold blood."

(ii) Preservation of energy—the horse's riding life is lengthened.

(iii) The carriage of the horse and its appearance are improved.

(iv) The horse becomes a really good and reliable ride.

(v) The horse's natural talents and qualities are accentuated.

GUSTAV GRACHEGG.   6 January 1939

HACKNEY STALLIONS WHICH MADE THE BREED.

THE modern Hackney horse dates back to the Norfolk Cob, famed as a trotting sire about 125 years ago. The Norfolk Cob got Bond's Norfolk Phenomenon, foaled 1825, and sold to go to Yorkshire in 1836; and the Norfolk Phenomenon got the horse known as Theobald's Old Champion, or Hewison's Champion, foaled in 1836. From this last our Stud Book Hackneys trace their descent, so wrote the late Sir Walter Gilbey, who in his day at Elsenham owned many of the finest stallions in this breed.

Ramsdale's Performer was another famous old sire. He begat among others the dark chestnut Lund's Merrylegs (449) out of a Sportsman mare. This horse was foaled in 1830, his breeder being Mr. W. Lund, of Bielby, who had him until 1835, when he became the property of Mr. R. Denison, of Kilnurch Priory. Merrylegs was the sire of Brigham's Merrylegs, Matchless, Gant's Merrylegs and Rickell's Merryman.

Redhead's Alonzo the Brave (22), foaled in 1866, was a bay with black legs. He was bred by Mr. Henry Redhead, of Leverington, and after doing good service in England was sold to Mr. Richard Evans, of Plasnewydd, Cardiganshire, in whose hands he proved most valuable in improving the breed of Welsh Cobs.

D'Oyley's Confidence (158) by Prickwillow (614), foaled in 1867, was a famous sire. Bred by Mr. Wm. Rose, of Dukebeck, near Wymondham, he changed hands thrice during his career. Mr. Henry D'Oyley, of Kempnall, Long Stratton; Mr. Wm. Dunham, of Wymondham; and Mr. H. B. Spurgin, of Northampton, owning him in succession. D'Oyley's Confidence was a black brown; he had little success in the show-ring, a fact which perhaps accounts for his being put to mares of very ordinary quality.

Even thus mated, Confidence showed himself an impressive sire; all his progeny inherited his peculiar dash, a quality which made them much in demand. He sired at least twenty-two stallions of real merit, and the number of his progeny registered in the Stud Book falls little short of 600. Confidence died in December, 1892.

Bourdass's Denmark (177) by Sir Charles, dam by Merryman, was a chestnut, foaled in 1862. Denmark had a very successful showyard career, winning first prizes at Scarborough in 1865, 1867, and 1869, and at Bridlington in 1869, 1871, 1874, and 1875. His dam, when twenty-three years old, took first prizes at Driffield and the Great Yorkshire Show in 1862. She was shown with Denmark at foot, and won as the best mare for breeding Hackneys.

This horse was the sire of numerous good stallions, the most famous being Danegelt (174), purchased for the Elsenham Stud for £5000 in 1890. Of Denmark's other stallions mention may be made of Charley Denmark, Moore's Confidence, Brigham's Denmark, Worrington, Duke of

The Royal Box at the International Horse Show at Olympia, London in 1907.

Parma, Fordham, King Christian, and Foster's Sir Charles Denmark, died in 1888.

Triffit's Fireaway (249) by Hairsine's Achilles out of Nancy by Rover Performer, was a dark brown, foaled in 1859, bred by Mr. William Triffit, of Holme, in Yorkshire. This horse had a most successful showyard career, and during a quarter of a century he travelled in Yorkshire, covering mares not of the best class, begetting, nevertheless, stock for which there was always a keen demand. His progeny were distinguished for size, bone, action, courage and temper, good looks, and soundness. Fireaway's get had not quite the quality of Denmark's but they were all good. The mating of Denmark's stock with Triffit's Fireaway's always has produced many of the finest examples of the breed.

Lord Derby II. by S. Leake's Lord Derby (415) deserves a few words. The horse was foaled in 1871, his dam Nancy by Achilles. He was bred by Mr. J. R. Burnham, and was a great success as a show-horse, winning thirty-seven prizes in Yorkshire.

Danegelt by Denmark out of Young Nellie, a dark chesnut, foaled in 1879, was bred by Mr. F. Rickell; by him he was sold to Mr. G. Bourdass. Of his progeny it has been quite justly said of him that he hardly got a bad foal. Among Danegelt's best sons were Ganymede, a stallion with which Mr. Mitchell gained many prizes, Astonishment II. and General Gordon, Lord Milton, Saxon, and Royal Danegelt.

Sir Horace by Little Wonder II. out of Dorothy Derby easily takes first place among Hackney pony sires. Until the sixth show of the Hackney Horse Society the small Hackneys had been exhibited among the full-sized animals. At the show of 1890 pony classes were formed for the first time to meet an increasing requirement.

Col. G. T. Hurrell, Past-President of the Hunters' Improvement Society.

Sir Horace, bred by Mr. Christopher Wilson, was the winning pony stallion in 1895, and for several years held his own against all-comers, heading the list in 1897, 1898, 1899, 1900, and 1902. The show of 1903 was the means of producing significant evidence of Sir Horace's value as a sire. The old pony was first in his own class, and the second, third, and fourth prizes were taken by his sons. The first prize winners in four out of the five remaining pony classes were by him, and several second prize winners.

21 April 1939

THE STORY OF LINDSAY GORDON.

ADAM Lindsay Gordon certainly lived out of his time and out of a country which would, to-day, have hailed him as the out-door man's poet. But what England lost by Lindsay Gordon quitting its shores an early and as then undeveloped Australia gained. There to-day his name is deeply loved and honoured, and his poems likened unto the best of anything the old country has produced. The claim has been made by a literary man of note that "Baily's Magazine" discovered Lindsay Gordon and proclaimed his real merit as a poet years before anyone else in Britain believed in him. Born in the Azores on October 19th, 1833, Lindsay Gordon was, at the age of seven, sent to Cheltenham—on the very day the college opened its doors. After a year he disappeared, and we find him again six years later as cadet of the Royal Military

Academy at Woolwich. He was the friend and fellow of Gordon of Khartoum. At the end of three years he left. Then he was sent to the Royal Grammar School at Worcester. When there he rode in a steeple chase. Then he had another year at Cheltenham, when as a result of something which upset his people he was sent to Australia; passed through a lot of ever-changing phases, failed, and died in poverty. He had stood for Parliament as a squatter's candidate, and had been returned at the head of the poll because he was the best rider and horsebreaker. In Parliament he bored the House with speeches full of classical quotations, and he himself became worried by the slowness of procedure. Horse-racing losses drove him to writing, and that he combined with a livery stable at Ballarat. This was a failure, but in 1867 appeared his two volumes. "Sea Spray and Smoke Drift" and "Ashtaroth." During the next two years he won steeplechases and wrote many poems. He was publishing "Bush Ballads" and "Galloping Rhymes" about this period, and having seen them through the press he went off to see some friends who might give him some permanent position. They happened to be out, and in a fit of desperation Lindsay Gordon shot himself. Gordon had a distinguished ancestry; he was descended from the Cavalier Marquess of Huntly, who died more finely for his King than Montrose himself; from the great Lord Peterborough, whose conquests in Spain Macaulay enshrined in an essay; and from Thomas Bowdler, whose outrages on Shakespeare have added a word to our language; he was a collateral of Lord George Gordon of No-Property fame, and he was a descendant of all three principal branches of the Gordon family—the Dukes of Gordon, the Marquesses of Huntly, and the Earls of Aberdeen. Gordon wrote hunting and racing poetry quite on a par with that of Whyte Melville or Egerton Warburton.

SCOT. 30 June 1939

"BONNIE PRINCE CHARLIE" WAS A SPORTSMAN.

PRINCE Charles Edward, "Bonnie Prince Charlie," was one of the best all-round sportsmen of his day—he was born in

1720—and this fact emerges from a study of his career, apart from the praise that was lavished upon him due to his rank. He started at six and a half to show surprising skill with a crossbow. He had a stable of riding ponies when seven; played "the golf" at eight; then took on tennis and shuttle-cock; and at fifteen had built up a frame which could stand up to much fatigue. In Italy, he hunted game of every kind, from wild boar and red deer to snipe and woodcock, and when sixteen fought under the Duke de Liria with the Spanish forces at the siege of Gaeta on the Italian coast. When in the isles of Scotland, with eight English vessels searching for him, he enjoyed himself shooting grouse. He is said to have shot flying so very well that his prowess was a novelty as well as an eye-opener to the Highlanders. He shot a stag in South Uist and assisted in the preparation of the meat for supper. Prince Charles was essentially a creature of the open air, and in after years he could be heard of in Lorraine, and at Bouillon, where good shooting could be got, deer and wild boar prevailing on the last-named estate, which belonged to his cousin, the Duc de Bouillon, and was near Evreux. He pursued wolves and bears in Luxemburg. When he went back to Rome, a broken man, in 1766, on the death of the Old Pretender, he was a mere shadow of the gallant light-hearted youth who had landed in Scotland in 1745. He spent much time shooting in the neighbourhood of Albano and Frascati, and in a letter to his brother Cardinal York in 1767 he com-plained that he was no longer amused with quails or any amusement whatever. "The nasty bottle," as the Cardinal described it, had helped to close a career in gloom and misery.
HUNTER.   19 January 1940

COMMENTS ON MARTINGALES.

BORN, not made, is an adage which is only half true. I have heard it variously applied to artists, sculptors, musicians, writers (save the mark), huntsmen, jockeys, lady hair-dressers, and plain unvarnished horsemen.

Now I do not think that good hands are sent direct from Heaven; some of us possess Chifney-like ones, others are inclined to be heavy, while some are frankly bad. But one can

The late Mr F. V. Gooch on Mr Walter Winans' His Highness, several times champion hack at the International Horse Show at Olympia in the early years of the show.

improve them so much by plenty of continuous practice, the suppling of the wrists, the recollection of watching some first-class horseman at work in the show-ring, the constant riding of different horses where the key to the mouth has to be found, that heavy hands can often be turned into moderately light ones. The latter are, of course, a horseman's gift, but, as I have said, they can be improved upon beyond all knowledge with a little care.

For the novice—for whom these lines are principally written—there are, of course, various supplementary and artificial aids to good hands, and into this category comes the question of the martingale. At one time it was practically unknown in the hunting field, and by the earlier writers it is scarcely mentioned except as a perquisite of the Turf. Even "Nimrod," who knew as much about horses and riding as any man, does not say much about the employment of the martingale. The hard fact of the matter seems to be that in those hard-riding days, which knew not wire and hunting was the prime sport of our nation, sportsmen did not like these appendages round their horses' necks, although, strangely enough, they seem to have had no objection to using breastplates, as may be seen from the pictures of Herring and of Ferneley. Dick Christian, so far as we know, never used a martingale, and they were scorned by such a bruising customer as James Pigg, even when he had to "leap ower the dyke backs" full of snow. It may be that our hands have deteriorated, for practically every horse wears a martingale to-day, often when it is not necessary, for in the gay 'nineties and the brilliant and all-too-short Edwardian era martingales were unknown at Melton Mowbray. The Duke of Portland tells us that in that era of the covert-hack and the smart pony-trap, when second horsemen wore livery and cockades, they were an excuse for bad hands. That may be, but times have changed.

Before dealing in detail with the various types of martingales it may be said with perfect truth that in nine-tenths of cases their employment is quite unnecessary provided you have plenty of time for the schooling of the horse. If you have fairly good hands this is a long job; in fact, I have been told that you cannot produce a well-balancad, perfectly-collected horse under two years. This is a long time for the novice to wait before experiencing the joys of the saddle. It is all hands and hard work is this same schooling, and in an age of speed is hardly practical politics. So the martingale is the life-line for the novice. He or she perhaps wants to be able to ride in some degree of comfort in as little time as, say, a month; therefore the martingale must be used to reinforce the aid of the hands.

But what sort of martingale should the novice employ? It is a big question if one does not know the facts of each individual case, but it may be answered by certain broad and well-defined arguments. Martingales then are divided into three types—the running martingale, the standing martingale, and the Irish martingale. Sometimes they are called "rings" and a "pair of spectacles" in the tack-room. It should not be forgotten that each can help the young and bold horseman or woman, even though they are inclined to abuse them when they have reached the years of discretion and managed

Horses and driver
wearing gas masks
during the First World
War.

to learn a bit about collection and balance through the medium of the hands.

Now as to the action of martingales. The running martingale is the one generally used, and it certainly has a check on a keen horse. I like to use it when properly adjusted—there should be a rubber ring between the neck strap and the martingale proper to keep it in place—with a snaffle bit, for it is an excellent check for a horse that is inclined to take hold of a bit. It can, too, keep a horse's head in place, and it is largely used by nagsmen when schooling—the sort of hard-bitten lean and hardy men, with caps well down and straws in mouth, as pictured by the genius of "Snaffles"—where it serves a very useful purpose. It is a good thing, too, to use upon a horse which is inclined to stargaze, or one of those irritating animals which persists in tossing his head up and down. I have dealt so far with the snaffle, but when the running martingale is used with a double bridle I am not so sure that I can either advocate or sanction its use. True it prevents the reins from going over the horses's ears, and if it is correctly adjusted it sometimes serves the purpose of steadying the horse over a big country. But to which rein should the rings be placed—snaffle, bridoon, or curb? Here again one is writing in the face of criticism; but just as personal opinion, proven by a certain amount of varied experience, let me say that the curb rein should be run through the rings of the martingale, never the bridoon. The rings, by the way, should never be more than three-quarters of an inch in diameter; if they are much bigger they will catch in those of the bit, and you will then realise what a riding accident can be like.

The reason why I advocate this course is that the function of the snaffle is to raise the horse's head, that of the curb to lower it, and as the whole essence of the utility of the martingale is to keep the horse's head straight and steady I cannot see why your own object should be defeated by using the bridoon in conjunction with the martingale. But as has been observed, not everyone will agree with the statement; anyway, it is always as well to have two sides to a question.

So much for the running martingale. Now as to the standing martingale, which requires a lot of adjustment. The novice should watch an expert doing this before attempting to do it for him or herself. Roughly speaking, a horse should be able to stretch his neck to the level of its eyes when using a standing martingale. Now to my mind the standing martingale is the only permissible one to use. It keeps a horse sighted at timber or a blind ditch and steady at gates, for the standing martingale does not allow a horse to poke its nose about. Furthermore, and this is important to the hacking novice, it keeps the head in the desired position, and so gives poise and balance. It has, I may point out, been used for years at polo, and here you have the highest balance combined with the maximum of speed. Still further, I am convinced that its use teaches a horse to know his "foot drill" in a shorter time.

There are people who contend that a standing martingale is dangerous for jumping. Such an argument, as inaccurate in conception as it is weak in practice, can be refuted by much good cause and effect. There is no chance of a horse catching the key piece in his mouth, or running backwards, or doing all sorts of other unpleasant things which so often happens when a running martingale is used.

Moreover, the standing martingale achieves one great purpose. It keeps the horse's head straight. Now in jumping, however good a horseman you may be, in the final strides it

is the horse that decides, but he can be materially assisted in this direction by the standing martingale, for he can stretch his neck in describing the parabola of the leap. And it should not be forgotten that when a horse does this he uses his neck as a sort of balancing pole, keeping as much weight as possible off the forehand. The horse, too, will be on the look-out for any sudden jab in the mouth, and his defences, so to speak, against severe bitting—more often due to bad hands—are to poke his nose in the air and draw in his neck towards the chest, which is, of course, as unsightly in appearance as it is quite wrong in practice. The forelegs, too, take the shock of landing—they are attached to the body by muscles and are better for this purpose than the hind leg, which is one of propulsion—so it is as well to have the head as free as possible. If a novice not quite so sure of his capabilities should be inclined to jab the horse in the mouth on landing, a fault often seen, then it is a good sound plan to leave the reins quite slack and hold on to the necklace of the martingale. Thus you save the horse from an unpleasant shock. I wonder how many horsemen and women have been saved a nasty fall by employing this method, or conversely, how many good horses have been ruined and sickened of jumping by being jabbed in the mouth with continuous regularity?

Mrs Glenda Spooner, Chairman of The Ponies of Britain.

The standing martingale having been advocated for the novice, I must say something of the Irish martingale, which, it may have been noted, is also known by other titles. Now to me the Irish martingale is used by two people, and always on a snaffle bridle. One is the nagsman and the other the steeplechase jockey. It is useful in a way, as it prevents the reins from coming over the head in the event of the rider "hitting the mat," and I have been told that it does something to stop a puller over a big country. I could never quite see it through those eyes, and I would not say with any confidence that it is likely to be much help to the novice in times of stress. There I will leave the question. In writing this I have been well aware that there are many people who loathe martingales, but to strike a middle course I would say that they are a very useful aid for those who have not the time, nor the necessary experience, to thoroughly school their horses and so render the martingale a useless piece of horse-furniture. They do save you a lot of trouble—perhaps many a wet shirt—and that upon my life is something in these days.

WILLIAM FAWCETT.   10 January 1941

"SKITTLES"—A REMARKABLE LADY RIDER

SIR,—In a book, "Rum Ones To Follow," by a Melton Rough Rider, published in 1934, I read as follows about a lady whose nickname was "Skittles":—"See that fence? I once saw a lady jump it. They called her Skittles. I never

84

knew her proper name. She were not what you'd call a 'lady,' but she was a fine rider, went like smoke, and was very quiet and well-spoken. A merry lass she was, and as pretty as a peach. Open-handed lady she was; did a wonderful lot of kindness to the poor. One day she had a fall, and her skirt got left hung up on the saddle. Real murderous things they wore then, long and heavy, not mere aprons, as they are now, and underneath they wore white frillies. There was a lot of chaff among the gentlemen as to who should go to her rescue. They all asks for a married man."

The author was writing about the Fernie country, and the period seems to have been about 1865, when Mr. Tailby was Master.

In a book about Wilfred Scawen Blunt, by Edith Finch, published in 1938, quite a lot of information is given about "Skittles," as well as her portrait. Her name was Catherine Walters, and she was born in 1839. She was one of the most renowned demi-mondaines of the late nineteenth century, and her bright chestnut hair, delicate, clear-cut features, slender figure, and sensitive hands made her very charming. In early life she was in Paris, and later in England. Her receptions in South Street, Park Lane, were frequented by the then Prince of Wales and others famous in the public life of England. Even Gladstone came alone to take tea with her, having sent her beforehand 12lb of Russian tea.

In public she was to be seen roller-skating in the fashionable rinks of London and Tunbridge Wells, driving the ponies of her phaeton in Hyde Park, or riding in Rotten Row a horse that no one else could ride and which had finished second in the Grand National. She was interested in modern art, knew something about music, and liked serious reading, even on religious subjects. Her letters, although illiterate and nearly illegible, were highly entertaining. Even those who ceased to be her lovers remained her devoted friends. Of the German Kaiser she wrote in November, 1914:—"I knew him so well when he was Crown Prince. He gave me his photograph and a jewelled sunshade. The latter I have sold for the Red Cross. He was most charming to me, and went cracked about my riding. He looked well on horseback, and had a handsome face."

In later life she was known as Mrs. Bailey. She died on

August 4th, 1920, and was buried in the churchyard of the Franciscan monastery at Crawley, and the grave-stone is lettered "C. W. B."

H.L.   17 January 1941

WHAT MAKES A GOOD HUNTER?

IT is interesting to look through the records of hunters one has owned over some two score years and read when, where, and how each was bought, prices, and remarks. The first thing that strikes the writer is that with a few exceptions the most expensive did not usually give the most satisfaction. Also that the majority of horses which turned out the best buys were those which had been bought in March or April after a hard season's hunting. They may have been lean, rough-looking, and over-hunted, lumped and bumped, but after a good summering and attention one's eye liked them even better than at time of purchase.

On the other hand horses bought in the late summer or early autumn proved so often sadly disappointing. These had been "dolled up" and well rested. Among some of the older ones bought looking in full bloom at this time of year it was not infrequent, after a hard day's hunting, to suddenly find a little "heat" in a tendon or a foot which evidently was an old patched-up trouble! The fat, sleek five year old bought in August definitely rode well and looked a nice horse, but often, with harder work and longer days' hunting, he began to "melt." His back did not look so powerful, and his quarters visibly shrank. He had been fattened, but never muscled-up. What is more, this five year old who had been admired so much in August, and who had jumped the little made-up fences so neatly and was so handy, was very green when out hunting and clumsy over rough ground. After the first hard day those clean legs began to show windgalls and later threw out splints. This horse was bought as a "made" hunter and at the price of the made article, but was barely more forward when it came to hunting than a colt that had had but four months' breaking for all practical purposes.

Among three and four-year-old colts and fillies bought, unless coming from a good dam, and she herself from a good

86

Music Hall, winner of
the Grand National of
1922 (L. B. Rees up)
with owners Mr and
Mrs Hugh Kershaw
and trainer Owen
Anthony (at horse's
head).

line of performers, few turned out really grade A. When they
came of age to join the hunting stables, although their original
price as youngsters seemed low, after allowing for accidents,
wind going wrong, and the expense of some years' keep and
breaking, those which turned out really good ones stood at a
high price. All the above rather goes to prove that a good eight
or nine-year-old hunter who knows the game, whose action
is fresh, and his limbs hard and clean, is a good and economical mount to buy even at a high price.

The best hunters the writer remembers, which did the
most work and lasted the most years, were chiefly clean of
limb and unblemished to the end of their careers. On the
other hand he recalls many excellent blemished hunters.
Somehow or other quite a number of these blemished horses,
bought as such, would get cuts and blemishes again, good
hunters though they were. There is no doubt that among
horses who are equally good hunters some will be neater with
their feet and cleverer and more controlled in their action
than others, and they will somehow not knock themselves
about as much as others. Many people miss a good horse because they think him not big enough. It is not the size of a
horse which determines what weight he can carry—it is much
to do with his action. A horse first has to carry his own weight,
and it is what he has left over after this which carries the
rider. How often has one seen a big horse which would be

termed "up to 15st" barely able to canter up a hill with only a light weight in the saddle, while a 14st farmer on a 14-hands game pony will gallop up the hill past him like a rocket!

Sir Albert Muntz, who died many years ago, commissioned the famous hunter dealer John Henry Stokes to buy him the best weight-carrier he could find, no limit being put to price. Sir Albert rode 17st, and was one of the hardest men in those days across the Midlands. Stokes sent him on a blood mare he bought for him in Yorkshire. On seeing the mare Sir Albert was very annoyed, and sent word to Stokes that she was but a 13 hands 7in huntress. The reply came that he had bought her for a man who rode 18st, and that for the past three seasons he had been at the top of all the most gruelling hunts the Holderness had had on this mare, and that therefore, whatever her size was, she must be up to his weight.

"Good-winded" horses are always a joy to ride; by this I do not necessarily mean a horse which is certificated so. There are "sound-winded" horses who will pass the examination of all the veterinary surgeons of the realm, but who will blow up in a fast hunt, while others who are called "whistlers" will not blow a candle out when pulled up after a real "elbows and legger"! I think the sinews of a horse probably play as much a part as anything else to make outstanding hunters. Whyte-Melville said if he had to choose a horse by one thing only he would choose "the eye." Looking back on his old favourites the writer thinks if he had to choose a horse by one feature only it would be "the hock." Mr. Jorrocks was also very partial to that part of the equine structure.

SHEEPSKIN LEGGINGS.   7 March 1941

REMINISCENCES OF HUNTING PARSONS.

SIR,—The recent death of a sporting clergyman recalls to memory a select company of past clerics who have worthily represented their cloth in the hunting field, and even as judges on the flags at Peterborough and in the Dublin ring. In Cuthbert Bradley's "Hunting Reminiscences of Frank Gillard" the artist-author depicts in a sketch of a run with the Belvoir in the 1890-91 season the Rev. J. P. Seabrooke on Top-bar giving a lead over a formidable post and rails to a waiting field. Nearer the home of this scribe the prowess

A London Fire Brigade horsedrawn fire engine.

of the Rev. Edgar Milne, Master of the North Bucks Harriers from 1895 to 1900, and of the Cattistock Foxhounds from 1900 to 1931, must be well known to many readers of "Horse and Hound." The West Country has always been the home of sporting parsons, both good shots and good riders, and there is a story that years ago a Bishop visited for the first time the church of a newly-inducted incumbent. After hearing him preach he remarked to a farmer-churchwarden—"I liked your rector in the pulpit to-day," and received the unexpected reply—"Ah, my Lord, but you should see him in the pigskin!"

"Well, if you go and put me into 'Baily' they'll never make me Archbishop of York" was the comment of the Rev. Cecil Legard. When his portrait appeared within the green covers nearly fifty years ago, to be followed by an excellent cartoon of him in Major Guy Paget's "Rum 'Uns to Follow," "Baily's" record of Mr. Legard's career as a sportsman up to the age of fifty-three includes the winning for two years in succession at Cambridge of that much-coveted trophy the University Challenge Whip. But it was as rector of Cottes-brooke that he came at the end of the 'eighties into prominence as one of the leading authorities on horse and hound in the

89

kingdom. There were few of the great shows of hunters at which his services were not frequently requisitioned, including the monster one at Dublin, in which one class alone contained over 250 horses! At Peterborough he officiated once with Lord Coventry and Mr. Tom Parrington when the first prize for unentered hounds was awarded to Lord Willoughy de Broke's Harper, subsequently one of the greatest stallion hounds of the day. At the request of the Committee of the Master of Foxhounds Association Mr. Legard undertook about that time the authorship of the "Foxhound Kennel Stud Book," which involved the picking up of the thread of some seventy of the principal packs from 1863, where volume one terminated. The task, however, was a congenial one, and the volumes published by him at five-year intervals proved of the greatest use to existing and future generations of Masters, huntsmen and foxhunters generally.

The county of Devon has in the past supplied a succession of sporting clerics to the hunting field, and in Snell's "A Book of Exmoor," published in 1903, there is a characteristic sketch by the late F. C. Gould of "Two Passuns." Mounted on shaggy, long-tailed Exmoor ponies they are depicted as scampering over the moor wearing peaked cloth caps, leather gaiters and unclerical-looking jackets, holding their whips in front of them like a conductor's baton, but both keen stag-hunters, however, by the look of them. In three successive chapters in this book the author recounts briefly several good stories about the Revs. John Froude, Jack Russell, and Joseph Jekyll, all of whom lived on Exmoor from the second half of last century onwards. No parson, he records, ever gave occasion to so many good stories as Froude, of Knowstone, who kept a pack of hounds there when Jack Russell was a curate at George Nympton. He hunted three days of the week and shot on the others, when he could walk most men off their legs. His huntsman was Jack Babbage, who appears in the well-known engraving riding behind Mr. Fenwick Bissett, in which anything but justice is done to the little man who, though ugly, was not quite a man-monkey. The relations between Froude and his huntsman were, we learn, most comical. "When the man had the misfortune to offend the Master he was always addressed as 'Mr. Babbage,' and if he waited on Froude for instructions with regard to meets would be answered shortly—'Go where you please, Mr. Babbage.' The huntsman accordingly would arrange the fixtures, send round the notices, and at the proper time take the pack to the trysting-place. In these circumstances it was not often that Froude could resist the temptation of turning out, but he would ride at a great distance behind or follow the sport from the opposite ridge. All this so that Babbage might be impressed with the enormity of his offence and his Master's deep displeasure."

The redoubtable "Henry of Exeter" (Bishop Philpotts) highly disapproved of Froude's foxhunting activities, and on one occasion came to Knowstone to communicate his views and displeasure to the vicar. Froude was forwarned of the visit, and upon the Bishop's arrival his old housekeeper Jane met him at the door and in response to his lordship's request to see Froude, the former was informed that the Master was ill in bed. "'Tis a faver of some soart, but I can't mind what the doctor call'd it." "Not scarlet fever, I hope?" "Worse than that, my lord." "Typhus?" enquired his lordship, no longer able to hide his look of alarm. "Iss, that's it; 'tis a whist job, fai!" The Bishop clutched his hat and with little ceremony took his departure. When fairly out of sight Froude put on his long gaiters and went hunting for the rest of the day!

On another occasion when the two met Froude was accompanied by a greyhound which in Devonshire is commonly styled a "long dog." "And pray, Mr. Froude," enquired the Bishop, "what sort of a dog may you call that?" "That? Oh, a lang dog, my lord, and if you was to shak yewr appern to 'un, he'd go like a dart." The Bishop's reply is not recorded, but it is safe to conjecture, records the chronicler, that being sensible of his position and all that went with it, he did not take the hint.

Jack Russell's record and career are so well known as to render repetition at length unnecessary. Born in 1795, he was the son of the Rector of Iddesleigh, North Devon, and after serving as curate at George Nympton, became successively Rector of Iddesleigh and Vicar of Swymbridge, where he was buried in the spring of 1883 at the age of eighty-seven. Russell's father kept hounds, and his son followed in his footsteps. He began early keeping hounds at Blundells School, and by reason of his untimely indulgence narrowly escaped expulsion. Notwithstanding his devotion to sport, records of the period show that it was never brought home to him that he ever neglected his duties as a clergyman, and although it was alleged by some that he sometimes confounded the parts of parson and hunting man, it is extremely doubtful whether all or any of them were founded on fact. On this point his biographer observes:—"Much has been said of the active service which Russell expected from his curates in the hunting field, but of course some of the stories told in that respect were utterly untrue. One for instance describes him as testing the voices of rival applicants by making them give view-holloas, and then accepting the one whose voice sounded the most penetrating and most sonorous. A capital story no doubt, but as a matter of fact it is one which rests on as baseless a fabric as the fleecy clouds that float through the sky."

Russell kept up his foxhunting and staghunting to a period far beyond that at which most men, whether they will or no, are forced to retire. In 1877 he received a visit from Frank Goodall, the Queen's huntsman, who came to see what sport on Exmoor was like. On this occasion Russell found it convenient to drive to the opening meet at Cloutsham in a gig, and although then in his eighty-first year, the sight of the fine old man out of the saddle struck all beholders, and, to quote Mr. Snell's book on Exmoor, one old staghunting farmer remarked: "Zee, there he go'th; Passen Russell in a chaise; never zeed un avore off a horse's back, never. But there, us must all come to 't; you can't have ten forenoons to one day." Russell, however, was able to demonstrate then, as well as afterwards, that he could still ride to hounds with the best.

Mr. Charles Palk Collyns, author of "The Chase of the Wild Red Deer," a keen staghunter for more than forty-seven years up to his death in 1864, and of whom the Hon. John Fortescue speaks admiringly in his "Records of Staghunting," as does Kingsley in a happy allusion to him in his "Water Babies," refers to hunting parsons as follows: "For myself I will say that, without wishing to see the dignitaries of the Church again maintaining their kennels of hounds, I should feel regret if I were to miss from the field the familiar faces of some of the clergy who join in the sport of the country and whose presence is always welcome at the covert side."

H. R. TATE.   4 July 1941

BRAINS OF THE HORSE.

Coaching enthusiasts of 1923 standing in front of the Old Berkeley stage coach which ran from the Berkeley Hotel, London, W.1, to Box Hill (changing horses at The Bull, Sheen), returning the same day.

Sir,—I do not want to deny that a horse has brains, but whether he can make use of them by reasoning is open to doubt. By reasoning I mean as opposed to intelligence and teachability, which a horse undoubtedly has. I can only say that, having had a lifelong experience of horses of all kinds, I began with the idea that a horse had some power of reasoning, but experience has taught me something very different. Instinct is quite a different thing. He has that on the day of his birth, and it tells him to get up and find his milk. I would describe a horse as a bundle of nerves, with a wonderful memory, aided no doubt by the extraordinary development of his sight and sense of smell that a horse never forgets. If he used his brain would he, think you, submit to the treatment he meets with every day? The answer to such a question must be in the negative. We used to read the stories of cavalry horses who, when their riders had been killed, kept their place in the ranks, and when they heard the sound, "Retire," were always just where they would have been had their original riders been on their backs.

I think this is a proof of routine established by a strong memory. Arising out of this, I was asked how does the horse's homing instinct compare with that of a homing pigeon. I agree that both possess the same desire to return home—perhaps, in the case of the horse, a lost companion is a more important feature; but both have not the same means of doing so. A homing pigeon, on being released miles away from its loft, will fly straight up into the air, mounting higher and higher in ever-increasing circles until he comes into contact with the wave, or beam, or whatever the wireless calls it, which he knows by previous experience leads him to his loft. Not so the horse. I do not think a horse, taken a long distance by rail or road transport, would be capable of finding his way home. The result would be different if he had traversed the road on foot, and if he escaped, and was in the mood, I verily believe he could do so whatever the distance, providing he was given the time and met with no interference, even through towns. Such is his unerring recollection of a route once covered. I think a tribute I once heard paid to the German shepherd dogs lies in the fact that these dogs have not been bred for the show points that have made our other breeds into monstrosites. And they retain more of the form and character of their original canine ancestors than any other breed of dog.

FRED UNWIN.   12 February 1943

SATURATION AND TELEGONY.

SIR,—The following may give the believers in telegony thoughts for reflection. In April, 1939, I heard of a cart-mare belonging to Mr. Ben Gritton, of Lawrenceburg, Kentucky, having given birth to living twins, one being a mule and the other a horse-foal. At the same time photos of this rare occurrence appeared in some of the newspapers. The best known shows the cart-mare, her owner, and the twins. To get some authentic information of this very rare case I wrote on April 29 Mr. W. S. Anderson, Emeritus Professor of Genetics, Animal Industry Group, University of Kentucky, for confirmation, and the following is a copy of Mr. Anderson's reply, dated May 11, 1939: Sir,—I have been waiting to answer your letter of April 29 until I saw how the photographs came out. I had gone to Lawrenceburg on April 27 to investigate the

Sir Walter Gilbey
(right) judging the
turnout of riding club
members in Hyde Park
in 1933.

twins—one a horse and the other a mule. I found them in a remote section of the country, foaled by a grade Percheron mare. This mare had been bred the previous year to a Jack, and twenty days later to a Percheron stallion. She foaled on March 31. The horse-foal is a male, and a very vigorous, well-formed animal, with no characteristics resembling the mule. The mule is a female, and at the time the photographs were made she was rather delicate, but well-formed, and much greater in height than the twin horse-foal. The explanation is that two eggs were liberated, and by the laws of chance mating was so made that each became fertilised by different sires. In 1917, in Marion County, Kentucky, I found twins of the same kind, and photographed them. An account of this, with their picture, was published in the "Country Gentleman" at the time. So far as I know these are the only cases in which a horse and mule twins have been foaled by mares, and both twins living. It is rather rare for a mare to produce twin foals both of which are perfect enough to live.

BUCKAROO.   16 April 1943

RACING AND GENETICS

IN the article headed "Genetics Up-To-Date," by J. M. Rendel, in your issue of September 6, it is stated that the following sentence is a misconception: "An animal inherits nothing from its parents; everything it inherits comes from the grandparents."

95

Believing this sentence to be an extremely important point in the mating of thoroughbred animals, I append some quotations from books of recognised authorities on this subject.

The Cell in Development and Inheritance (Second Edition 1900) by E. B. Wilson. Page 13. "The child inherits from the germ cell, not from the parent body and the germ cell owes its characteristics not to the body which bears it but to its descent from a pre-existing germ cell of the same kind. Thus the body is, as it were, an off-shoot from the germ cell."

Mammalian Genetics (1940) by W. E. Castle. Page 11. "This shows that the germ cells derive their genetic potentialities directly from the fertilised egg, not from the soma since different soma may be substituted for the natural one, without altering the potentialities of the germ cells."

The Marquess of Exeter, K.C.M.G., MFH, President of The British Horse Society in 1963.

Page 91. "At sexual maturity germ cells will begin to be produced by the germ plasm but the chromosomes and genes in these germ cells are not derived in the final analysis from the body of the parent (somatoplasm), but from the same source from which the body of the parent has come, viz., the fertilised ovum or zygote."

Breeding and Improvement of Farm Animals (Third Edition 1942) by V. A. Rice. Page 277: "Any organism receives the determiners for all its potentialities from its ancestors through its immediate parents."

Animals Breeding Plans (1943), by J. L. Lush. Page 46. "Thus the parent gives to each offspring only a sample half of its own inheritance."

The Principles of Heredity Applied to the Racehorse (1906) by J. B. Robertson. Page 7. "On this inner layer, a few cells are set apart and reserved unchanged to form the germinal layer of its testes, or ovaries. Thus, in a few hours' time, after impregnation, all the characters that the individual will be able to transmit when it reaches maturity, are already fixed in its reproductive system. These characters are necessarily derived from its sire and dam, and may differ materially from the combination of characters present in the somatic or body cells which form the individual itself. This has a most important bearing on the practice of mating; for it may safely be asserted that no horse or mare ever reproduces exactly the same combinations of characters as are present in the somatic cells, hence the practical necessity of paying more regard to the four prospective grandparents than to the two individuals you propose to mate."

The facts surrounding the breeding of Racehorses are to be found in the General Stud Book and the Racing Calendar, and any genetic explanation must conform to these facts.

H. E. KEYLOCK.   20 September 1947

BREEDING MODERN FOXHOUNDS
BY A. HENRY HIGGINSON

IT seems to me that it must be a very puzzling matter for a young man taking on a pack of foxhounds to decide what type of hound to breed which is best suited to the country which he has taken over. For there is no denying that to obtain the best results, hounds should be bred with a view to the conditions which obtain in the locality in which they are to be hunted.

In the old days, the famous packs of Great Britain were, many of them, fortunate in being ruled in an autocratic manner, by one Master over a long period of years, and even up to that period which was marked by the outbreak of the First World War, there were many "family packs" where the Mastership descended from father to son, sometimes over several generations. Under such conditions, the chances that the policy of breeding remained more or less the same were great, and certain packs, bred in the country for work suited to that country, acquired characteristics which were familiar to any student of hound breeding and hound conformation.

To-day, except in the case of very few of what I may term the "family packs," which possess very marked pack characteristics, there are many which have suffered from short Masterships, and have changed their characteristics half a dozen times in the last twenty-five years.

What is the objective to be attained in the breeding of a pack of foxhounds in these modern days? Is it to show a fast burst to a hard-riding field with perhaps a lost fox at the end of it? Is it to show a slow hound-hunt to a lot of people who appreciate good hound work, perhaps marking a fox to ground at the end—or if lucky, killing him? Is it to win on the flags at Peterborough or Aldershot or Honiton? Is it to kill foxes? Or is it a combination of two or more of the above? I think, myself, that the third qualification ought not to be seriously considered if, as is sometimes the case, it interferes with the one which to me—particularly in these modern days —is all-important.

Perhaps it is because I have been a Master of Hounds who has hunted his own pack for a number of years that this is so. I know from experience that unless foxes are killed—not merely "accounted for"—the farmers in the country will not be satisfied, and that, it seems to me, must be the first consideration.

In America, it is otherwise. Foxes are not sufficiently numerous to be a serious menace to farmers—or even to poultrymen—but in Great Britain, they are a real menace if not properly kept down, and it is absolutely essential for the welfare of the country to let it become generally known that if a fox is causing serious loss, he will be summarily dealt with if the Hunt is advised of the fact. The riding man who wants a gallop must be considered, but after all, your true foxhunter with the interests of the pack at heart, should be —and usually is—content to take his sport as it comes, and to remember that his individual tastes cannot be considered of paramount importance. If then, the killing of the fox is the first consideration, one is faced with the problem of how best to breed a pack of hounds suited to one's needs in the country which it hunts in.

We must remember that conditions have changed enormously in the last sixty years, and are changing even to-day. Wire fencing, motors with their attendant tarmac roads, the electrification of railways, all make it more difficult to accomplish the desired result. The long, slow hunts are a thing of the past, and the modern foxhound has to work under much less advantageous conditions than did his forebears. To-day, I am willing to wager that eighty per cent of the foxes killed are killed within forty minutes from the time they are found, and if one breeds a type of foxhound that can "burst" his fox in the first twenty-five minutes, one is much more likely to kill in the end.

In order to do this, one must breed hounds which are quick, and can be gotten away close behind their fox when he is found; hounds which will push him hard from the outset,

A Royal Mail van,
January 1939.

and yet possess nose enough to be able to press their advantage with a failing scent and get him in the end. It does not seem important to me to breed a hound whose sphere of usefulness extends beyond his fourth or fifth season. I shall be criticised for this statement, but I cannot see the use of sacrificing efficiency in the field to longevity.

We are told that many of the great hounds of the past "hunted at the head of the pack right up to the end of their seventh, eighth, or ninth, or even tenth season." I am glad they did; but does it not often strike one, in reading of these feats of prowess, that the pace of that pack must have been comparatively slow? What racehorse that has ever been bred retained his speed after middle age? What man has ever been able to stand hard physical strain after he has passed his prime? Why should a Master of Hounds wish to keep a foxhound after he has done four or possibly five seasons, except for breeding purposes? The strength of a pack lies in its second and third season hunters, and a Master, if he is a knowledgeable breeder of foxhounds, should be able to produce a first-class entry year after year. If one grants the above, what is the use in sacrificing certain qualities to obtain longevity?

Any man who has had to do with hunting must be aware of the fact that a different type of horse is needed for the level, open pastures which one finds in the Shires, as compared with the hilly going which predominates in many of the provincial countries, and this fact applies to hounds as well as horses. A new Master coming into a country with which he is not familiar, should always bear this fact in mind, and see to it that he breeds hounds which, in conformation and scenting ability, are best suited to the country in which they are to hunt. If one cannot produce something better—not as good, but better—each year, he is a failure as a breeder. But if he produces something better, the old must make way for the new.

It seems to me that constitution, combined with nose, voice, and drive—with speed as a matter of course—and good looks and uniformity as a very pleasing, but not essential attribute—should be the goal sought after, and that the most important thing, which must never be lost sight of, is that a pack of hounds should be bred that can kill foxes regularly and in proper style.

18 October 1947

HUNTING—A KILL IN THE COMMONS

On Friday, February 25, the Private Member's Bill entitled Protection of Animals (Hunting and Coursing Prohibition) Bill, introduced by Mr. Seymour Cocks (Soc., Broxtowe), lost its second reading in the House of Commons by 214 votes to 101. The following is an abridged version of the debate.

IN moving the second reading of his Bill Mr. Cocks said he was trying to speak for creatures which could not speak for themselves, and to appeal for protection against the thoughtless cruelties of man. He introduced the names of several prominent people who supported the Bill, and caused loud laughter from Opposition members when he came to that of Prof. Laski.

Referring to a report that foxhunters were to ride down Piccadilly in protest against the Bill, he said he thought it might have amused the late Mr. Oscar Wilde to see the unspeakable pursuing the uneatable in the vicinity of Leicester Square.

Mr. Cocks quoted extracts from an article in a Sunday newspaper describing coursing and how greyhounds went for the entrails of the hare, but was interrupted by Brig. Head (Con., Carshalton), who said that anybody who has had dealings with greyhounds knows that that statement is utterly untrue.

Mr. Cocks said the only defence of coursing he had heard was that it helped to keep down the number of hares, but that was disproved by figures issued by the British Field Sports Society which showed that very few hares coursed were killed.

Supporting the Bill Mr. Carson (Isle of Thanet) said he had been down to his constituency to find out what the opponents of the Bill were saying, and organised distortion of what it sought to do had been put forward. It was his belief that it was fundamentally wrong to chase these animals, putting the fear of God into them and then to have them killed by dogs in the name of sport. He would not be right in sacrificing one of the basic principles of what he believed to gain a little easy popularity.

Mr. Maurice Webb (Soc., Bradford Central) asked for the rejection of the Bill. The fact that there was a strong feeling in the countryside against the Bill was something of which the House must take note. There was angry opposition to the Measure not only in the countryside but in many industrial districts in the North where coursing was a pastime to which people have given their support for many years.

The "chasing of animals by a handful of idle playboys" was not a true picture of the situation. It was something with which the ordinary people in large numbers throughout the country have occupied themselves for many years.

Opposition cheers greeted his remarks that "as the Mother of Parliaments it is not our business to stop children doing everything just because they are doing it. It is not our business to say, 'Go outside and see what the people are doing and tell them not to.'"

He could not think that here there was any abuse or mischief which was intolerable and offensive to the public interest. There was gross exaggeration of the degree of cruelty that existed and he was convinced there was no cruelty in hunting which could not be covered by the existing law. Mr. Webb concluded: "I do not want to eliminate completely sections of wild life which must be kept going. I should like to think there will always be foxes in this island. Nature effects a kind of balance, but I am convinced that hunting by man is an essential element of nature affecting the balance in wild life."

Sir Jocelyn Lucas (Portsmouth, South) said one reason why he did not support the Bill was that the anti-sport societies backing it had said openly that it was intended as a first step towards the prevention of hunting, shooting and fishing. The essence of sport in field sports was that the animal hunted should have every possible chance of escape.

Mr. Kenyon (Chorley) suggested that if members had to watch hare and rabbit coursing the sport would be quickly ended. It was the most revolting, cruel and degrading so-called sport in the country. He was interrupted several times when he alleged he had seen hares torn to pieces on the field.

"I was amazed at the speech of Mr. Webb," he added. "The overwhelming feeling of our movement is in favour of this Bill."

Mr. Manningham Buller (Daventry) said instances of alleged cruelty had been unable to give the date or place of one incident he quoted. He regretted the livid accounts that were published and were found to be quite untrue. If the case for the Bill was a good one there would be no need to bolster it up by untruths. He maintained that killing by hunting was the least cruel method.

Mr. Manningham Buller quoted from a bulletin issued by the National Society for the Abolition of Cruel Sports in which it said that for tactical reasons foxhunting was excluded from the Bill. These people will next attack other sports if they get it on the Statute Book, he said.

Mr. Stubbs (Cambridgeshire) opposed the Bill, and said the stories they had heard had come from people who did not understand country life. Our bloodstock industry was an important one and our horses which were used not only for racing but for foxhunting earned us dollars by their sale to the United States.

The late Col. "Taffy" Walwyn, one of the founders of the British Show Jumping Association, on Stuck Again.

Mr. Richards (Wrexham) spoke on behalf of the Bill and remarked that years ago his party passed resolutions to abolish blood sports and added: "I am sorry to find that they are apparently intending to alter their attitude now they are the Government of the country. A party which changes its policy on the grounds of expediency is not a party for which any of us have any deep respect.

Mr. Vernon Bartlett (Bridgwater) opposed the Bill and said he had received requests to do so from over 170 of his constituents, and only 19 requests to support it. They had no more right, he stated, to over-rule the feelings of people from rural areas than to impose a ban on any of the amusements of the people in the cities.

Mr. Thomas Williams, Minister of Agriculture, said he yielded to no one in detesting unnecessary cruelty and referred to his support of a similar Bill in 1925. One should never be ashamed to own that sometimes one may be wrong.

"Since then I have learned a good deal not only about hunting but about governing people to the advantage of many of my hon. Friends."

He was satisfied that to abolish hunting without providing

an effective alternative (and the Bill did not provide one) would mean there certainly would be more rather than less cruelty in the country.

This controversy endangers our food production drive, and any interference with these sports except on grounds of national emergency, might have serious consequences to the nation. He read a letter from a chairman of a county executive committee which stated:—

"Hunting is often the only form of recreation for farmers in the winter and most farm workers take an interest in the hunt, and take every opportunity of watching the hounds when they pass near their homes. I have just been told that certain hill shepherds have said that if hunting is stopped they will not remain in the out of the way places."

Mr. Williams continued: "Another disquieting feature is the feeling that this is a townsman's attack upon the life of the country, and that the arguments of cruelty are merely a cloak. This feeling is there and the psychological reaction could not be in the national interest.

"They read about football matches with 80,000 people and know special trains are put on and that thousands of cars are at present all using dollar petrol. They read of greyhound racing collecting 20,000 to 25,000 people, and know that theatres are full and cinemas bursting with people, yet so far as I know, they make no complaint.

"I have read articles about 'Sadists in fancy dress' and am surprised a Londoner should use that sort of language. It may get the headlines but it is not an argument for or against the Bill.

"The primary purpose of hunts is recreation and the joy of the chase and 19 out of every 20 who follow the hunt never see a fox and certainly never see a kill."

The kill is usually instantaneous and if the decision is to be based on cruelty no case has been made out for the Bill.

The Bill left it to the Minister to specify alternative methods of destruction, and Mr. Williams said he could sanction hunting if necessary.

"Very nice, thank you," he commented. "To-day they are hunting the hunters. To-morrow they will be hunting me." He said it was no part of Government policy to nationalise packs of hounds, in case some Minister of Agriculture in the

Capt. M. P. (now Col. Sir Michael) Ansell jumping his horse Leopard without reins at Aldershot in 1932.

future may consider it the best way to deal with excessive concentration of deer, hares, rabbits, or something else.

For nine years our people had had to forego many liberties and put up with measures of austerity, he concluded. Was this the right moment to make another attack on freedom of action?

Earl Winterton (Horsham) submitted that the Bill carried inconsistency to a point where it was indistinguishable from gross hypocrisy.

"Can any Member say that a salmon caught by rod and line fighting for 20 minutes with a hook in its mouth and then landed with a gaff feels less pain than a badger or hare?" This was not dealt with in the Bill because Members below the Gangway were afraid to lose the votes of thousands of fishermen.

He said the crown of absurdity should be awarded to the Royal Society for the Prevention of Cruelty to Animals, which thinks it right to hunt foxes but wrong to hunt otters which are just as destructive. In no other country could such a body get away with that without being ridiculed out of existence.

Among the less desirable elements behind this Bill were the "Bloomsbury Boys" who invented the satirical phrase, "huntin', fishin' and shootin'." Their patron saint was Oscar Wilde, who he did not expect Mr. Cocks would have wished to cite as his supporter. The "Bloomsbury Boys" opposed these outdoor sports because they required courage, endurance and physical fitness—every quality which was anathema to them.

He recalled a case in which a man was charged with cruelty to a cat by throwing a stone at it. It was reported that 15 women in that court fainted at this cruelty.

"Would they faint if they were told of some of the horrors put on human beings behind the Iron Curtain?" he asked. "Not one of them. A cat must be protected but not a human being."

Earl Winterton concluded by saying that the Bill should be rejected because it was dripping with dishonesty, evasiveness and inefficiency.

Mr. Symonds (Cambridge) said that the people who ought to see psychiatrists were those who supported blood sports because the very violence of their opposition to any form of social control suggested a guilty feeling.

The late Mr Reg Hindley, Captain of the 1952 Olympic Three-day team.

Supporters of the Bill appreciated that there was cruelty in nature, and that there may be cruelty in any form of reduction of pests, but they saw no reason why cruelty, even if necessary and inevitable should be made into a public festival and holiday, and even less reason why pests and vermin should be specially preserved for hunting.

As he saw it, if it was wrong to set dogs on a cat, it was not right to set dogs on a deer simply by calling them hounds. As an alternative to hunting, shooting was to be recommended and the effect would be a steady reduction in the number of pests to be controlled.

Mr. Symonds quoted a letter he had received from the delegates of the North Devon Divisional Labour Party stating that the Division protested strongly against the Government withdrawing its support from the Bill, and said he was sure a large part of the suggested strong feeling in the country was not genuine.

Major Legge-Bourke (Isle of Ely) asked Mr. Symonds why he thought it more suitable to quote from a Labour Party resolution in North Devon when the Cambridgeshire National Farmers' Union, 2248 strong, asked for the Bill to be opposed.

When Mr. Symonds said he did not represent Cambridgeshire, Major Legge-Bourke commented: "Or North Devon."

Viscountess Davidson (Hemel Hempstead) opposing the

Bill, said those who had been brought up in the countryside knew how difficult it had been to make townspeople understand problems of the countryside. To-day there was a better relationship between the two communities than in the past and it was a disastrous moment to undo the good which had been done.

They had been told there was a general desire to lift controls and to abolish unnecessary interference with the individual, but here was a case where those without any personal experiences and knowledge were attempting to force the countryside to accept something with which they did not agree.

Mr. Collins (Taunton) submitted that the Bill was not one to abolish hunting, but a Bill for the promotion of cruelty to wild animals. So far as he could judge 95 per cent. of people in his constituency (which included Exmoor) were opposed to the Bill.

If the League Against Cruel Sports denoted a small proportion of the time, money and energy at present spent on inaccurate and ill-informed propaganda, on research on the best methods of humanely controlling deer and foxes they might have a case. They might eventually find that properly controlled hunting was the most humane.

In his Division, he said, they had more than ten Hunts and he had never heard a single complaint against hunting from any farmer.

Mr. Anthony Greenwood (Heywood and Radcliffe) supporting the Bill, said it was moderate and of very limited scope. He did not agree that if otter hunting were stopped the otter would be exterminated, and also considered that the damage done by deer was grossly exaggerated.

He concluded "Nine chairmen of country agricultural executive committees have told my right hon. Friend that he can forget about cropping targets if this Bill goes through. Are we, the Parliament of this country, to be dictated to by nine chairmen of county agricultural executive committees? This party made a mistake in 1931 when it surrendered to the bankers and we shall be making a mistake in 1949 if we surrender to a handful of chairmen of committees who have been appointed by my right hon. Friend."

The House divided: Ayes 101; Noes 214.

5 March 1949

OUT TO GRASS

THE end of the hunting season varies according to the locality hunted. For instance, on moor or downland the season ends later in the year than in what is known as 'in-country', the main reason for this being that in the former country there are no early sowings or young crops liable to damage.

Before hunters go out to grass, they are roughed-off in stables. This operation consists of cessation of clipping, discontinuance of grooming, whereby the grease remains in the coat giving additional warmth, light exercising only, and when at this nibbling at grass should be indulged in, the periods increasing daily.

Reduce the corn ration by gradual means until it is eliminated altogether. Feed dampened bran and chaff and a liberal ration of hay to which it is advisable to add some green meat. These items should form the main diet, bulk being required to prevent loss of flesh.

This is often a trying time of the year for horses, when winter coats are being shed with the consequent liability of loss of condition. Ventilation should be increased by gradual methods, first by opening the windows day and night and later by opening the upper halves of stable doors, reducing the number of rugs worn and as the grease accumulates in the coat discarding the rugs altogether. Prior to this final phase of de-rugging the hunter should have been acclimatised and hardened to the increased ventilation.

Some people like physicking before putting out to grass, others do not. Physicking is said to be good for horses which have been on exceptionally high living and also cooling for the blood and system. If this procedure is carried out, it should be done early on, and before the main part of roughing-off comes into operation.

Another item is blistering. The legs should be carefully examined; a hard season renders them liable to knocks, bruises, blows, strains and sprains, thus it may be necessary to blister in order to strengthen the limbs in preparation for the time when the horse is next brought into work. It is advisable to carry out this process a week or so before putting the animal into the fields.

Lady Wright, a well-known and successful show jumping rider between the wars, seen here on Toby.

Removal of the shoes and paring down the hoofs should be done by the blacksmith on the morning of the day the animal is being put into the fields, and it is as well to have a blacksmith's examination once a month during the grazing period.

The best time to turn out is at the end of April or early May. This is governed by the state of the weather and the condition of the grazing. Some horsemasters prefer to allow their charges to graze for a few hours daily before finally turning them out altogether—this by way of acclimatisation, which is no doubt beneficial, though often followed with a lot of botheration in recapture for return to the stable.

Choose good grazing. There is a variety of grasses for selection: cocksfoot, Timothy, meadow foxtail, hard fescue and others; avoid coarse, souri and broad grasses. Observation and enquiry will usually give the desired information.

Drinking water is another matter for consideration. Spring water is best, and if not available endeavour to obtain a field wherein there is running water.

Roomy fields affording shade and protection are desirable; avoid those fenced with barbed wire and pocked with rabbit holes. Sloping fields have their points, for they catch the breeze and so blow the flies away; on the other hand they need shelter as a protection during heavy storms.

Opinions vary as to the duration of grazing in the summer season. In this respect much depends on the work done and what will have to be done, and also the condition of the grazing. Hard and fast rules cannot be laid down.

Some are of the opinion that grazing is not necessary for the hunter, which fares better if kept in a roomy box. It is contended that a big horse is not so liable to do well out at grass, and if it gets pulled down it is a long and difficult business to bring it back into hard hunting condition, whereby it will be ready in time for the season. Also there are ideas that grazing is bad for the wind, due to the size of the larynx in big and small horses being the same. This latter opinion were better left to the scientific expert rather than to the amateur owner.

QUOI HAI.   21 April 1951

ARABS AND THEIR BREEDING
BY LADY WENTWORTH

Two hundred years ago the pure Arabian breed was universally recognised in all countries and by all nations as the most celebrated, best, biggest, fastest and most beautiful, as well as the oldest of all light breeds and the synonym for speed. It is only quite recently that it has been the fashion for modern writers to treat the Arabian as a made-up breed dating from as late as A.D. 600, originating anywhere except in Arabia.

All facts, historical, genealogical, pictorial and osteological, unite in proving that the Arabian is a foundation breed and not a derivation from anything at all. It represents quality, speed and beauty, which belong only to the hot-blooded division of the two main foundation stocks of the world—cold and hot—from the admixture of which all other breeds are developed.

The Arabian is the oldest breed of which we have any detailed records. The survival of his type throughout the centuries, unchanged, is one of the most notable of his many remarkable characteristics and the breed has spread all over the world infusing quality everywhere. In actual speed the

Twenty-four year old Broncho, owned and ridden by the late Brig. Malise Graham, a fine show jumping combination of horse and rider, winners of King George V Cup in 1925 at Olympia.

Arabian's specialised progeny have left him behind, but he is still the fastest of unspecialised natural breeds, and still unrivalled in staying power and stamina by any breed, improved or unimproved.

The unique prepotency of pure Arabian blood is now as great as ever: it imparts "class" together with stamina and soundness, but it must be remembered that Arabs of degenerate weedy conformation will not improve anything and care must be taken to select sires with the breed characteristics strongly marked. Evidence of pure descent is shown in several main points:

1. Gazelle head, broad forehead, undulating profile tapering to a small muzzle with large nostrils. Extremely large eyes placed low in the head, and small delicately shaped, pricked ears.

2. Arched neck, crest and arched throat set into wide jaws.

3. High set, high carried tail and level back; free, sprightly action and great pride of carriage. Heavy bone is not characteristic of either the Arabian or the Thoroughbred and is not allied with speed, but legs should be straight and strong and not tied in below knee or hock.

No Arab should have a long, narrow head, small eye or ewe neck. Degeneracy first shows in the head and common faults are shortness from hip to tail and pinched narrow quarters, slovenly carriage of tail and slackness of action.

Arabs should have large flat hocks and good hock action. This hock action is very important. The front action should be shooting out from the shoulder, not up and down knee action. Shoulder well sloped and withers well marked—the ordinary good points of a good horse apply equally to Arabs. They are horses not ponies and must be judged as such.

It is a common fallacy to think Arabs will deteriorate and become "soft" unless kept on short rations and exposed to hardship. On the contrary, the better fed and sheltered from rain, wind and cold in winter the better they will thrive and develop.

The late Col. Jack Hance.

The conformation of a horse can be marred to the point of distortion by so-called "hardening" during the first three years of its life. Irregular growth, resulting in overgrowth of head and undergrowth of limbs, will overweight a starved body and do damage which can never be repaired. The lost development is lost for ever and nothing you can do will be of any avail after the bones are set.

In the last century the Arabian breed was considered the ideal for polo owing to its fast sprinting speed and astonishing apitude for quick turning. It is a pity that the abolition of the 14 hands 2in limit turned the game into a semi-professional contest between the few owners of big expensive horses, instead of the old army game of India which was the joy of the many less wealthy owners of small Arabs and which was popular everywhere.

Surely a game confined to the 14 hands 2in limit could be popularised once more in addition to the game for the "highbrows"? This would create an admirable market for the smaller Arabs and one in which our younger riders could enjoy something more exciting than parading up and down a show ring, too much of which is apt to be boring to spectators.

Harness is almost obsolete except in the shows, but Arabians make first-class light harness horses and can trot a great pace and keep it up for long distances.

As hunters some of them are good, but I prefer Anglo-Arabs, which have more size and a longer rein and a bit more speed and are not quite so impetuous. They are also better than Thoroughbreds being sounder in legs and wind. In fact

I consider Anglo-Arabs of the first and second generations, and some cross-breds by Arab sires, among the best hunters and hacks which the world can now produce.

The excellence of Arab crosses on ponies is amply proved by the outstanding super champion Pretty Polly, bred in Ireland from an Arab of pure Crabbet blood and now sweeping prizes off the board wholesale in England.

America is breeding some very good Arabs, chiefly from importations from England and their leading all-Arab show musters up to 300 horses.

There has been some controversy lately as to what percentage of Arab and Thoroughbred blood constitutes an Anglo-Arab, but mathematical calculations are useless to define it. When we consider that the grey colour of the Alcock Arabian is as potent now as it was over 250 years ago, it may be said that a cross of Arab blood is indelible and its influence may re-appear at any time however mathematically diluted it may be.

The Thoroughbred was established under that name 100 years ago and any Arab cross since then is inevitably Anglo-Arab, for it is neither Thoroughbred nor Arab.

14 July 1951

NEW ZEALAND RUGS

So many readers seem to have trouble both with the fitting of the New Zealand rug and the care of the animals using it that it is hoped this article, based on a good deal of practical experience, may help them.

To the needle-women of the horse-world I suggest "Make your own." It is *not* difficult. All you want is the green water-proof canvas that garden-chairs are made of, some carpet-felt, a thin soft old blanket, a few yards of three-inch webbing, four buckles and straps (any saddler will stitch these on for you), a strong tailor's needle, waxed thread and, if you have a sewing-machine, it saves time binding the edges.

During the first year of the war I had disastrous results with a borrowed N.Z. rug owing to a mare resenting the straps swinging between her hind legs and galloping into a pond, where she nearly drowned before we got her out. So I set about inventing one and made five during the war years. They were a complete success.

The rug also has the advantage of being much cheaper, much warmer, never slips back or moves when the horse is rolling *and* you can make it to fit your own horse.

Spread the canvas on the floor and lay a rug that fits your horse on top. Cut out, allowing for a triangular gusset inset where the withers go and at least three inches more depth all round for tucking under tummy, covering quarters well and over-lapping round chest. Use carpet-felt as inner-lining and thin blanket as outer, and bind all three materials together at edges.

Make two surcingles out of webbing, fit rug on horse, and safety-pin one into place immediately behind the withers and the other about six to eight inches behind the first to keep the rug down over loins. Sew these firmly halfway down each side, allowing the remainder to hang like a girth.

Then make a breeching-band from the webbing and sew on each side of the back edges. The tail is, of course, pulled over band when rug is adjusted.

Get your saddler to stitch two buckles and straps (over-lapping) as breast-straps and buckles and straps on the two surcingles and your rug is finished. If wanted for a trace-clipped horse in bad weather, then omit the carpet felt.

The novice owner must realise from the start that the New Zealand rug is an economy in *labour* only. Any animal doing hard work or fast work off winter pasture should have all the oats he can eat and, if left out, a hay-net, stuffed with the best seed-hay procurable, hung on a railing or a tree at night.

If appearance is a secondary consideration, then it is an immense economy in labour, as it eliminates mucking-out entirely, to a large extent grooming, as the horse is better left with the grease in his coat and all exercise between hunting-days if he has good range at grass.

If the oats are fed on short grass he will pick up every one without being able to bolt them, which eliminates the hardest labour of all—chaff-cutting.

The toil of mash-making can be almost forgotten, too, as, even on winter grass, a horse will find his right medicine without the laxative of damp bran and boiled linseed. In cold weather it is advisable to give gruel or chilled water in the

The late Mr Horace Smith, well known with his daughter Sybil as riding instructors, at their Cadogan Lane riding school. They taught several members of the Royal Family.

stable on returning from hunting and the main feed after half-an-hour of walking about the field grazing and rolling.

Horses seldom "break out" or sweat under their rug like this, and I have found that the most highly-strung, excitable animals who stand quivering in the stables or rushing to the door after hunting, instead of getting on with their mash, will graze at once and lick up the last oat of their evening feed.

Being the natural way of keeping a horse, as against the artificial, coughs and colds are very rare. Horses are quieter, but just as fit, and the elimination of road-exercise is an enormous saving, not only on shoes, but all foot troubles and many leg troubles, too.

I have never seen a case of azitorea or kidney trouble at grass, and lice should never put in an appearance if the animal is well fed and the rug well shaken out and aired in the sun or on a hot pipe when he is at work.

To those that can afford to turn out spotless and shining at the meet, the New Zealand rug is hardly a necessary or a practical proposition, but to the hard-up brigade who prefer to spend their all on forage—they are invaluable.

W. GEARE.   5 January 1952

OUR GREAT VICTORY AT HELSINKI

BY LIEUT.-COL. MICHAEL ANSELL

AT Helsinki, on August 3, the Olympic Grand Prix des Nations for the World's Jumping Championship was held. The competition was timed to start at the early hour of 8 a.m., which necessitated horses and riders preparing themselves for the long day about 5 o'clock. Twenty nations were represented by 58 riders.

The course was large, as expected, but not such a formidable proposition as that at Wembley in 1948. The arena in the main stadium was the size of a football ground; and although the going was good, it was undoubtedly slippery during the first few hours. About 840 yards long, the course necessitated two changes of direction. It consisted of 13 obstacles, which totalled 16 individual efforts or jumps.

The first fence was a brush with a white rail about 4ft 3in high, which was immediately followed by a triple bar 4ft 6in high with a 6ft spread, with a wattle hurdle under each rail. These two were hardly touched throughout the day. The rider then circled left along the end of the arena and across to the left diagonal, where he met three fences. First came the parallel bars (4ft 8in, with a 5ft spread) with sloped trusses of straw underneath. This was followed by a post and rails at 4ft 9in, and then a wide spread fence made of parallel yellow planks (4ft 8in high with a 6ft spread). A fence that made the horses "look," this was, perhaps, the first which offered any serious problem to high-class horses.

Circling right and coming down the outside of the arena, the rider then met a treble, the first fence being a wattle gate 4ft 7in high followed by a wattle jump 9ft wide at 34ft 6in distance, and then the third fence at 34ft distance from the water, a log wall 5ft high. This caused little trouble as the distances were correct. However, the water (or what one might legitimately call a puddle) seemed rather senseless.

The next fence, No. 7, a triple of brush at 4ft 11in with a 7ft spread, for some reason caused difficulty to a number of horses. The reason probably was the second rail not being sufficiently high. During the morning a number of horses

The last American polo team to visit this country before the Second World War. From left to right, Eric Pedley, Michael Phipps, Stewart B. Inglehart and Winston Guest.

refused at this fence and caused endless delays, as surprisingly in so important an event the organisers did not appear to have sufficient spare material. One horse in particular was kept waiting in the ring for over 20min whilst repairs were made!

The rider then circles right, across the end of the stadium, to return on the right diagonal. This provided one of the deciding factors of the competition. The first fence met was a double—parallel rustic gates 4ft 7in high with a large spread of 7ft. This was followed by another spread—parallel rustic poles, with brush in the middle, 4ft 6in high with a wide spread of 4ft 6in. The distance between these—24ft—was measured from inside to inside, and was correct for one long non-jumping stride with a horse galloping on. Should a horse jump this slowly he had to take two short non-jumping strides, and this lack of speed made it difficult to jump the two large spread fences.

Fence No. 9 was a formidable cream straight wall, 5ft 3in high and only 69ft from the double. Following rapidly came a bank of flowers with a white rail (4ft 10in), only 46ft from the wall. These last two were not difficult if the double was jumped correctly; but for the horses faulted there the wall was a severe test, as the stride would then be incorrect.

The rider then rounded the end of the arena, bearing left

to the outside lane, where lay the second great problem of the course. This was the open water (16ft) followed by a large gate at 5ft 3in; but this was only 90ft from water. Only one horse throughout the day jumped these two fences without fault—Aherlow.

The competitor then turned left for the final obstacle (No. 13), a bank of green flowers with parallel bars standing 4ft 11in high with a 7ft 6in spread.

Fences were all at least 15ft wide. Rails were painted white, and for the spectator the course looked rather "naked" and lacking in colour. The obstacles were certainly large and formidable, and necessitated great jumping; but one is accustomed to seeing courses as large in Nations Cups.

First British horse, Aherlow, ridden by Lt.Col. D. N. Stewart, entered the arena about 8.40 a.m. The mare jumped the first two fences perfectly, and perhaps her rider took a risk in not giving himself sufficient room when approaching the parallel rails and straw, where the mare put in a short stride and hit the fence.

Jumping well, she reached the double, and here again the mare failed to stand back, hit the first and was all wrong for the second, which she also hit. Col. Stewart then jumped the next two perfectly, cleared the water and gate with ease, and completed the course with 12 faults. A satisfactory beginning, when no horse had as yet made less than eight faults.

Mr. Wilf White with Nizefela jumped a really brilliant round. He is a rider of extensive experience and, with Nizefela, there is no more reliable combination. With perfect precision, he completed the course with only the gate down. His riding at the water roused the admiration of all, as on each occasion he brought Nizefela so close that he hit the bottom of the take-off fence and so jumped the wide spread with ease.

When each team had sent in two horses in the first round the scores were : Italy 12, Britain and Portugal 16. We were thus well placed at this stage. However, sensations were soon to come.

The name of Lt. Piero d'Inzeo was called. After a lapse of some 10min it was announced that he had been disqualified as he was not ready. This was a blow for Italy, then in the lead; but as events later turned out it made no difference to

Col. Harry Llewellyn on his famous show jumper, Foxhunter, the horse whose name is now world-renowned as that given to the popular novice show jumping competition.

the final result.

Next sensation was that of Foxhunter. Lt.-Col. Llewellyn entered the ring with the horse looking superb and calm. It is our custom to expect Foxhunter never to fail, and it should be remembered that all are liable to make mistakes; but indeed it was a tragedy that this brilliant horse should do so on such a day. He jumped the first four fences without fault, then faulted behind at the parallel planks. He appeared to approach the double too slowly, but with awkward jumps got over although obviously unbalanced.

The great cream wall he cleared with a supreme effort, almost from a standstill, and in so doing unseated his rider; but by the grace of the gods he managed to remain on the horse. Struggling back, having refused at the bank of flowers, he then jumped it with a fault and cleared the water with ease only to hit the gate, finishing with $16\frac{1}{4}$ faults. This was a bitter disappointment to Harry Llewellyn and to all those who have such complete confidence in this great pair.

At the end of the first round the scores were: U.S.A., 23; Portugal, 24; Argentina, 28; Brazil, $28\frac{1}{2}$; Germany, 32; Britain, $32\frac{3}{4}$; Egypt, 33; Spain, 35; France, Sweden and Mexico, 36. F. Thiedmann jumped a brilliant, clean round for Germany, and led in the individual placings.

The second round commenced at 3.15 p.m. in brilliant

sunshine, before a packed stadium of some 70,000 excited spectators. Certainly one was offered a contest the drama and excitement of which probably has never been equalled.

The danger from Argentina was settled in the first round, when Don Juan, ridden by Sagasta, appeared to hit himself halfway round. Although lame, he completed the course with $20\frac{1}{4}$ faults.

Lt.-Col. Stewart, riding probably one of the greatest rounds of his life on Aherlow, faulted only at the "puddle" in the centre of the treble, and this only because Aherlow jumped too big over the wattle gate. No praise can be too great for Duggie Stewart. He came in at a critical time and with great courage and determination put us really in the battle.

By the time each nation had jumped one horse for the second time Britain had held the U.S.A. at their same lead, as McCashin on Miss Budweiser had made only one mistake; but France, thanks to a brilliant clean round by d'Oriola on Ali Baba, had gained on us. However, we had moved up to second place.

Wilf White on Nizefela again jumped a really brilliant round and, like Duggie Stewart, had only four faults. These he got at the big water jump, which was difficult to under-stand as he again hit the bottom of the take-off fence and seemed to jump it exactly as before.

The critical time came with the entrance of Russell on Democrat, the U.S.A. second horse. He faulted at the yellow planks, wall, the water and the last fence for a total of 16, and this put Britain in the lead for the first time, with only one horse each to jump.

The task of securing the victory was thus left to Fox-hunter. He entered the ring and appeared to realise how much depended on him. It was a different horse and rider we saw in the afternoon; it was indeed Foxhunter in his usual form. Fence after fence he cleared with ease to jump a clear round and so ensure the first Gold Medals that Britain has ever won in an Olympic equestrian event.

The third Chilean horse, Pillan, ridden by Mendoza, also jumped clean, giving Chile second place with $45\frac{3}{4}$ faults and the U.S.A. third with $52\frac{1}{4}$.

For the Individual Gold Medal five riders were equal with eight faults for the two rounds. These jumped off over the

first six fences, some now raised to 5ft 11in. In the event of further ties time was to decide.

Ali Baba (France) jumped a superb fast round without fault to give d'Oriola the individual prize. Christi (Chile) on Bambi was second with four faults; third was Thiedemann (Germany) on Meteor with 8 faults, in better time than Menezes (Brazil) on Bigua. Nizefela had 12 faults.

No praise can be too great for the three British riders. At half-time we had set ourselves a severe task. With great determination and courage our riders and horses fought their way into the lead, and Foxhunter made ample amends for his earlier failures with that wonderful clear round.

Mr. White was undoubtedly the team's "full back." He was indeed unlucky not to have won the individual Gold Medal, for no horse and rider gave two more convincing displays.

Aherlow, after a shaky first round, was ridden brilliantly in the all-important second.

All the riders and horses went to, and returned from, Helsinki by air.

For four years the B.S.J.A. have worked and planned with this Olympiad in view. At times there has been some criticism, but all these critics surely must now be proud of this great achievement.

Our riders and horses have proved the supremacy today of British jumping throughout the world. This has only been achieved by careful planning and the loyal support of the many who have lent horses so generously and subscribed to the funds. These may well feel satisfied.

It was indeed a proud moment to see them standing on the daïs in the centre of the vast stadium, receiving the greatest of all honours whilst the massed bands played God Save the Queen.

9 August 1952

THE FOUR QUEENS

THE Queen's undisguised love of racing, inherited perhaps from the long line of her Royal ancestors, has greatly endeared her to the large section of her subjects who share her enthusiasm. Dimly, maybe, they are aware of the traditional support which royalty has given to racing since the earliest days. It is well now to recall that Her Majesty is the fourth queen to occupy the throne whose pleasure it has been to encourage our great sport.

Count Robert Orssich.

Elizabeth—Queen Bess of romance—and two of her Masters of Horse—the Earls of Leicester and Essex—showed their enthusiasm for horse-breeding (we hesitate to call it bloodstock breeding) by precept and example, crystallized by numerous enactments calculated to encourage horse breeding to suit the requirements of their time. The Hampton Court Stud, with which our Royal Family has had an almost unbroken association, was one of the earliest studs owned by the King, and it is odd that, although eclipsed in Elizabeth's day by the Royal Studs at Malmesbury and at Tutbury, it has outlived them both.

Elizabeth, however, seems to have taken a livelier interest in her racing stables at St. Albans and Windsor and, more especially, at Greenwich. Here she kept some forty "coursers," with their attendant trainers, stable hands and two jockeys, or "ryders."

Queen Anne's reign was all too brief for her to have made any notable impression on the Turf, either as a breeder or as a racehorse owner. The early part of the eighteenth century was, however, a period of progress and expansion. It was the period when some of the great founder sires were imported, such as the Darley Arabian, and when Flying Childers was foaled. The Queen had frequently visited Newmarket with her father as a child and maintained her racing establishment, with the notorious Frampton Tregenwell as her trainer.

She and her Consort were generous donors of cups and other trophies, some of which are still in existence. One of them is the Saltby Gold Plate, a beautiful two-handled cup. Another trophy (like all Queen Anne's racing trophies, collectors' pieces) was the Hambleton Gold Cup of a hundred guineas, won by the mare Penelope. Cups and plates were also given to Newmarket and elsewhere, but none more historic than the plate inaugurated for the famous race on Ascot Heath on August 11, 1711. The Queen and her ladies and gentlemen were there to see the first race run on the Heath's wide expanses; three years later she won a stakes with her own horse, Star.

Queen Victoria, a graceful horsewoman in her youth, was not a racehorse owner, although she thought fit to visit Ascot and other meetings on special occasions. As early in her reign as 1838 she drove along the New Mile at Ascot and honoured the meeting with her presence. It was she, too, who presented the first Ascot Gold Vase, first run for in 1839. She visited Ascot, Epsom and some of the country meetings, although it was Edward VII who built Sandringham and who, towards the close of her reign, made Newmarket his own.

Victoria, none the less, maintained the royal plates and, above all, the royal paddocks at Hampton Court. Records of her personal interest in the Hampton Court Stud are at present very slight, but the fact remains that, as a breeding establishment, the stud was not only run efficiently but with intelligence and, for one glorious period, with remarkable success. The Hampton Court Sales took rank with the most important of the season's functions; the roll of horses bred there, and of mares either imported or reared there, contains names illustrious in Turf history.

None is more illustrious than the filly, foaled in 1872, who was so appropriately named Quiver, daughter of Toxophilite. This wonderful mare, incomparably greater, as a foundation mare, than Sceptre or Pretty Polly have as yet been able to prove themselves, bred not only the classic sisters Memoir and La Fleche, but Maid Marian and Miss Gunning II. It is no small matter that La Fleche became the dam of John o'

Gaunt, and thus the grandam of Swynford. Maid Marian became the dam of perhaps the still greater sire Polymelus, who has had such an enormous influence on English and French breeding for more than a quarter of a century. Miss Gunning, through her daughter Silent Lady, made her notable contribution to the widely known "U" family, so successfully exploited by the Aga Khan and represented, in its latest degree, by Palestine.

St. Albans (1857), his son and grandson Springfield (1873), and Sainfoin (1887) were all Hampton Court products, and from them, in the direct male succession, we have had Tracery and his classic sons Papyrus and The Panther; later in the line came the Two Thousand Guineas winner Flamingo. It is, however, to the Hampton Court mares that the General Stud Book owes so much.

The restoration of the stud, after a series of changes following its break-up in 1937, dates from 1851, when the tenant, General Peel, having surrendered his lease and sold most of the stock, was made aware of the Queen's wishes to resume her ownership as a breeder—it is believed on the advice of the Prince Consort. The hoped-for successes did not materialize until twenty-two years later, but from that date—1873—Hampton Court became world-famous.

Wedlock, Eglentyne and Pampeluna all figure in the stud's records in the year 1874. Wedlock became an important ancestress in the G.S.B., although not in the classical school. At any rate we owe to her important winners like Fourfold, Lindos Ojos and Lapel (dam of the recent Jubilee winner Durante). Eglentyne gave us the family which produced The Tetrarch and, much later, the Gold Cup winner Supertello. Pampeluna was destined to play perhaps a still more important role.

A daughter of The Palmer, she bred Navaretta, the dam of Altoviscar. Altoviscar, perhaps forgotten nowadays, was a wonderful founder mare, from whom have descended, first and foremost, the great Foxlaw, plus the Derby winner Call Boy and the One Thousand winner Dancing Time. Of more importance to our story is that Pampeluna became the ancestress of Alope and so of Aloe and Feola, precious members of the Royal Stud, of whom Peola became the most valuable product. Her daughters Angelola, Hypericum and Above

Board all earned distinction in our time; Angelola is still more of present interest as the dam of the Queen's good colt Aureole.

30 May 1953

RUNNING A P.C. CAMP

MOST Pony Club branches go to camp for a week in August or early September. During this period the members are constantly with their ponies, and they are able to gain much valuable and concentrated instruction. To ensure that all activities will go smoothly and the maximum of benefit and enjoyment be derived from the camp, it is imperative that everything is well organized beforehand.

The first step is to find somewhere to hold the camp. The ideal situation, I think, is a park belonging to someone who is sympathetic to the local branch of the Pony Club and interested in its functions. Most country houses owning parkland have good stables attached, and these may sometimes be used for members' ponies. Alternatively, the ponies may be picketted in long lines in a shady spot near a stream or water-trough.

If possible the children can be accommodated for the week under canvas or they can travel daily from their homes. Personally, I believe the former suggestion is much the most beneficial—and enjoyable—for the children, although it means more for the District Commissioner to organize.

But travelling daily necessitates some parents continually driving back and forth from home to the camp site, and the children are not at hand early in the morning to attend to their ponies. Most children love sleeping in tents, and it is worth the small added expense and trouble that is needed to arrange this.

A hard-working and efficient staff are the backbone of the camp. They must be young, energetic and full of enthusiasm, prepared to work hard and help the children enjoy a happy and instructive week. They should make it quite clear to members on the very first day that discipline will prevail and all orders must be carried out without any shirking.

If the timetable states that the children are to feed and water at seven-thirty in the morning, see that every member is up and attending to his or her pony, not bribing someone else to do it for them. If bedtime is nine-thirty, see that they really are all in their respective tents and not eating sweets and talking in someone else's.

Generally speaking, six staff should be able to manage thirty children. Most important, of course, is the District Commissioner, who naturally has the most responsible position in the camp. To him all queries, suggestions and complaints will come. Though he probably will not have to wash a dish or sweep a stable once during the whole week, he must tactfully see that his staff are carrying out their duties and that every child is happy.

The D.C. should have at least two competent assistants capable of taking the children on rides, checking tack, etc. It will be helpful, also, if they are able to give short lectures or instructional schooling when necessary. In addition, one or two Associate members should be persuaded to come. Then there is the cook, a very important member of the staff.

For the last two years we have had an ex-army cook at our camp, and he has proved excellent. He was used to dealing with numbers and working on a field kitchen. He loved the children and was always cheerful and willing.

Calor gas or a range can be managed by two voluntary helpers acting as cooks. They will save the Club a little money, but personally I should infinitely rather pay an experienced cook than have amateurs who are unused to dealing with numbers and unfit for the heavy work.

The cook will work in conjunction with the housekeeper, who is responsible for planning all meals. He, or more generally she, would appreciate a helper, as there will be a lot of dish-washing, potato-peeling, laying of tables, etc., to do. Even with our hardworking cook there was still always a lot for our housekeeper and her assistant to attend to.

Two of the staff should sleep under canvas near the children while the rest would, I am sure, appreciate accommodation over the stables or in a nearby house. There should be at least two cars at the camp. It may be necessary to fetch milk or stores daily, and there may be emergencies like illness for which a car is indispensable.

Send round a list of essentials for members to bring to camp. For example, a pair of Wellingtons, a complete change

126

Nicolaus Silver
(H. Beasley up), winner
of the 1961 Grand
National.

of underclothes, two jerseys, and a mackintosh. Also grooming kit and tack-cleaning outfit.

If a rough estimate of food needed is made out by one competent housekeeper who has been to camp and catered for the week, then the same list can be used year after year with small modifications or changes according to camp site and ease of obtaining stores.

You may not get the same voluntary help next year, and it is a great help for the new person to have something to work on. Parents are very kind on these occasions and last year we were given fourteen dozen eggs (all we needed), some extra bacon, and a dozen rabbits.

A typed list of the day's routine should be pinned up some-where where all members can refer to it at any time. Lecturers should if possible come over every day to instruct the child-ren. At the end of the week most camps give a short performance to parents and friends. This often takes the form of a jumping display or musical ride, followed by a gymkhana. This last is, I think, important, because all the members get an opportunity to ride before their parents—not just the star turns.

Do not encourage parents to come over during the week to see how their children are getting on. Tell them that they will all be made welcome only on the final day.

Remember to arrange some indoor games and lectures in case of weather emergencies. These could take place in a garage or nearby barn. I have purposely not given an outline of a day's routine at camp because it will have to vary according to circumstances. For example, whether the ponies are stabled or picketted, the children travelling daily or sleeping under canvas and the range of country available for rides.

Given a reasonable amount of luck in the way of kind weather and freedom from illness and accidents, there is no reason why the camp should not be a tremendous success from the point of view of both members and staff.

V.H.   8 August 1953

The late Col. V. D. S. Williams, O.B.E., President of The British Horse Society in 1953 and one of the founders of the British Show Jumping Association.

BREAKING YOUR PONY

START to break a pony as soon as the foal is old enough to go out into a field with his mother by having a small soft leather head-stall made for the foal with a small tag hanging that you can catch him by. And whenever you go into the field take a few oats and give them to him so that he learns to come up to you, catch him by the head-stall and lead him about, and stroke him, making him thoroughly used to being handled, picking up his legs, etc., so that he becomes tame and un-afraid.

As a yearling I should bring him into the stable and put a surcingle on to make him used to something round his middle. When he is used to this, put a snaffle in his mouth and walk him about; having done this for ten days or so and got him thoroughly used to them, turn him out again. If you have a field near a road where there is traffic so much the better, as this will get him used to it.

128

As a two year old you can have him up again, put a saddle and snaffle on and lead him about the roads. When he is going quietly put the stirrup irons on, letting them hang loose at his side. When he is used to these, long reins may be attached to the cavesson, driving him straight on from behind.

To start with, an assistant should walk at his head to lead him when necessary and to give confidence. Later on this assistant may be dispensed with. After a fortnight of this he man be turned out again.

The next year he should be brought in and have the dumb-jockey put on, with a mouthing bit. To start with, the straps from the bit to the dumb jockey should be quite loose and gradually tightened. Be very careful that these straps are even on both sides. Then draw the top straps up until the colt's head is raised, so that his jaw is about on the level with his wither, then draw the lower straps in till the nose is brought into line with the top of his head, thus making him carry his head up and bent at the poll.

If you have the top straps loose, and lower tight, it will make him bend from the centre of the neck with his nose bent in, and if you have the top straps tight and the lower loose it will make him poke his nose, both being wrong.

Having adjusted this correctly, walk him about in a school or some enclosed place. Do not hold on to him; moving un-restrained will keep him from leaning on the bit and getting dead-mouthed, because as he walks he will relax his jaw and give to the bit. Be careful that your tackle is kept oiled and soft so as not to rub.

Do not keep this on too long. Start with six minutes or so, and next day to ten minutes, and so on up to thirty minutes. This exercise is very tiring for the muscles of the colt's neck till he gets used to it, so do not overdo it.

Having got the colt going well, carrying himself properly flexed, you can give him some work on the long reins. If you can use two reins properly do so, but if you are not certain of yourself use one lungeing rein, fastened to a ring on the cavesson.

Teach the colt to walk round in a ring, keeping him out at full length of rein by use of the whip. An assistant may be needed to start with. Teach him to trot and canter in this way, changing direction every few minutes. Bring him up to you by pulling in the rein every time your change direction. Be very careful not to frighten the colt.

Having got him quiet and going steadily at this, you can put a saddle and snaffle bridle on him the next day, and lunge him in that until you have his back down. Then get an assistant to lead him with a separate leading rein on the ring of the cavesson, get quietly on to his back, let him stand still till he is used to your weight and then walk him on.

If he plays up, your assistant must be sure not to let him go, and at the same time not to hold on too close. Give him a little rope. You may use any means you like to sit on him. Hold the saddle, but be careful not to hold on by the bridle. Let him have his head unless he tries to get it down between his legs; then you must raise it.

Keep this up till he is walking quietly along with you. Do not stay on too long, and do this every day for a week. At this period do not feed too many oats. When the colt goes quietly he may be turned out again.

I have shown above the quickest way of getting a colt backed, but if time is no object, before backing him or putting him on to the long reins I would take him into a school with a double bridle on, and after having got him used to being touched anywhere with a whip I would take the bridoon rein over his head, leaving the bit rein lying on his neck, catch the bridoon rein short just above the colt's nose, with my left hand raising the head.

Then with a whip in my right hand and standing facing him, tap him on the flank where the rider touches with his heel, viz., just behind the girth, till he moves away from your whip, making sure that he is moving up to his bit.

His forelegs should move on a small circle at the same time as his quarters move on a larger; make him move one step at a time, bringing the hind leg on the side you touch, up and across the hind leg on the opposite side; do this on both sides by changing whip to left hand and reins to right, thus making your colt used to the leg aids before you have even backed him.

Then take the pony to the side of the school, with both reins over his head, taking the reins in your right hand under his chin, with the bridoon rein between forefinger and thumb, and right curb rein between second and third, and left

between third and little finger evenly, so that by turning your wrist you can tighten the curb. Then hold the ends of reins in the left hand, with a long whip level to your side keep the pony's head up with the right hand and make him walk out by touching him behind with your whip.

This lesson teaches the colt to flex and to keep well into his bit, and when you have him walking round the school freely without having to touch him with the whip, you can stop.

I should then teach him to back, still keeping him against the wall and holding the reins in the same way; bring a steady pressure on the bit till he takes a step back, and then release it and pat him, continue this till he backs as you wish, but do not back too far at once.

If he shows obstinacy and declines to move backwards touch him with the whip on front of each fetlock till he lifts each leg in turn and puts it back. If he wants to swing his quarters towards you when backing check him with a touch of the whip. The wall stops him from swinging away from you.

Do not try to back a colt by standing in front and facing him. Firstly, it is not what you can do when riding, and secondly, you can not then prevent him swinging without roughness to his mouth.

Having taught the colt these lessons thoroughly, you have him more than half made before you back him. He can now be turned out again and kept fat and well till he is a four year old. Then if he is to be a polo pony you will school him for polo.

If he is to be a hunter I should give him a few weeks in the school, doing more or less the same as with the polo pony, making him change on the turn, go well up to the bit and flex properly, teaching him to move in all paces correctly balanced, etc., and if you give him the same schooling as the polo pony without making him do all the very sharp turns, etc., which are unnecessary for a hunter, you will find him a very much more pleasant ride.

Naturally the average breaker has not the time to do all this, but where possible it makes a hunter more valuable.

F. JACKSON. 7 August 1954

SHIRES IN LONDON

THE sight of a pair of majestic Shires drawing a fully-loaded brewer's dray has always been one to warm the heart of the lover of heavy horses. During the Christmas holiday period parties from several branches of the Pony Club had the opportunity of spending an afternoon in London visiting some of these animals in their stables and learning something of the inside story of their work and history.

Organized by Messrs. Whitbread and Company the visits were made to their premises in Chiswell Street, in the heart of the City. In addition to seeing the horses the members were shown the coopers working at their ancient craft of cask-making. Among the branches who took advantage of the company's hospitality were the Old Surrey and Burstow,

Surrey Union, West Street, Woodland, Romney Marsh, Enfield Chace, Perivale, Wimbledon, N.W. Kent and Mid-Surrey Draghounds. The keen interest of the children was borne out by the many questions put to the guides.

At present the company has 28 animals, all Shire geldings, and although this number has fallen considerably since the advent of mechanization—there were 412 in 1914—no further reduction is contemplated.

The horses, of which a high proportion are greys, are mostly obtained from stud farms in the Cheshire area and join the company's service when they are about five years old. By then they have already put in useful work in agriculture and know the feel of the shafts, but they have to learn how to get accustomed to the hustle and bustle of London's traffic. Thus for the first few months a novice is sent out in pair with an older, more experienced horse.

Each horse is named when it first arrives at the stables and in any particular year these names start with the same initial letter. This alphabetical procedure is adopted so that the stablemen may know exactly how long each animal has been in service.

Their work consists of delivering beer in cask—a fully-loaded dray weighs four tons—and, as it would not be economical to use them over long distances, they are generally confined to an area within 3–5 miles of the brewery. Longer trips are undertaken, however, some pairs going as far afield as Lewisham or Tottenham, a total journey of some 15 miles.

Life is not all work for the Shires. Pairs are frequently sent out to give displays at shows during the summer, but as they are all true working horses the policy is one of exhibition rather than competition. Four horses toured Belgium in 1954, taking with them a replica of the type of dray in use two centuries ago.

For more than a hundred years it has been the tradition for the company to provide the horses to draw the coach of the Speaker of the House of Commons. By a happy coincidence the pair selected for this task in the Coronation procession were named Royal and Sovereign.

Last year, for the first time, these Shires took part in one of London's oldest ceremonies, the Lord Mayor's Show, six of them pulling the Lord Mayor's coach. Early in the New

Year he paid an official visit to the stables and met the horses and also the men who had acted as his driver and postilions.

At the end of their working life, which lasts 7–10 years, the Shires are "pensioned off," the majority being found light work on farms where they can end their days in quiet and peaceful surroundings.

The men who work with the animals are all true horse-lovers. Long service is the rule among them and, although they are given the opportunity of promotion to other departments, most prefer to remain with the horses they know so well.

At the conclusion of their tour each Pony Club party was entertained to tea. Thanks were tendered to the company, not only for arranging the visits, but also for their policy in maintaining this link with the past in spite of present-day economic conditions. Further visits are being arranged for next holidays.

H.A.C.   21 January 1956

BREEDING OF WEIGHT-CARRYING HUNTERS

SINCE the breeding of heavyweight hunters is a topic of such great importance these days, I feel my experiences in this direction may be of assistance to others.

Shortly after I came to my Shropshire farm from Australia in 1935, my veterinary surgeon suggested that I mated a Belgian mare I had to a Thoroughbred horse, and as a consequence I have been breeding half-breds ever since.

I have bred 60 half-breds, mostly from Shire mares, and ten three-quarter-breds. I have purchased, broken and hunted two three-quarter-breds, two cobs, six Thoroughbreds and 30 half-breds.

All my half-bred horses have been good hunters and could gallop. All have won money at hunter trials and show jumping, and in ten years I have taken 500 rosettes, mostly with four year olds or under. I kept only two over five years old— Lady Jane I and Prince Charlie.

My teams of three ran 14 times in hunter trials, winning 11 and being placed in the other three, and there were different

young horses in nearly every team. I have been amazed at the
success of these horses, and had no idea this would happen
when I started breeding.

Gilpin, brother to Lady Jane I, which I sold to an M.F.H.,
won six times in nine hunter trials as a four year old, several
of them on time. Prince Charlie appeared to be a slow horse,
but in no hunter trial was he more than 2sec slower than
the fastest; he covered the ground with big, long strides.

All my horses do farm work in harness. Lady Jane I
harrowed ten acres of cabbage the day before I took her to the
Royal Show at Oxford, and jumped and sold her.

When I mated my first draught mare to a Thoroughbred
stallion, my waggoner disapproved. He thought the resultant
foal would be "neither one thing nor the other," and I have
met this strong prejudice ever since. Yet three half-breds
which I can quickly call to mind are the famous Nizefela,
Craven A and Dumbell.

I would not be interested in any horse that did not have a
Thoroughbred sire or dam; I do not think it matters which
way. Three-quarter-breds are easy to sell up to two years old,
but the most successful horse in the hunting field on stiff,
Midland clay is the half-bred.

I prefer the Shire for the dam to any other breed; it has the best feet, limbs and movement. The half-bred Suffolk or Percheron is easy to sell, but I have not been able to win much with them in hunter trials or show jumping. I had one half-bred Shire who won several gymkhana events and a jumping competition the same day. The fastest horse I have ridden was a half-bred Shire—and I have ridden about 4000 horses (Thoroughbreds included) in Britain, Canada, New Zealand and Australia.

I attribute a large part of the success of my horses to their hybrid vigour. They have the strength of the Shire, and have worked alongside Shires all day on the farm. They have speed and endurance. Hybrid vigour has played an important part in the breeding of beef cattle and the best dairy cows, and of sheep for mutton and pigs for bacon.

I must add that my three-quarter-bred horses have been shown successfully in the ring—Sunday's Quest and Sultana being two notable winners in the last season.

But when it comes to selling these horses, the half-bred commands a better price than the three-quarter-breds, even though the former would not be placed in the show-ring because of its feather. But due to its superior strength and staying power it is more valuable as a hunter.

One of my three-quarter-bred horses. No Star, carried a huntsman for two years and was sold for £350 at Leicester. About the same time Porlock, a half-bred, fetched £410. In three years, 14 of my horses were sold for over £350 each; all but No Star were half-bred. I picked up these facts in my travellings, and from reading *Horse and Hound*.

It should be remembered that, because of this cross-breeding, there has in the past been a large variety of ponies and hunters available, giving people the chance to select a mount just to their weight, size and strength.

In my opinion, emphasis should be laid on keeping some Shire stallions in the country, for you cannot have Shire mares without them. It is of course far more difficult to keep stallions on the farm than mares because of the need for experienced horsemen to look after them.

As regards the keeping of Shire mares, a local farmer whose family has bred these horses for many years once said to me, "Noel, if you will find a little money to keep the Shire

At Kirby Gate, Melton Mowbray, when the Quorn Hunt celebrated its 200th anniversary.

horse classes going at the country shows, we will be able to keep the brood mares you want." The Shire is a show horse which appeals to the eye and, I think, can continue to exist in the same way that the Hackney and Arab breeds have.

NOEL WARD.   8 February 1958

STUDY OF AN ARTIST

PAINTINGS of the horse, and of sporting activities which include the horse, are peculiarly "English," yet, paradoxically, this country has produced comparatively few exponents of the true equestrian portrait.

This is perhaps the more understandable when it is realised that equestrian portraiture is a highly specialized form of art. The landscape painter has only to cope with his landscape and the portrait painter with his portrait; but the equestrian portrait painter must be skilled in landscape work, portraiture, and animal anatomy.

One young man who is making his mark in this sphere is Richard Dupont, whose recent work has included portraits of several hunters and well-known racehorses, Light Harvest,

Matador and Pinza among them. He is now working on a presentation portrait to be given to Major Pearson, retiring Master of the Suffolk Foxhounds.

Born in 1920 and son of a doctor, Dupont started to draw almost as soon as he could hold a pencil and, since much of his time was centred upon the family ponies at his Frome (Som.) home, horses were his inspiration and motif from an early age.

A habit derived from these childhood days—when he would take pencil and paper down to the stables "to get things right"—stands him in good stead today, for he frequently makes "on the spot" notes in his sketch-book when out hunting with his local pack.

At the age of 16 he was taken by his parents to see G. D. Armour and later to Lionel Edwards. The kindly remarks of both these eminent men persuaded young Richard's parents that their son had talent and were largely responsible for his taking up art as a career.

In 1938 he was accepted for entry into the Royal Academy Schools, which, though in no way well equipped to teach animal anatomy or horse painting, have had famous members specializing in this form of art—George Stubbs, Sir Edwin Landseer and Sir Alfred Munnings.

On the outbreak of war Dupont joined the Dorsetshire Regiment and, after service in Burma, was withdrawn and made an official war artist for the South East Asia theatre, covering all aspects of the conflict there, on land, on sea and in the air.

Many of his sketches done between fighting were seen by Lord Mountbatten and, as a direct result, an exhibition of his war drawings and pictures was shown at the Royal Water Colour Society after hostilities had ended. These works were all in pencil or water colour, since oil painting under jungle conditions was impossible.

On demobilization he re-entered the Royal Academy for a further four years of study, finally qualifying for the Diploma in the School of Painting. He has spent years studying and painting straightforward portraits, for he fully believes that "if the rider's not right, it matters not how well you paint the horse."

In 1952 he was commissioned to paint two portraits in

The late Mr Arthur Portman, owner of *Horse and Hound* for many years. Well-known contributor under the pseudonym "Audax".

138

Sweden, but further contracts followed and he stayed on for two years, visiting Denmark as well. Amongst the horses he painted whilst in Sweden were several which subsequently represented Scandinavian countries in the Olympic Games. A large part of the Swedish Army is still horsed and the 300 animals in the cavalry barracks of the Norreland Dragoon Guards presented opportunities for hours of study.

Further equestrian commissions followed on his return to England and he later made a holiday visit to the United States, where he was able to study and paint American hunting at first hand.

Returning to England once again he set up residence and subsequently opened a studio at Dedham, Essex. Nearby is the home of Sir Alfred Munnings, who has always been Dupont's inspiration and whom he describes as "one of the greatest—if not the greatest—equestrian portrait painters of all time."

Sir Alfred was President of the Royal Academy when Dupont was a student and from him he received his first box and easel. He freely admits that without Sir Alfred's kind criticisms and help in the past he would still be learning much that he already knows.

24 May 1958

WHEN DRIVING WAS A JOY
BY LT.-COL. H. M. LAMBERT

LOOKING back over the years one can remember traffic congestion even prior to the First World War, especially in the City and West End of London, but not, of course, so acute as the stoppages are today all over the country.

But in those dear old days, almost before the infernal internal combustion engine arrived, one did have real joy in driving about, either in town or country, especially if one was, perhaps, fortunate enough to be travelling in a high dog cart or phaeton behind a high-stepping Hackney.

The roads then were different from to-day in that each "turn-out" was individual. "Good sorts" were driven by those who could handle the ribbons both with private and commercial vehicles.

Business concerns had good animals and well-turned-out

vehicles in different colours, thus giving the roads, in spite of the mud, a much more cheery appearance.

Then one saw the gloriously matched carriage horses, and even today, when I remember them, I recall again how cruel some of the owners and especially the coachmen were. They not only had tight bearing reins but really cruel curb port bits with curved bars on their poor beasts which would be driven up and down, while, for example, their owners were at the theatre, the coachmen flicking and annoying the horses with their whips.

These were perhaps exceptions because, by and large, owners and drivers loved and well looked after their animals and had real knowledge of animal management.

Hyde Park and the West End roads in those pre-war days were certainly sights with the lovely carriages and their fine pairs. Then there were the commercial undertakings with their smart carts and vans. In my humble opinion, James Buchanan and Co., Ltd., took pride of place with their spotless vans, painted blue body with red wheels, and with the name of the company written on the sides in gold leaf lettering. The coachman wore a top hat and smart livery, and the harness shone.

However, these were closely followed by many others, including the smart little, well-trimmed cobs of Meredith and Drew, with their chocolate-coloured box vans; the sedate single-horse vehicles of Derry and Toms; the dashing, two-wheeled, striped-painted, hooded carts of John Barker; and the vans coming out each morning from Cadby Hall.

The Army and Navy Stores, if I remember correctly, had green hooded vans drawn by two well-groomed mules, their drivers taking such tremendous pride in their animals.

Charrington, Sells, Dale and Co., the old-established coal merchants, with their chocolate and black quarter-lock nicely designed vans, had some beautiful animals, as did Rickett, Smith, Walter Moore and others of that trade.

The brewers, many of whom still use horses, always produced tremendous animals in their drays, many four-in-hand teams then being on the roads.

Finally, there were the many omnibus concerns, their vehicles being painted in their own distinctive individual company colours. I suppose the most famous were the Times,

Anne Duchess of Westminster, with her great steeplechaser Arkle, winner of many big races.

belonging to Thomas Tilling. These were painted light green with white wheels, I believe, picked out with green, and were mostly horsed with greys.

The General Company had many routes, all the omnibuses being painted different colours for particular journeys and drawn by powerful animals; also the Road Car Company, whose vehicles, if my memory does not fail me, had little Union Jack flags flying on a small pole in front of the off-side; Birch Bros., and Jones Bros., who I believe had only one route but owned some lovely up-standing coach horse type of animals and smart vehicles.

Harry Turner ran many omnibuses which were drawn by well-turned-out light cobs, rather like those used by Meredith and Drew. They were smart and went along at a good pace. Competition between the concerns was keen, and a certain amount of racing occurred, much to the concern of elderly passengers!

Yes, they were wonderful times; all classes of people seemed to be more cheery even if money was very scarce in some quarters, but people did laugh in those days.

6 December 1958

GREAT RUNS WITH THE ATHERSTONE

Sir,—I have recently been asked by Mrs. M. C. Inge (her long hunting record—77 consecutive seasons—was referred to by "Observer" some weeks ago) to send you the accounts of two great runs of the past with the Atherstone Hounds, of which she is a former Master, as was her husband.

She feels sure that all hunting people, especially those bred and born from the old hunting families, will be interested to read these accounts, which are taken from the hunting diaries of Mrs. Oakeley (Mrs. Inge's mother) and Mrs. Inge herself.

Mrs. Inge has checked these accounts and says she believes them to be as near correct as is possible. She tells me that her father always maintained that the Atherstone Great Run of March 22, 1873, was the greatest in hunting history.

Atherstone Great Run, March 22, 1873 (from Mrs. Oakeley's hunting diary): "Found in Meriden Shafts, ran by Millison's Wood, Royal Close, between Blackwaste and Stoneymoor Wood, Kenilworth Chase, The Boot at Honiley, Beech Wood, Wroxall Warren, Haywood, Lowsonford, and killed beyond Preston Brook, near Henley-in-Arden. A 14-mile point. Time, 2hr 10min. Distance, approx. 28 miles.

"The only people who got to the end of this great run were Mr. and Mrs. Oakeley, Mr. and Mrs. Henniker, Col. Madocks, Mrs. Wilson, Castleman and Sam Hayes. Drizzling rain."

Willesley Great Run, December 12, 1900 (from Mrs. Inge's hunting diary): "Willesley Osiers blank. Found in Willesley Wood, a good fox, and ran by the Railway Covert, across Willesley Park, leaving Packington on the right, through the gardens at Coleorton, on by Griffy Dam, then bearing left by Worthing, turned right with Osgathorpe on our left to Grace Dieu, leaving this on the right and Belton on the left by Shepshed and killed in the open (on the football ground) three fields from Piper's Wood. A nine-mile point. Time, 1hr 50min, and 15 miles as hounds ran. Distance, 23 miles.

"Only seven at end were W. F. Inge, Mrs. Inge, Mrs. C. H. Morris, Mrs. F. Manley, two Misses Harris, C. A. Brown, C. Ingram, W. Orvis and Fred Knight."

Some of the Heavy Horse teams giving their popular display at the Horse of the Year Show at Wembley.

Further interesting information about this hunt is given to me in a letter from Mrs. Inge, in which she states:

"I can ride every yard of it again now. Hounds did slip the field a way from Willesley Park, but we always had Whitmore's red coat in sight, and several of us were with hounds before they got to Coleorton. They checked on the road near Shepshed, where the fox had lain down in a ditch, but Champion put him up and the whole pack raced him across a big field and killed him on the sports ground.

"I believe the two Misses Harris and W. Orvis were not actually up when the fox was killed, but came up immediately afterwards.

"If it had not been for my husband, who had hounds to himself after Grace Dieu, we should none of us have been there. We all rode the same horses all through the run, and they went home quite cheerily and were none the worse."

MICHAEL C. S. SADLER, M.R.C.V.S. 14 February 1959

VALUE OF H.I.S. PREMIUM SCHEME
BY MAJ.-GEN. SIR EVELYN FANSHAWE

ON March 11 the Thoroughbred Stallion Show of the Hunters' Improvement and National Light Horse Breeding

Society returns to Newmarket after an interval of 40 years. This has been made possible through the great kindness of Messrs. Tattersalls in offering the use of their Sales Paddocks and their services free to the society.

It is interesting to recall that the late Mr. E. Somerville Tattersall was a founder-member of the society and its first treasurer in 1886. This therefore seems to offer an opportunity to record a few remarks on the history and working of the society.

Founder members with Mr. Somerville Tattersall were Sir Walter Gilbey, Messrs. E. F. J. Preston, J. Rooke Rawlence, W. H. Fife, Tresham Gilbey and Wyndham B. Portman (who himself founded *Horse and Hound* in 1884). President in the inaugural year was the Earl of Coventry.

The premium stallion scheme was initiated by the H.I.S. in 1887, and this section of its activities was subsequently taken over by a Royal Commission on Horse Breeding, then by the Ministry of Agriculture, and finally by the War Office until 1929–30, when the Hunters' Improvement Society took complete control.

The first stallion show was held in London in 1894, when 29 premiums of £150 each were offered. The show continued in London until 1939, with the exception of the years 1918–19, when it was held at the Park Paddocks, Newmarket (hence its return this year to Racing Headquarters).

No stallion shows were held from 1940–46, but the scheme was continued in a modified form until the resumption of the show at Derby Racecourse in 1947, where it remained until last year. Possibly one of the outstanding memories of visitors to the Derby shows is the severe climatic conditions that prevailed on so many occasions!

Although the H.I.S., like any other private or public body, is always the butt for a certain amount of criticism—much of it from those who are not too well informed—it has in the past done a very great deal of good for the riding horse in general, and will continue to do so. Those of us whose interests and pleasures are linked with the horse should be forever grateful to the society for its past and present activities.

In almost all foreign countries the breeding of the riding type of horse is not only Government subsidized, but is organized and based on State studs. In most Continental countries many more horses are used in the normal daily working life than here on our island, where commercially we are almost totally mechanized.

This is, of course, a great handicap to the breeding of any horse other than the Thoroughbred. In our country there is no help, financially or otherwise, from the State. The breeding of the light riding horse is chiefly in the hands of the Hunters' Improvement Society, which is financed entirely voluntarily from two sources—the Racecourse Betting Control Board and members' subscriptions.

With great generosity and far-sightedness the Racecourse Betting Control Board donates a large sum every year, and has done so annually since 1935. This grant makes it possible for the H.I.S. to award the premiums to stallions and mares.

The society and everyone connected with light horse breeding have reason to be grateful to the R.B.C.B. for this generosity. On the other hand, it is to be hoped that the Board gains some reward and compensation for its "investment" in the following ways:

First, the H.I.S. scheme encourages a quite considerable market in stallions, in that members purchase horses out of training with a view to competing for premiums at the show. Secondly, these stallions are themselves the sires—through the scheme—of quite a number of winners in National Hunt and point-to-point races. Thirdly, they produce hunters and other riding horses, and so in turn encourage the love of riding in general. Fourthly, they get quite a fair number of "event" horses and show jumpers to swell the ranks in those sports. And lastly, all of these together go to make up a "nursery" for young men and women who will ride and go racing in future years.

The second source of revenue, through members' subscriptions, offers a practical method whereby everyone connected with horses can support this great work.

The administration of the policy and finances of the H.I.S. are in the able hands of its Council, the members of which have always been men of great practical experience in the breeding, production and use of the riding horse.

One often hears the question asked: "Where do all the animals go that are sired by H.I.S. stallions?" The answer is quite simple and exactly what is wanted. Apart from those

who make their names racing and jumping—they go hunting!
It is a thousand pities that more people who hunt and ride do
not take a greater interest in the breeding of their horses, for
this information would be of the greatest value in gauging the
extent of the society's work.

In this age of mechanisation it is a really cheering fact to
all those interested in the breeding of hunters and riding
horses that they can in any part of the country have the services of a Thoroughbred stallion for the absurdly low service
fee of £5. This is due to the premiums allotted by the society,
and there is little doubt that, were it not for these subsidies,
many of the selected stallions would be standing at around
£50.

28 February 1959

FOXHUNTER—THE WONDER HORSE

LAST Saturday Britain lost her greatest show jumper of all
time when Lt.-Col. Harry Llewellyn's mighty and courageous
Foxhunter died in retirement at the age of 18 at Llanvair
Grange, Abergavenny. During his highly colourful and
spectacular career between 1946–56, Foxhunter jumped at
the world's greatest shows and was in the British Olympic
team that won the bronze medals at Wembley and the gold
medals at Helsinki in the Grand Prix des Nations, and by
1954 had competed with the British team in 34 Nations' Cups.
He was the only horse ever to win three times the Royal
International Horse Show's most coveted award, the King
George V Gold Cup, and he finally retired in 1956 with 78
international wins to his credit in ten seasons' jumping of the
highest class.

Foxhunter's magnificent performances at home and
abroad quickly caught the imagination of the public, and he
played the star rôle in raising the prestige of British show
jumping at a time when, primarily through the medium of
T.V., the popularity of the sport was growing by leaps and
bounds.

Foxhunter's name became a "household word." In his
prime at his appearance in the show ring spectators awaited

146

George Barker with the Quorn Hounds near Thorpe Satchville.

in tense excitement for him to do the seemingly impossible, and he rarely let them down!

Foxhunter was bred by Mr. K. Millard, of Nether, Norfolk. A 16 hands 3½in bright bay gelding, he was born on April 23, 1941, by the premium sire Erehwemos out of Catcall, by Step Forward out of a pure-bred Clydesdale mare. Foxhunter was the only foal of Catcall, a brilliant hunter who died from tetanus. Both she and his sire were very placid.

As a foal he was made to jump in and out of his barn over a solid 18in rail, and later was turned out in a field with 12ft dykes, and he loved showing off over these and other obstacles. He was a gay, active and playful youngster; in fact, he got a slit in his left ear due to his being over-friendly with a cart-horse!

Foxhunter was sold unbroken to Mr. Norman Holmes, of Thrussington, Leics. who hunted him with the Quorn as a four- and five-year-old before bringing him out as a novice jumper in 1946, and winning first prizes at the Peterborough and Beaufort Hunt shows. In 1947 he won at Newark and the Notts County shows before being sold, at the beginning of July, to Col. Llewellyn. From then on he seldom competed other than in international horse shows. He was very bold, adored jumping and naturally jumped clean. To the end he remained a placid, calm performer in the ring and a very great pet outside, being especially friendly towards children.

Foxhunter's first journey abroad was to Ostend show in 1947. The following winter he was trained in elementary dressage by Lt.-Col. Joe Dudgeon in Dublin and this subsequently proved of great value. In the summer of 1948 he represented Britain (whose team was third) in the Olympic Games at Wembley, and was equal seventh in the individual placing. He then went on to the International Horse Show, where he won his first King George V Gold Cup before winning at Dublin.

Mr C. N. de Courcy-Parry, the oldest of contributors to *Horse and Hound*, who writes under the pseudonym "Dalesman".

He started the next season by winning the international Grand Prix indoors at the Paris Palais des Sports, and then went on to win the Grand Prix de la Ville de Nice and, jointly with Monty, the Grand Prix de France there. In July he strained his back while competing for the King's Cup, in which he was fourth, and this kept him out of the ring until the Horse of the Year show at Harringay. There he won an international class and also the individual prize in the team event with two clear rounds. He then went on to win classes in Paris and Brussels in October and at Geneva in November.

Foxhunter's first show in 1950 was at Lucerne in June, when he won the Prix Burgenstock, the Grand Prix, and also the individual prize in the Prix des Nations, which was won by Britain. After winning the Puissance at Vichy, he came home to take the King's Cup at the White City for the second time, as well as the Puissance, in which he cleared 6ft 6½in. He was in the British team that won the Prince of Wales Cup and later, the Aga Khan Cup in Dublin, where again he put up the best individual performance.

He went on to the Horse of the Year show, where he won two classes and the final championship. He later jumped with the British team in America. He won in New York, but showed his best form in Toronto, where he won two international classes and helped our team to win a third with two

clear rounds. Including team events, he was first in 19 international classes in this season.

In 1951, although he won the Puissance at Nice in April
and an event at Rome in May, he did not show his best form
until the International Horse Show in July. Here he was
unbeaten on five of the six days, winning the *Daily Mail*
Cup. White City Cup and Welcome Stakes. He was one of
the three British horses to set up a record when winning the
Prince of Wales Cup (incidentally for the third year in
succession) with a no-fault score.

At Dublin he won a class as well as the individual prize in
the Aga Khan Cup, which Great Britain won for the second
year running, and then kept up his form to win the Grand
Prix d'Ostende, the individual prize in the Nations Cup at Le
Zoute, and the Grand Prix de Rotterdam. At Harringay he
won the Puissance, and then scored at Zurich before falling
heavily at the bank in Geneva, after which, fortunately
uninjured, he was retired for the season. Altogether he won
18 international events that year.

At his first show of the 1952 season, Foxhunter was equal
first in the championship at the Western Counties show. He
then won on the last three days at the Dublin Spring, and
followed up this with three wins at Lucerne. Here he won the
Grand Prix for the second time, and therefore outright for
the first time in its history. He was then a member of the
British team which won gold medals at the Helsinki Olympic
Games, and also of the team which won the Prince of Wales
Cup for the fourth successive year at the White City, where
he also won two other events. Half-way through the Horse of
the Year show, Foxhunter was retired with bad corns.

After a long rest, he had his first 1953 show at Brighton in
June, where he won the South of England Championship
jointly with Fanny Rosa. He went to Germany and throughout
the Aachen show hit only one fence. Then he returned to the
White City and was undefeated until the very last day when
he was second to the Italian Merano in the *Daily Mail* Cup.
During this show he became the only horse ever to win the
King George V Cup three times, and he was a member for
the fifth successive time of the British team which won the
Prince of Wales Cup.

He then jumped with the team in Dublin, which won

Britain the Aga Khan Trophy outright as it had been won by our team for three successive years. A few weeks later he won the National Championship at Shrewsbury, thus becoming the first horse ever to have won both that event and the King's Cup. After an early win he fell heavily on the last night of Harringay, getting a pole between his fore-legs, and this and other painful accidents in Harrisburg and New York caused him temporarily to lose confidence. Although he won the Drake Trophy in New York, he did not come back to form until the Royal Winter Fair in Toronto, where his final clear round helped Britain win the International Team Trophy for the first time in history.

Foxhunter's visit to Rome and Lucerne in the spring of 1954 proved that he had not regained his full confidence, although he was placed second at the latter show. By the White City in July he was back in form, but Col. Llewellyn injured a riding muscle and was unable to ride him until September. He then won the testing Olympic Trial at Dunster with the only clear round, and the horse was retired for the season.

The following year Foxhunter was placed every time out in Ostend and won in Rotterdam, his only shows. In 1956 he was in great form at Dublin and won the final Committee Trophy. Although again consistently placed at Ostend, he appeared bored and so Col. Llewellyn finally retired him from active competition.

Since being "grounded," Foxhunter has made public appearances from time to time. His last was at the Horse of the Year show at Wembley last month, when, as usual, he was there to greet the winner of the national novice championship named after him.

28 November 1959

A DAY IN THE LIFE OF A SHOW COMMENTATOR

IT's just after 9 o'clock in the morning on a typical English summer day. Despite the pouring rain, however, the car-parks are filling rapidly, for it is Show Day. Suddenly a car with its windscreen covered in labels hurtles up to the stock

Credit Call (ridden by Joey Newton) seen leading over the water on the second circuit before winning the *Horse and Hound* Final Champion Hunters Chase Cup at Stratford-on-Avon in 1975.

gates and the officials, evidently bewildered by the "Doctor," "Press," "Official," "Priority," etc., let it through to the ground. The hired Show Commentator has arrived, late as usual.

You are already one up, having defeated the gate stewards, thus saving yourself the mile walk from the car-parks, advertised rather whimsically as being adjacent to the show ground. The aim is now to get your car as near the commentary box as possible, in case a hasty retreat is called for. The one label a commentator never puts on his car is "Commentator," because he is liable to find his tyres let down, or worse, for saying too much, or too little, about the exhibits.

The red-faced military gentleman pacing about in the ring is obviously the chief steward, and has been looking for you for hours; avoid him at all costs and slip into the commentary box. You are greeted with "Good morning, I thought you were never coming; I've announced the first class." This from your assistant, the local gentleman who has been doing this job for 25 years; indeed, it is your unlucky day.

Thank heaven most grand rings, unless of course it's some mad jumping show, are oases of calm in the mornings, with just a few hunters and cobs being run up by their owners and run down by the knowledgeable onlookers.

You can now sit back and read the morning newspapers, or take a free cup of coffee at one of the trade stands.

Believing thoroughly that an army marches on its stomach, most commentators, course builders, and other itinerant horse-class stewards can usually be seen sliding off to lunch shortly after mid-day. They know from bitter experience that there are only 20 portions of salmon in the tent, and if they are not quick their goat, pig, honey and flower contemporaries will have snaffled the lot.

Coming back from the salmon, you are confronted with a pile of lost-child notices, and you suddenly notice the grandstands beginning to fill up. "Bird-watching" is popular amongst the showing fraternity, and you're glad you remembered the binoculars.

"Third block from the left end, fourth row up . . . COR!"

In the ring the course builder, Derek Fixer, is being slapped on the back by last week's winners and avoided by the losers. Funny, isn't it, that one jumping course can be both marvellous and lousy.

"Look out, we're off." "First to jump, Josephine Doolittle on Block-Buster," you announce. Now's your chance to shine, out with the card index . . . only to find you haven't got the perishing horse listed.

Time drifts slowly by. The chief judge is asleep and so is nearly everybody else—except the competitors.

"Clang" goes the 'phone, Oliver Twist says, "Pat Blythe had a brick off the wall." Panic in the box! We're all awake now, even the timekeeper. "Did you see it?" "No, did you?" "No." "Quick, fetch Fixer." Fixer has also been having a little nap, but being a sharp thinker says she did. "Correction, Pat Blythe had four faults." The crowd is rather displeased and show it by rocking the commentary box.

Rosette time at last, and this is where the committee has its little joke with the commentator, for the dignitary making the presentation is never who they say it will be. "See the chap with the carnation, that's Lord Tomnoddy; if he refuses I'll ask old Mrs. Bluebottle, the vicar's wife—that's the one in that hideous violet suit."

In fact, out comes an undersized chap with an oversized chain round his neck. You announce: "The rosettes are now being presented by the Mayor of Bradwell." Perfect, except

Miss Jane Bullen on Our Nobby, members of the gold medal winning team in the 1968 Mexico Olympic Games.

that this is Brightlingsea. If the citizens are patriotic this might be the moment to cut your losses and bolt.

The most sinister words on any programme now appear as the next item: "Grand Parade with Commentary." In theory all the prizewinners parade in catalogue order, the champion hunter leading the horses and the champion bull, the cattle. In practice, the military gentlemen in charge of the horses have had a little difference with the gentlemen farmers in charge of the cattle over the order of precedence. This usually leads to one of two things:

(a) Both sides will hurl their charges into the ring from opposite ends. Result: utter chaos, and the only thing to do is read the results rapidly in pidgin English and go to tea—you will have plenty of time.

(b) Both sides will sulk and the grand parade will consist of the goats and the childrens' ponies, who never can resist a show. The only possible thing to do is as in case (a).

Your first sight as you climb the stairs after tea is a massive pair of No. 11's. The law is back with more lost kids. You broadcast: "Will John and Terry Smith join their mother at the band-stand," and "The police have a little girl wearing a gymslip and a squint."

Give up, nobody can hear you. The motor bikes are roaring round inside the ring and the native ponies are roaming around outside. Ghastly thought! Native ponies are next on the agenda, if they can ever be caught again. The trouble is, to the non-native they all look the same. The only safe thing to say is that they go back thousands of years and are extremely hardy. Of course, you can also be a little poetical with "See them flitting through sunlit glades, or tripping daintily o'er the heather." With a bit of luck, this sort of thing may see you through.

The shades of night are falling fast. "Will John and Terry Smith's mum and dad leave the band-stand and join their children at *home?*"

The last class is for novice jumpers, 50 of them, and looking through the binoculars you see that some are already being taught a thing or two over poles, which seem to be going up and down like see-saws.

The chief judge suddenly remembers an urgent appointment and departs. Now you must whip up the excitement in the crowd—two men, a rather disinterested dog, one policeman and the little girl with the squint. You observe "You will notice Miss Doolittle rides Bronco only in a sheepskin noseband." A hearty guffaw from the policeman indicates that you have, once more, made a slip.

As darkness draws in you can only tell the whereabouts of the collecting ring by two familiar voices raised in song. Mr. Wallace Hobday demanding the class be cancelled (he obviously hasn't got a clear round), whilst Mr. Oliver Twist, senior, is demanding the jump off (he has obviously got at least one clear round).

A deputation approaches across the ring. Don't look for help, the gentlemen farmers and military gentlemen have long since departed for the bar, and the noise indicates they are still there. The jumping judges have noticed the advance with something akin to panic and the last words you hear as they, too, depart for the bar are: "Tell them to divide."

Never mind, another day is over and you can now cadge coffee from some show jumping caravan and catch up on the latest gossip. Just one last word, always remember the motto of the Microphone Clutchers Union: "When in doubt, give the microphone a clout"—you can always blame the sound engineer.

Good night.

Ex-COMMENTATOR.   5 March 1960

SHOW JUMPING—A WAY OF LIFE

"SHOW jumping has become more than a sport," remarked someone who should know the other day, and added, "Now it's a way of life." It is. Its devotees, who multiply annually, are a dedicated community. For eight months of the year they seek to fulfil themselves by wandering like nomads, ever in pursuit of clear rounds.

On the highest plane, show jumping entails transporting oneself, perhaps certain members of one's family, possibly half of one's stable and certainly the greater part of one's wardrobe on a protracted tour of those cities that have been accorded the privilege of staging their country's C.H.I.O. Thus encumbered, and with the possibility of other (usually equine) appurtenances being acquired *en route*, the international rider embarks on a pilgrimage that leads to many glamorous Meccas.

His caravan may come to rest in Nice, Rome, Lucerne, Lisbon, Madrid, Aachen, London, Dublin, Ostend, Le Zoute, Rotterdam; possibly in New York and Toronto, and perhaps in Davos, Paris, Algiers, Brussels, Bilbao and Palermo.

Show jumping on this scale means living in hotels of comparative comfort, and enjoying the pleasures of a round of receptions, dances and cocktail parties. Evening apparel is as important a part of the wardrobe as are breeches and boots. Press photographers and autograph hunters contribute to the apparent grandeur.

It is virtually show business, with horses thrown in. With the possible exception of the polo world, the life is indeed the most luxurious that the horse accords to its pursuivants.

155

This is the lot, however, of the lucky few. At the other end of the scale the picture is very different. The travelling is just as incessant, but for the Grand Tour of the Continent one substitutes a trail through the provincial towns. There are no military bands or national anthems. Hotels are forsworn, for the most part, in favour of a caravan, towed precariously behind a horsebox that hides it completely from the vision of the driver, its hopefully intending occupant.

Frying pan replaces evening dress as the most important item of equipment, and social life is confined to chats over cups of tea infused on a Primus stove—or at best whisky and water drawn from a jerrycan. Luxury is *non est*, and even comfort depends very largely on the weather.

Mr Fred Winter, former top steeplechase champion who is now a most successful trainer.

Yet 90 per cent. of the show jumping fraternity elect to spend their summers thus. The life must have its merits—or is it simply that as a nation we take our pleasures hard?

On arrival at the showground there is a certain jockeying for position. The loose boxes that have been allocated to the horses are almost invariably in the most inaccessible and inconvenient places, so we will not dwell on this point save to mention that it is seldom possible to change them. The owner of six horses may well find them scattered in pairs about the horse lines, and it is impossible to exercise them without running a gauntlet of squealing pigs, cows being milked, and threshing machines that are demonstrated from dawn till dusk and emit a continuous din.

The frustrations involved in getting the horses settled, however, are as nothing compared with finding a congenial spot for the caravan. Familiarity breeds contempt just as prolifically in the caravan lines as it does anywhere else. From previous bitter experience the show jumping rider has evolved a lengthy list of undesirable neighbours who, in the interests of harmony, are to be avoided at all costs.

There is the caravan in which hilarious parties take place until well into the small hours. There is the one whose occupants retire at dusk, and resent even a subdued chuckle after 10 p.m., but arise to salute the happy dawn with a conviviality as vociferous as it is undoubtedly (in the jaundiced view of late-night celebrants) misplaced.

There is the caravan that boasts a record player and a veritable library of long-playing rock-and-roll records, and

156

the one inhabited by four whippets whose concerted voices are raised to the heavens in protest to decry a singer's claims to popularity.

Yet camaraderie seems to flourish in adversity. Many a good party has been held outdoors in the rain after a show, or in a caravan festooned with steaming coats and breeches, with the guests removing their gumboots at the door. When the caravan is bursting at its seams, late arrivals stand outside and join in the festivities through the open windows.

The horses, meanwhile, munch hay happily enough in their awkwardly-sited boxes. They are the most equable animals on the showground, so used are they to travelling and strange sights. They adapt themselves remarkably well to their métier and if, in the sophistication that has been forced upon them, they ever wonder what all the journeying and jumping is in aid of, they quite probably stumble upon the answer too. Show jumping *is* a way of life, and there are many that are less agreeable.

P.M.-M.   16 April 1960

HYPERION IS GONE—BUT HIS RADIANCE WILL REMAIN!

HYPERION, who was put down on the Friday of last week, was not the greatest racehorse—there were many with superior records and, in fact, no fewer than 30 others have shared his dual Derby and St. Leger triumphs; but he ranks with the greatest stallions who ever set foot on a stud farm and his name will be spoken of long after those of his generation, and many that followed, will have been forgotten.

Bred by the late Lord Derby, on April 18, 1930, Hyperion was got by triple-crown winner Gainsborough from the Chaucer mare Selene, a winner of 16 races, who was out of Serenissima by Minoru from Gondolette by Loved One. This was classic breeding of a high order and it was not altogether surprising that he turned out to be a champion.

But Hyperion, like his maternal grand-sire, Chaucer, was only a small horse (he measured 15 hands 1½in before his Epsom victory) and there was some head-shaking about his prospects. Even his trainer, George Lambton, did not know what to make of him at the outset of his career, for he was also a very lazy colt and "showed nothing at home."

On the racecourse, however, Hyperion was another horse altogether and he proceeded to win nine races (one dead-heat) and get placed in three of the other four in which he ran. His victories were in the New Stakes (Ascot), Prince of Wales' Stakes (Goodwood), dead-heat, Dewhurst Stakes, Derby, St. Leger, Chester Vase, Prince of Wales' Stakes (Ascot), March Stakes and Burwell Stakes; his placings included a short-head defeat, giving the winner 29lb, in the Dullingham Stakes, and a third in the Ascot Gold Cup.

Taking up stud duties in 1935, Hyperion had immediate success, and with winners from his first crop in 1938 such as Heliopolis (later a great success as a stallion in the U.S.A.), Casanova, Titan and His Highness, he finished 15th on the sires' table. The following year he came second and then in 1940, with his oldest stock only four, he was at the top.

Hyperion remained supreme for the next two years; he then had a third and a second and was top again in 1945 and 1946. During the next seven years he was twice runner-up and never lower than tenth. In 1954, he reached the top again.

By this time he was in his 24th year, an age when most stallions have departed to another realm, but Hyperion remained on at stud for another two years and then, on the announcement of his retirement in 1956, he was found to be so well that he resumed his activities with a limited number of mares for a further three seasons. His record for 1960 reads: six winners of six races value £7207, and this brings his total number of races won up to date to 744 and the stake-money to £564,854.

Hyperion's success as a sire abroad, of course, is quite phenomenal, particularly in America and Australia, and he made his mark as a sire of dams of winners, a section which he headed in 1948 and 1957 and in which he was runner-up in 1949, 1950, 1952, 1953, and 1959.

It is only possible in the space available to mention but a few of the star performers got by Lord Derby's little chesnut horse, but these alone present quite a pageant of the Turf from the late pre-war days to the current year when his daughter Opaline II finished up the best two-year-old of the season and his son Aureole took the premier position on the

A Point-to-point Steeplechase by the late Sir Alfred Munnings.

sires' list. Those which come readily to mind are:—

Admiral's Walk, Hypnotist, Stardust, **Godiva** (Gns, Oaks), His Highness, Heliopolis, Hyacinthus, Hyperides, Pensive, **Owen Tudor** (Derby), **Sun Castle** (Leger), Sol Oriens, Orthodox, **Sun Chariot** (Gns, Oaks, Leger), Dèvonian, **Hyeilla** (Oaks), **Sun Stream** (Gns, Oaks), Rockefella, Sweet Cygnet, Gulf Stream, Khaled, Midas, Radiotherapy, High Stakes, Rising Light, **Hypericum** (Gns), Run Honey, Avila, Babu's Pet, Double Eclipse, Hyperbole, Leading Light, Saturn, Judicate, Mister Cube, Caerlaverock, Eastern Emperor, Choir Boy, Aureole, Hornbeam, Ommeyad.

17 December 1960

TRIUMPH OVER IMPOSSIBLE ODDS
BY AUDAX

FROM Agincourt to D-Day, France, I suppose, has been the scene of more brave deeds by Englishmen than any other country in the world. Mostly, of course, they were inspired by the horrid waste of war, but sport in its less serious tragic way, can also lift a man to heights of daring and achievement, and as Fred Winter and Mandarin came back last Sunday after winning the Grand Steeplechase de Paris, I like to think that the ghosts of long-dead English horsemen rode beside them, glad and proud to know that the flag for which they fought and died still flies, even in this sad, dull mechanical age.

To win at all would have been a famous victory—to win as Winter and Mandarin did was an heroic triumph over odds so steep that no normal man or horse could have been blamed for giving up long before the end.

None of this, of course, could even be guessed at, as, in the atmosphere of a Turkish bath, the 14 runners swept gaily past the stands for the first of three intricate, twisting circuits.

So far as one could see in the friendly but chaotic tangle that serves Auteuil for a parade ring, the French horses were not a wildly impressive sight. Nor, to someone who had never seen him before, would Mandarin have been, but to the large band of English supporters, the sheen on his coat, the hard muscles writhing over his quarters, and the way he pulled "Mush" Foster round the paddock, all told their own encouraging tale.

Sure enough, after flicking neat and fast over the pre-liminary hurdle jumped on the way to the start, Mandarin was soon upsides in front and passed the stands pulling, as usual, like a train. He has always been a "heavy-headed" ride with precious little feeling in his mouth—and always runs in a rubber-covered snaffle to save his lips and jaws.

At the beginning of last season, a brand-new bridle was bought—and Mandarin had worn it only half a dozen times, including both his victories in the Hennessey and Cheltenham Gold Cups. But the trouble with rubber bits is that a fault on wear can develop unseen in the steel chain—and this, no doubt, is what had happened now.

After the first, sharp, left-hand bend the Grand Steeple course comes back towards the stands and there, going to the fourth, a soft but staring privet fence the best part of six feet high, the bit snapped clean in the middle, inside Mandarin's mouth. I remember thinking at the time "he got a little close to that one," but for another full circuit none of us in the stands realized the dreadful truth.

In fact, of course, Fred Winter now had no contact what-soever with the horse's mouth or head. The reins, kept to-gether by the Irish martingale (or "rings") were still round

Riders in the Great
Hall at the Spanish
Riding School, Vienna,
performing the
quadrille on their
famous Lippizzana
horses.

Mandarin's neck—and they, together with the thin neck-strap of the breast-girth, were Winter's only hand hold.

To visualize the full impossibility of the situation you must remember first that when a racehorse, particularly a hard-pulling 'chaser, is galloping on the bit, much of the jockey's weight is normally balanced, through the reins, against that of the horse's head and forehand. Now, for both Fred Winter and Mandarin, this vital counterbalance was gone completely. The man, with no means of steering but his weight, had to rely entirely on grip and balance—the horse, used to a steady pressure on his mouth, had to jump 21 strange and formidable obstacles with his head completely free—a natural state admittedly, but one to which Mandarin is wholly un-accustomed.

Small wonder then that, at the huge "Rivière de la Tribune"—the water in front of the stands—he fiddled awkwardly, landing only inches clear of the bank and disaster. Thereafter, save for another nasty moment at the same fence next time round, the little horse jumped unbelievably well—and Fred Winter, sitting still or driving on as the need arose, matched his every move with the sympathetic rhythm that is nine-tenths of horsemanship.

But the fences, needless to say, were only half the problem. Walking the course that morning with Winter, Dave Dick and Joe Lammin, Fulke Walwyn's head lad, we had all wondered afresh at the many turns, and countless opportunities for losing your way. The Grand Steeple is, roughly, two figures of eight in opposite directions and one whole circuit outside both. There are at least four bends through 180 degrees, and to negotiate them all as Winter and Mandarin did, without bit or bridle, was, quite literally, miraculous.

The answer lies, of course, in many things—in the matchless strength of Winter's legs, in Mandarin's own good sense —and in the absolute determination of them both never to give up while there was one shot, however forlorn, left on the board.

It is also, I think, only fair to give some credit—and our thanks—to the French jockeys, several of whom could, had they pleased, have taken advantage of the disaster and, without much risk to themselves, got rid of the biggest danger. Instead, at least one—Laumas on Taillefer—and probably several others, actually did their best to help, proving gloriously that the comradeship of dangers shared can, in *some* sports at least, count far more than international rivalry.

Throughout the race, save for a moment on the last bend, Mandarin was up in the first four—and, as he jumped the Rivière for the last time, the full horror of his situation dawned upon us in the stands.

From that moment on, the nerve-racking suspense, the wild impossible hope, plunging to black despair and back again, were like nothing I have ever known on a race-course —or for that matter anywhere else.

Mandarin cleared with ease the tricky post and rails at which he hesitated fatally three years ago—and came to the junction of the courses close fourth—close enough to lift the hearts of those who knew his and Winter's invincible finishing power.

But now disaster almost struck. Before the last right-handed turn a large bush must be passed on the left—but can with equal ease be passed on the right. Mandarin, on the inside, with no rail to guide him, could not know until the last moment which way to go. For a few heart-stopping strides he hesitated, Winter threw all his strength and weight into one last desperate swerve—and somehow they were safe.

But priceless lengths had been lost and now, round the final bend, with only two obstacles to jump, Mandarin was only fifth, some six or seven lengths behind the leader.

On the turn, of course, Winter could hardly ride at all, but

A lineup of
Andalusian brood
mares bred in the area
surrounding the
Guadalquivir River in
Spain's deep south.

then, facing the Bullfinch, in a straight line for home at last, it was a different matter. From the stands we saw the familiar crouching drive of the shoulders, and Mandarin, responding as he always has and always will, thrust out his gallant head and went for the Bullfinch like a tank facing tissue paper.

None will ever know what the little horse felt or thought between those last two fences. I have always believed he knows just what it means to win—and now none will ever convince me otherwise. In a hundred desperate yards he passed three horses as if they were walking and, as he landed in front on the long run-in, my eyes, I am not ashamed to say, were half-blind with tears.

But it was not over yet. Mandarin was deadly tired and Winter, the reins gathered useless in his left hand, could do nothing to hold him together. He could only push and drive —and how he drove. Even so, inch by inch, Lumino, the only French horse able to accelerate, crept nearer and nearer.

In the final desperate strides, not knowing the angle, not one of us could really tell who had won. Fred Winter thought he had got up, but *he* could not speak, so for several ghastly moments we had to sweat it out. But then, there it was—number one in the frame—and as Mandarin came back, mobbed as no film star has ever been, head down, dog-tired, sweating

—but surely happy—a cheer went up such as I have never heard on any racecourse.

For Fred Winter it was not the end. Riding a dream of a race, he went on, 40 minutes later, to win the Grande Course de Haies on Beaver II. I have neither time nor space to describe that race and, triumph though it was for Beaver's trainer, Ryan Price, it only served as the perfect ending to an historic afternoon. For on Sunday, Fred Winter and Mandarin had earned themselves a place among the immortal names of sport. I have never seen a comparable feat, never expect to—and can only thank God that I was there.

23 June 1962

Col. the Hon. C. Guy Cubitt, D.S.O., T.D., D.L., one of the founders and past Chairman of the Pony Club.

THE HORSE WITH THE GOLDEN SMILE

ALTHOUGH horse dentistry is not new, it is rare, and perhaps the best-known example is the remarkable dental operation that was carried out in Geneva on the renowned international show-jumper that has garnered so many laurels for Italy in the world's arenas, Major Piero d'Inzeo's Pioneer.

This case is particularly interesting, for no fewer than eight experts took part in the operation.

Dental surgeon René Habib and veterinary surgeon Araldo-Edmond Mastrangelo had to fix a bridge on three broken front teeth. This was necessary because Pioneer had been in very bad shape for some time after taking a fall in which he broke the teeth.

It was Dr. Mastrangelo of Geneva, who was looking after Major d'Inzeo's horses, who decided that dentistry was necessary. He had indeed successfully carried out a similar operation a few years earlier.

The actual operation lasted two and a half hours. One hour was spent filing down the dental roots, it took half an hour to take the impression, and then another three-quarters of an hour to drill the ducts. Sealing the bridge took no more than ten minutes.

Before the operation started, it was necessary to treat the broken teeth to ensure that they would support the bridge solidly. It was also necessary to ascertain that once the bridge

164

was fitted the horse would suffer no pain.

Pioneer had to be kept quiet and calm throughout. It was decided that, as his own muscular strength would be needed during the operation, he should not be put to sleep. So he was given a small quantity of tranquillizers which at least assured that he would not panic or react violently to the filing down of the roots.

The bridge itself was made specially out of a metal called randolph, which is saliva-resisting and looks like gold. Unfortunately the mechanic ran out of the metal, so stainless steel piano string had to be used as well.

The operation was a complete success, despite all the difficulties, and no more than three days lapsed before Pioneer was again in training.

H.K.   23 February 1963

TEARS AND FULL THROATS GREET
TRIUMPHANT ARKLE
BY AUDAX

SATURDAY, November 6, 1965, Sandown Park, Esher, near London, England. The date and place are worth remembering.

The sky was clear, cold blue and at 2.48 p.m. or thereabouts the sun hung low already over the racecourse stables. Around the empty unsaddling enclosure a sea of faces spread and grew, fed by a stream of men and women running, pell-mell from the stands.

They ran, uphill, with thumping hearts and eyes alight—as if the devil was behind them or the Holy Grail in front.

And, in a way, it was.

For, however great or small the part played in their lives by racing, there was not, I believe, one single soul in that whole motley, rushing throng who did not feel, for certain, that he was living through a piece of history. Not war, not death, not politics—but history just the same.

The cause of all this fever-heat was walking calmly up the self-same hill, his long ears pricked, courteous as always to those who pressed to touch him, his heart, I suspect, beating no faster than theirs.

His name, of course, was Arkle and—perhaps I should have mentioned it before—he had just won the three-mile Gallaher Gold Cup.

He had won it, the history books will show, by 20 lengths from Rondetto, with Mill House third, four lengths away. But what they cannot show is the manner of his triumph and its meaning.

They can't record how we who watched him felt, the tears in many eyes, the choking lumps in many throats, the volume of our cheers—the overwhelming sense of greatness.

No doubt such scenes have happened before on English racecourses—but never, in my experience, quite like this. The only comparable moment in my memory is Mandarin's Grand Steeplechase de Paris—and even that was different. Then it was courage and skill in adversity which inspired us. Now it was greatness pure and simple.

That Arkle should win was no surprise at all—that he should win as he did, in record time, giving 26lb and 16lb to horses like Rondetto and Mill House, was more than even his most fervent worshippers could possibly foresee.

It established him, to my mind and, I believe, to the minds of the vast majority of those who were at Sandown, as the greatest steeplechaser there ever was or ever will be.

Perhaps, who knows, time and some other horse will one day call those words in question. But I write them now without fear of contradiction. They represent the facts as we know them at this moment. There is no longer any room for doubt.

For this unforgettable day nature had set the perfect scene. The turning leaves, the sky, the cold, clean wind—all conspired, as we packed like sardines round the parade ring, to produce a sense of almost unbearable expectation.

It showed in the applause which greeted both Arkle and Mill House as they appeared, followed them down to the start and—something I've never heard before—continued almost unbroken, though in various keys, throughout the race.

The first cheers were, deservedly, not for Arkle but Mill House. Achieving at once a perfect understanding with his new rider, David Nicholson, the big horse jumped from start to finish as well as I have ever seen him—which is to say as well as any horse can jump.

Border Incident (Ron Barry) pictured left holds a small lead over Snow Flyer (John Francome) at the fourth last fence in an Embassy Premier Chase qualifier. Border Incident had seven lengths to spare at the line.

Led by Candy (10st) over the first two fences, Mill House (11st 5lb) brushed him imperiously aside down the Railway straight—and each succeeding giant leap drew a roar of appreciation from the crowded stands and rails.

Some lengths behind him Arkle (12st 7lb) had, unusually for him, settled calmly in Pat Taaffe's hands. But clearly there's a compass in his handsome head for, swinging round towards the Pond, he suddenly decided it was time to go.

I can't remember a more obvious display of understanding in a racehorse. No one had told Arkle the distance of the Gallaher Gold Cup, but he knew Sandown—and would tolerate no leader up the well-remembered hill.

Sweeping over the open ditch before the stands he and Mill House were cheered again and realising that this was not, after all, the end, Arkle settled once more, saving his strength and letting his rival draw ahead.

This, of course, is hindsight. At the time, as Mill House stormed majestically down the Railway straight, recalling with every stride the days of his supremacy, there seemed, to us in the stands, a very real chance that he would win.

David Nicholson's orders were to press on from the water and, obeying them superbly, he gained a length at each of the three close fences. Was Pat Taaffe waiting—or had he perhaps, seen the spectre of defeat? We could not tell—but the answer was not long delayed.

For now, round the final bend, without coming off the bit, without, apparently, the slightest encouragement, Arkle unsheathed his sword. It flashed once, brilliant in the sunshine, and, before the Pond, for the fourth and surely the last time, poor, brave Mill House saw destiny sweep by.

I doubt if he has ever run a better race. No other living horse could have done more and, in that moment, sympathy and sadness mingled with our admiration for his conqueror.

But losers are, alas, too easily forgotten and now, with two fences left, there was only one horse at Sandown.

Going to the last Arkle was still, almost literally, running away. Landing over it Pat Taaffe just shook the reins and, unbelievably, he quickened. I seriously doubt whether the 300 yards of the run-in has ever been covered much faster— and certainly no winner ever came home on this or any other course, to a greater, more rapturous welcome.

Twenty lengths behind Arkle, Rondetto deprived Mill House of second place and deserves his full share of credit. It was the little chesnut's first race of the season and, until the water jump second time, he had been sailing along hard held close behind his two great opponents.

From then on, according to Jeff King, lack of an outing began to tell and it was, in the circumstances, no mean achievement to catch Mill House.

The latter had, of course, borne the brunt of Arkle's awesome challenge—and David Nicholson treated him humanely when all hope was gone. But nonetheless I am far from certain that Rondetto was not second best on merit at these weights —and their next meeting (without Arkle) is something to look forward to.

"Without Arkle"—how often, I wonder, are those words going to be thought or spoken over the next few years? For after all the tumult and the shouting died away last week N.H. racing found itself face to face with a situation unknown since the days when Judges used to call: "Eclipse first and the rest nowhere."

Flitgrove, No. 7 and Jeff King at an early fence before winning The Scilly Isles Novices' Chase at Sandown on Saturday, 5 February 1977. Bolus Head and John Burke can just be seen.

With 12st 7lb on his back—the heaviest weight the rules now allow him to carry—Arkle smashed the three-mile chase record at Sandown on Saturday by 11 **seconds**. The concession of 16lb to Mill House made not one ounce of difference and I am personally convinced that had Mill House carried 10st or even 9st 7lb the result, though possibly not the distance, would have been the same.

So where, it has to be asked, do we go from here? The Hennessy Gold Cup (for which the weights have already been published), the King George VI 'Chase and the Cheltenham Gold Cup—all these are, barring accidents, as good as over and done with. They won't be dull—watching Arkle could never be that—but they will, unless something quite unforeseeable happens, be both uncompetitive and repetitive.

13 November 1965

169

GUNS AT THE GALLOP

THIS summer for the first time, the famous King's Troop of the Royal Horse Artillery is to cross the Atlantic to give North Americans an opportunity to see one of the most thrilling events in the equestrian calendar: the Musical Drive, as performed at the Royal Tournament.

The performance is included in the World Horse Spectacular at Canada's "EXPO 67" in Montreal. Only twice before in history has the Musical Drive been seen outside the United Kingdom—at Copenhagen and Milan.

Few of us, including indeed experienced riders, realize the degree of danger involved in the culminating "scissor" movement in the Drive.

His Grace the Duke of Beaufort, K.G., G.C.V.O., P.V., MFH, Master of the Horse, President of the British Horse Society in 1958. President of the British Field Sports Society.

Each gun team is 20 yards long. Each gun and limber weights $2\frac{1}{2}$ tons. There are, literally, only inches to spare between the gun of the first team and the lead horses of the second. There are no brakes to help out of trouble if anything should go amiss.

In other words, there is no margin at all for error.

Not only must each man's judgment be 100 per cent, but his confidence in himself and his horse, *and in every other participant and every one of their horses*, must also be 100 per cent. This is the whole basis of training of the carefully-picked men and horses for this unique unit.

How *are* men and horses selected?

The riders, rather surprisingly, are for the most part chosen direct from civilian life. Each applicant wishing to join is invited to stay a few days with the Troop at St. John's Wood, London. During his stay, a man lives the regular life of any serving member of the Troop. The Army pays all his expenses.

Treated exactly like any serving soldier, he receives a fair insight into what life as a member of the King's Troop means —and a fair chance to judge whether he has what the job calls for.

If after this taste of it he still thinks he has what it takes, and still wants to prove it—and if he measures up to the authorities' demands—he can then sign on for the normal engagement of six or nine years.

If on the other hand he fails to make the grade, and/or decides it is not after all the life for him, he can go home, with no hard feelings anywhere. It has cost him nothing and the Army has not had to waste public money trying to train the wrong material.

The majority of men of the King's Troop are selected on this basis. The remainder are picked from the Royal Horse Artillery or Royal Artillery.

The horses? These are imported from Ireland, usually as five or six-year-olds, and untrained. The troop has to find about 15 annually and the main problem is matching.

With six horses to each gun, plus detachments, this is not always easily solved. There are two bay teams; one light-bay; two brown; one black.

As well as solving the problem of colour, there is also the question of deciding on the right type and size of horse for each position in the team in this very specialized art of horsemanship.

Aside from their performance in the Musical Drive, and on occasions such as the firing of salutes on royal occasions and the provision of a team of black horses for state and military funerals or other ceremonial, riders and horses of the King's Troop have a proud record in top-class equestrian contests.

For example, from these stables have come a number of champion competitors in horse trials and show-jumping events.

Notable among these were Savernake, a British National Foxhunter Championship winner at the Horse of the Year Show. Two distinguished entrants in the three-day event at the Tokyo Olympics were Sgt. Jones's Master Bernard, and M'Lord Connolly, ridden by Capt. Templer.

Britain's team captain at Tokyo was Lt.-Col. Frank Weldon, a former C.O. of the Troop, who, with Kilbarry, was a member of our gold medal trials team at Stockholm in 1956.

It surprises some people that the "King's Troop" has held that title only 20 years.

Under its former title of the "Riding Troop" the unit always engaged the interest of the late King George VI. In 1947 he visited St. John's Wood. On signing the Visitors' Book, without comment he quietly drew a line through the word "Riding" and substituted "King's," whereby its unique status was established.

In 1952 one of the Queen's first acts on succeeding to the throne was to write to the Troop's Commanding Officer and say that in memory of her father's special interest, it was her wish that during her reign it should still be known as The *King's* Troop.

PHILIP DREW.   20 May 1967

A NATURAL GENTLEMAN WHO SEES
THE VISION WHERE WE SEE NIGHT
BY JOHN LAWRENCE

"One who makes us each feel taller when we claim him as a
    friend,
Who to a rude age a natural gentleman did bring
Who gave the words like chivalry and loyalty a new ring,
Making such words mean again to us who know him
To us who are grateful to his sight, which sees the vision while
    we see only night."

WITH those words, written specially by Ronald Duncan in honour of Col. Sir Michael Ansell, Dorian Williams expressed, on Thursday of last week, the feeling and purpose of a unique and memorable occasion.

He was speaking at a dinner at the Dorchester, London, given by Walter Case, Editor of *Horse and Hound*, to celebrate Col. Ansell's recent knighthood, and his audience included H.R.H. the Duke of Edinburgh and many famous names from the worlds which, as Whyte-Melville admitted, owe "the best of their fun" to horse or to hound or both.

Mike Ansell has spent most of his life in those worlds, and it was to honour his extraordinary services to them that so many of his friends and admirers met last week.

Looking at the tall erect figure (a good hand taller than anyone else there) we remembered the dreadful wounds, suffered at St. Valery in 1940, which put an end to Mike Ansell's active enjoyment of the sports he loved—the show-jumping, polo and hunting to which he had devoted so much of his pre-war life.

For most men those wounds, which nine painful years later

172

Richard Meade riding
Barbara Hammond's
Eagle Rock over the
Wall Fence at
Badminton.

deprived him completely of his sight, would have meant the
end of much more besides. But those who knew Mike Ansell
also knew that it would take a far bigger handicap than blind-
ness to curb his restless, indefatigable spirit.

And so it proved, for no man ever better demonstrated by
his deeds the truth that obstacles are made to be overcome.
From the moment when, in 1949, Mike Ansell and the late
Tony Collings started the Horse of the Year Show, the name
of Ansell has been synonymous with the post-war revolution
that has carried British show-jumping—and riding in all its
forms—to a peak of popularity and success never previously
achieved.

But that is an old story, often told before. Last week at the
Dorchester there were many who have played leading parts
in it; and some of them, paying their personal tributes to the
man who made it possible, gave us fascinating details of his
extraordinary life.

Dorian Williams, for instance, proposing the toast of the
guest of honour, confirmed that, from the very beginning,

173

life with Mike Ansell has never been dull. They were, in fact, brought up together (Dorian's father had become Mike's guardian), and at an early age, it seems, the future commentator asked some advice from the future president of the B.S.J.A. on the pursuit, not of foxes but of the fair sex.

The advice, for all I know, may have been sound enough, but the result, intentional or otherwise, was that Mike Ansell got the girl!

The friendship was not, however, permanently damaged —and later survived a hectic misadventure involving two broken arms and an accommodating fox, the climax of which I will not repeat for fear of incurring displeasure from certain quarters. . . .

At one of the early post-war horse shows Dorian Williams was unwise enough to criticize the standard of commentating —and got the typical Ansellian response "Well, do it yourself then." He has been doing it brilliantly ever since and is a perfect example of the rule that no commander achieves true greatness without the ability to choose first-rate lieutenants.

Then followed a tribute from the other side, so to speak, though Dan Corry, doyen of the Irish show-jumping world, has been as much a friend and collaborator of Col. Ansell's in the improvement of the sport as he ever was an opponent in the ring.

The impact of these two upon their foreign rivals must, by the sound of it, have been formidable, particularly on the Canadian who, as a token of Anglo-Irish gratitude for his services, found himself the proud owner of the biggest Aspidestra in Montreal!

It had been borrowed from the hall of a hotel at dead of night, and by the time it was discovered—blocking the door of its recipient's room—Cols. Corry and Ansell were safe on the high seas. Not all that safe, though, for most of the ship's silver vanished in mid-Atlantic—to be discovered under Col. Corry's bed!

Col. Ansell, replying to the toast, did not actually admit responsibility for this incident—he didn't deny it, either— merely remarking that, while the first three members of every Irish team are picked for horsemanship, elegance and diplomacy, the fourth must be first and foremost a good drinker. And in his view Dan Corry qualified on all four grounds.

Capt. Mark Phillips on Great Ovation taking the Normandy Bank at Badminton.

Col. Mike went on to welcome some of the other principal guests with examples of their prowess in various fields drawn from his capacious memory.

He cited Gen. Sir Charles Keightley for initiative (in commandeering a train-load of someone else's Bofors guns for his own use); the Maharaja of Jaipur for meritorious service at night ("which only occasionally made him miss the ball in the morning"); and Col. Harry Llewellyn for courtesy (landing over the water jump in Rome during a vital round on Foxhunter, the colonel acknowledged a storm of cheers by raising his hat before the next fence—only to find that the Italians were applauding the fact that Foxhunter had *failed* to clear the ditch!).

I must draw a veil over what (according to Col. Ansell) Mr. Bob Hanson considers a horse's most vital statistic, and hardly like to mention the fact that Lord Knutsford, that noted arbiter of elegance in matters sartorial, once made 47 in a cricket match at Badminton, *wearing a pair of black brogues covered with dubbin.*

It was, in any case, a wonderful speech, worthy both of the occasion and of the wonderful man who made it.

Major Bob Hoare, replying for the guests, started by saying that none of his best stories could be told in front of Lord Knutsford—because he had told them all first. He went on to tell one or two in which his lordship certainly played no part.

Travel in the United States is not, it seems, an unmixed joy for the Master of the Cottesmore. One friendly native, hearing his identity, said, "Gee, I hear you raise dogs. You must meet my wife—she raises cats."

In Holland, on the other hand, the gallant major had a much warmer welcome, but the tale of his efforts to fraternize with the local population must wait for another day—and perhaps for a less respectable journal than *Horse and Hound*.

Enough has been said, I hope, to show that this was not only a memorable dinner, unlikely ever to be repeated in the variety and distinction, from a sporting point of view, of those who attended it, but also the greatest possible fun; and that, as all who know and love the great man in whose honour it was held, was primarily how it should be.

THE GUEST LIST IN FULL

H.R.H. Prince Philip, Duke of Edinburgh.

H. H. The Maharaja of Jaipur, The Marquess of Abergavenny, Brigadier W. A. C. Anderson, Mr. Anthony Ansell, Major N. G. P. Ansell, Mr. G. E. Aubrey, Colonel Lord Barnby, Mr. W. T. Barton, Mr. Denis Bates, The Duke of Beaufort, M.F.H., Captain Lord Patrick Beresford, Major-General C. H. Blacker, Major Peter Borwick M.F.H.

Brigadier Arthur Carr, Lieut.-Colonel J. Collingwood, Major Arthur Collins, Lieut.-Colonel Gordon Cox-Cox, Mr. Geoffrey Cross, Colonel the Hon. C. Guy Cubitt, Mr. Robert Dean, Mr. John Dennett, Mr. Peter Dimmock, Major-General Sir Evelyn Fanshawe, Major R. I. Ferguson, Lord Fraser of Lonsdale.

Colonel W. H. Gerard Leigh, Lord Grenfell, Lieut.-Colonel H. P. Guinness, Mr. Robert Hanson, Mr. A. E. Hill, Mr. J. R. Hindley M.H., Major Robert Hoare M.F.H., Colonel G. T. Hurrell, General Sir Charles Keightley, Lieut.-Colonel N. H. Kindersley, Viscount Knutsford, the Hon. John Lawrence, Lieut.-Colonel H. M. Llewellyn.

Lord Margadale of Islay, Lieut.-Colonel John Miller, General Sir Rodney Moore, Lieut.-Colonel R. B. Moseley, Lieut.-General The Lord Norrie, Mr. James Orr, Count Robert Orssich, Major-General C. E. Pert, Major David Satow, Major-General V. W. Street.

Field-Marshal Sir Gerald Templer, Captain R. E. Wallace M.F.H., Mr. Sanders Watney, Captain G. H. S. Webber, Lieut.-Colonel Frank Weldon, Colonel W. H. Whitbread, Sir Dymoke White, Bt., Mr. W. H. White, Mr. Dorian Williams M.F.H., Lord Willoughby de Broke, Mr. Fred Winter.

10 May 1968

SPEED AND STAMINA IN THE RACEHORSE
BY LT.-COL. R. C. KIDD

IT is always fascinating to visit a Thoroughbred stud and see the stallions and mares, many of whom have had distinguished careers on the Turf. If, however, the visitor is a breeder or has some knowledge of horses, interest may be accompanied by a little surprise that some of the mares should have been selected for stud.

Not all possess the physical conformation desirable for breeding, and a few may have such serious defects that they should be discarded instantly for such a purpose.

Studs which are run on commercial lines cannot, however, afford to refuse mares, nor will criticism prove very popular with the owners.

The very high price of a mare both beautiful and impeccably bred may preclude purchase by all but the very rich. Some owners who aspire to breed a winner may not themselves have much knowledge or experience of horses, and for these, and for those who must be content with a mare of more moderate price, it may be helpful to consider the general principles by which they should be guided.

Speed in the racehorse is dependent upon a combination of physical conformation and the energy transmitted to the muscles.

Of these two main factors, conformation can be seen and assessed by a practised eye, while the potential energy of a horse is hidden and is subject to a number of complicated processes, many of which are obscure. It is, however, useful to have a superficial knowledge of how this energy is produced.

It is customary to use the expression "blood-strain" to denote the inherited characteristics which influence a horse's energy, although the word "blood" in this connection is something of a misnomer.

Capt. Ronnie Wallace, MFH, Chairman of the Masters of Foxhounds Association

While the number of red and white corpuscles may vary slightly, there is virtually no difference in the nature of the blood of any horse, whether he be Thoroughbred or a carthorse. The function of the blood is to provide a means of introducing and dispersing the necessary chemicals to the muscles through the circulatory system.

During violent exertion in a race lactic acid is formed in the muscles in amounts far greater than can be disposed of contemporaneously. Unless counteracted the muscles would then seize up, somewhat in the manner of an engine lacking oil, but this accumulation is rapidly removed in the presence of oxygen.

The oxygen carried in the blood performs this function while the venous blood returning to the heart removes the waste products.

In steady, prolonged exercise, fatigue is due to a number of ill-understood factors, but in the main it is attributed to changes in the brain resulting from slight loss of oxygen.

The phenomenon known as "second wind" is familiar to athletes, but this again has not yet been satisfactorily explained. Does this ability to gain second wind affect the distance capacity of a horse?

Why can some horses expend a large amount of energy for a short period while others produce a smaller amount for a longer period and are thereby classified as sprinters or stayers? Science cannot provide a precise answer to these questions.

The exact part played by the nervous system in the production of energy is also uncertain. A runner will continue to run or an oar to row long after the chemical conditions required for the expansion and contraction of muscles have passed, and will automatically continue this exertion until unconsciousness supervenes.

In much the same way a courageous horse will refuse to accept defeat and will battle on with instinctive determination. The reason is not understood, but it will be noticed how every part of the body makes its contribution to the general effort.

The pulmonary "bellows" supply the oxygen and the heart sends the blood mainly to the parts which need it. The efficiency with which the whole of this intricate system works depends upon the successful blending of inherited characteristics by matings to produce the ideal combination of speed, stamina and courage.

The possession of long and detailed records of breeding and performance renders the Thoroughbred horse a most fruitful field for the study of genetics. It is proof of the difficulties which beset research that, in spite of all the data available, only certain general principles have been evolved to assist the breeder.

Various methods have been devised, of which the Bruce Lowe evaluation system is one, but in the main all that has been established is that certain blood-strains are pre-eminent and that some will produce stamina and others speed. Such progress as has been made has been by dint of experience and has continued by trial and error.

That magnificent chesnut horse Irish Elegance was a champion sprinter of his day, but his pedigree was not above suspicion. When put to stud his progeny were virtually useless. The heart of Brown Jack, one of the most outstanding stayers of all time, is believed to have been abnormally large.

From such, and similar, instances a little more information has been gained. From all this uncertainty and scanty knowledge of how energy is produced only two helpful conclusions can be drawn. They are that oxygen is essential and that "blood will tell."

Happily it is a little easier to determine the physical conformation which is desirable. It is true that horses do win races in all shapes, but it is significant that, unlike some of the mares, the stallions are rarely seen to possess physical defects.

These horses have been sent to stud on account of their good breeding and notable achievements on the race-course, and it is not unreasonable to suppose that their conformation has made a considerable contribution to their success.

Oxygen is obtained from the air and it is obvious that the flow must be unimpeded. A horse which develops ailments in the nerves and muscles of his throat is useless unless surgically treated. Similarly the lungs must have space to expand and the heart to work. The throat should be fine with unrestricted movement to the neck, the chest wide and the girth deep.

However brilliant, a horse which will not stand up to the rigours of training and racing will only prove a disappointment and expense.

Although the bone of a Thoroughbred horse is of finer texture than that of his humbler brother, the racehorse must possess limbs of reasonable substance, particularly below the knee.

A comparison of photographs of a horse when standing and galloping disclose that when fully extended in a gallop the fetlock joint is noticeably nearer the ground. This action of the pastern stretches the tendons of the leg, and the tension is accentuated if the pasterns are unduly long and sloping, the tendons becoming strained or "bowed."

While short, straight pasterns may lead to jarring of the leg, a suitable compromise between two extremes is required. A recession of the knee (back at the knee) will have similar effects.

Even abundant energy will not achieve its purpose unless provided with an efficient machine in which to work. The length and angle of the limbs must be suitable for propulsion. In this connection it is interesting to examine the conformation of other animals, such as the hare, the greyhound and the hunting leopard, which are noted for speed.

All have one characteristic in common. It is the exceptional length from the hip to the hock and from the shoulders to the knee, which increases the length of the natural stride. The racehorse should be built similarly both knees and hocks being near the ground.

It has been said that "a good big un is better than a good

In the Ladies Open at the Easton Harriers Point to Point, Mayland Lad, right (Miss J. Cyler), leads from Duffy (Miss D. Harland) at the last fence. However they were beaten for first place by Royal and Ancient (Mrs S. French), just visible on the extreme right.

little un." Hyperion, however, was a small horse, and within reasonable limits the actual height is probably not so important as correct proportion.

The stride of a horse is also governed to some extent by the length of the neck, since the fore-feet cannot meet the ground beyond a vertical line dropped from the point of the nose. A short neck is therefore undesirable, since it will restrict this movement, apart from having other disadvantages.

The action of the gallop requires a great effort in propulsion. A long back or hind legs which are noticeably behind the body do not provide the most efficient system of leverage. It is preferable for the horse to be close-coupled, with hocks set within the quarters.

This brief attempt to analyse speed and stamina does not pretend to produce answers to the intricate problems of selection of lineage, which is in itself the study of a life-time. It is intended only to draw attention to certain aspects of breeding which are important to the avoidance of producing misfits and useless animals.

Inherited characteristics are no less persistent in the equine than in the human race. A Grecian profile, a Hapsburg lip, good looks and length of limb all have their counterparts in horses.

It is unwise to send a mare to stud merely because she is half-sister to a noted winner unless she herself possesses reasonable conformation, since it is probable she will transmit her defects to her offspring.

Neither perfect conformation nor impeccable breeding will necessarily achieve success. All that can be said is that, given similar blood, a well-proportioned horse is more likely to win races than one whose conformation is faulty. It is a consideration which does not always receive all the attention it deserves.

H.R.H. the Prince of Wales.

7 March 1969

MAKING THE MOST OF MAY

A MONTH or so ago, I was bewailing first the miserable wet of January and then the bleak cold of February. Now suddenly it is May. It would be nice to be able to say that it is all that May should be. Nobody needs telling that this is not the case.

On the other hand we have had some very pleasant days, and more than once I have had some of those enjoyable peaceful, balmy experiences that I always associate with May.

Almost overnight the country appears green and lush. This year, of course, it happened so late that one began to despair of it ever looking anything but bare and barren.

But the warm sunshine of Easter did its stuff and, although the rain that followed was accompanied by a cold east wind, Spring seemed to decide that it had waited long enough and, suddenly, there it was, albeit a little reluctant.

Walks and groves and gardens which are normally a mass of yellow by early April suddenly threw off the drab appearance with which one had associated them all through the dead months of winter and proudly flaunted their daffodils and primroses, and in the warmer, bolder corners, their handsome tulips.

It is one of the most pleasant times of the year to be riding, yet probably fewer people are riding in the country than at any other time.

Hunting is finished—yes, even in the west, the point-to-points are coming to an end, show jumping is in full swing, of course, but by now it is mostly a rush from show to show.

Not many people seem to go hacking these days, and, of course, with hunting finished there are not the autumn and winter sights of horses being exercised.

If one is lucky enough to live near a racing establishment there is, of course the ever joyous sight of racehorses on the gallops to the endless and enviable delight of the artist.

Even the eventers are thinning out, though one still sees earnest figures going round in circles settling their novices for the next dressage hazard. What is more, these horses are often the best-looking ones to be seen anywhere nowadays, for it does seem that the best-looking and the best bred horses today find their way into eventing, rather than into the hunting field.

Certainly one sees plenty of really fine horses at these desperately over subscribed one-day events; horses that can really gallop and jump, horses with courage and balance, the two qualities that are more important in a horse than any others—or so it was suggested to me by one who should know from years of successful experience.

As it happens, having a young horse that I hope to show a little later on, I have been doing a certain amount of quiet riding ever since the end of hunting—and very enjoyable it has been, despite a few soakings.

April certainly lived up to its reputation. One would set off in glorious sunshine with only a few feathery clouds scudding across the sky, and then suddenly it darkens, a huge lowering blackness sweeps up. For a moment one thinks, or hopes, that with luck it will pass by on the other side of the valley, or over the hill or across the river, but then, whoosh. . . .

Down it comes and in a moment one is drenched, one's cheeks stinging with the lashing rain, one's hands, usually gloveless, numbed, one's knees sticky and uncomfortable.

In a few minutes it is all over, and surprisingly, although one has been so sodden, by the time one reaches home one is dry again, the sun and the blustery wind and the internal combustion from exercise all having done their stuff.

183

Next day one is out again, still without a mackintosh, despite the inevitable shower being virtually a certainty.

But how lush and lovely the country looks, especially after the shower, when the very air itself seems washed as though it were plate glass, and there is a clarity that one associates more with flying at 30,000 feet than with the riding on a dusty lane.

The green of the crops coming through is tantalizingly deceptive. It appears as though there is a sea of grass as far as once can see.

The hedges now turning to green blend into the picture, and one is confronted with a scene that must have been familiar to our ancestors two or three hundred years ago: no arable, no fences, and, because of the sodden foliage, an almost forest-like appearance, so different from the land-scape I recently described, with the stark leafless trunks silhouetted against the sky.

Closer inspection shows the grass to be less abundant than at first it seems. A cold blast with a knife-edge reminds one why.

One is thankful that it has been possible, though incon-venient, to delay the putting out of one's horses. Not only has there been little enough for them to eat, but their coats have been stary, and those which have been out have looked tucked up and miserable, the flesh that one has managed to put back on to them since the end of a testing season quickly falling away.

But now they should thrive, for now one feels that summer is round the corner. The lazy cawing of the rooks, the lambs playing, birds on their nests and the first sign of the burgeon-ing of the magnificient chesnuts, all betoken the warmer weather.

May is a serene time, and its serenity after the bustling winter, the hurry and scurry of the Easter holidays, that I spoke of last week, seems to seep into one's bones.

I enjoy riding through the country. I enjoy wandering down our lane and looking at our hunters out at grass. I enjoy the long evenings with all the sounds and contentment of summer. I enjoy the early summer highlights, Newark, Windsor, the Derby.

By the end of June it is all tarnished somehow. The green

The Duke and Duchess of Kent arriving with Walter Case at the *Horse and Hound* Ball at Grosvenor House. Behind are Mrs Hugh Brassey and the Duke of Beaufort.

has faded, the land is parched and arid—in theory at any rate!—the freshness has been replaced by a used-up look as though the goodness has been sucked out.

The atmosphere of hope has been replaced by a jaded weariness, quickly to be followed by the sadness of autumn, the finality of winter.

It is all too short, the mood of May. We must make the most of it.

LORINER.   9 May 1969

THE MEANING OF DRESSAGE
BY COL. V. D. S. WILLIAMS

BEFORE the first world war, the motor car was a rare bird; practically the only method of getting about the country was on a horse or behind one. The whole country was horse minded. At the end of the second world war matters were different. It is almost true to say the only people who rode did so to hunt or play polo, and a few for exercise, probably riding only for an hour or two at weekends.

The Pony Club which had been formed between the wars became increasingly popular, but instructors were hard to find. The main sources from which they had been drawn in pre-war days, namely Weedon, the Cavalry regiments or Horse Gunners or their wives and daughters, who had been instructed by these soldiers had ceased to exist.

With the ever increasing number of Pony Club branches the instructor question became more and more difficult. As chairman of the Pony Club, I visited many Pony Club branches and was appalled at what was going on.

Let me quote two instances: I saw a ride being taken by an elderly gentleman. He was trying to make the children do a figure-of-eight at the canter with a flying change. Hearing him curse a child on a woolly bear of a pony for not performing this feat, in rather a loud voice I suggested he should get on the pony himself and show them what he wanted done.

He couldn't refuse without losing face. He mounted and after a fine exhibition of leg flapping and rein jerking failed to get the pony out of a trot. Infuriated he resigned.

On another occasion, the instructor of the ride had a daughter riding a good sort of pony. To impress me with his offspring he had put up much too big a course, over which his child performed reasonably well, but most of the rest either refused or if their pony did jump it, fell off.

I came to the conclusion the only thing to be done was to have classes for Pony Club instructors. To start with I had the greatest difficulty in getting anyone to come to these classes, and where were the instructors of the classes to come from? The teaching of bad dressage is worse than no teaching at all.

Before the first world war I had taken a tour of the Cavalry Schools of Europe. I went with Colonel George Ansell (Sir Michael Ansell's father) who commanded my regiment, as he was proposing to make me Equitation Officer to it.

I think the thing that impressed me most was the similarity of the training that was practised at all the continental schools we visited, with the exception of the Italian School at Tor de

Quinto where they concentrated chiefly on jumping, following the Caprilli method of the forward seat.

There their early training seemed to be confined to jumping numbers of small fixed obstacles, many of them parallel bars. Their final results with the advanced horses were astounding.

All the French Cavalry horses were trained at Saumur. At the end of their training some of the best were retained for further training as officers' chargers and a very few of these, with exceptional ability, were handed over to the Cadre Noir (a small specially selected group of the finest riders in the French army) to be trained in haute école.

The Commandant gave us a show on one of these especially selected horses, after which he asked me if I would like to ride it. I told him I knew nothing about this type of riding. He replied "Never mind that, get on and ride it, but don't try any fancy tricks." I did and when I returned from my ride I said it was the most lovely ride I had ever had. His reply was: "If the ordinary practical rider doesn't feel that when he has ridden a horse I have trained then I have failed in my training."

Next day I rode this horse on their jumping grounds where there was every possible sort of obstacle, and said what wouldn't I give to have a horse like this to ride across Leicestershire.

I returned home, and with Colonel George Ansell's guidance I tried to teach what I had learnt on the Continent.

After the second world war, with the help of the late Henry Wynmalen, I started the British Riding Club, the object of which was to improve the standard of training in this country.

The late Robert Hanson, C.B.E., one of the greatest sponsors of show jumping horses.

Now we sought for a word to describe our object. In the Army the words Rough Riders were used; in civilian life they talked about horse breakers—words that seemed to give the wrong impression of what we wished to convey. We had to fall back on the word "training" but this had already been adopted by the trainers of racehorses and led to confusion, and we had endless enquiries about training horses for this or that race.

We adopted the word "dressage" as universally used on the Continent (and on reference to the dictionaries it will be found primarily to mean training) in the hope that it would gradually be adopted in this country in the same way that the words "chauffeur" and "menu" have.

But that was not to be, and although with a large number of people it is now understood, there are many others to whom it is offensive and they mix it up with haute école, although there is as much difference between ordinary dressage and haute école as there is between ordinary ballroom dancing and the ballet.

How hard it has been to get this word over.

One day, taking a ride of members of the Pony Club branch of the Grafton Hunt of which I was once Joint-Master, my huntsman Will Pope, who was not only a brilliant man across country but improved every horse he rode, was watching the ride and said to me: "Do you think this dressage does any good? I never learnt any of this sort of stuff but I can get across a country."

I lined the children up and told Pope to ride down and

188

open a gate, which was one that opened towards us, and I told the children that if they watched carefully they would see Pope perform as good a "turn on the forehand" as they could wish to see.

Have you also ever watched a good steeplechase jockey riding a horse that is inclined to run out to the left? If you have you will probably have noticed that he applies a slight "right shoulder in." Yet if you were to ask any of these brilliant horsemen to explain how to do a turn on the forehand or a shoulder-in, they would not know what you were talking about.

To teach these things to beginners they had to be given names, and as I have always tried to explain, by dressage we are trying to teach people today, who probably only ride a few hours a week, what these brilliant horsemen have learnt by a lifetime in the saddle under all conditions.

The trouble came when people tried to separate dressage from ordinary riding and instead of looking upon it as the practical training for all purposes of riding, talked about it as if it were some peculiar sort of foreign riding.

Dressage competitions should be looked upon as tests to show what progress is being made and whether the horse is ready for more advanced training, in a similar manner to end-of-school exams, and not as a means to an end.

Every time a good rider rides a horse he practises dressage, and improves its ride. A famous foreign horseman visiting this country once said to me: "No country in the world has better horses than you have and you have a number of fine natural horsemen, but for heaven's sake forget the words "Piaffe" and "Passage."

A great number of horses are spoiled in this country by their riders trying to obtain movements for which they are not properly prepared and the riders themselves have not the knowledge to teach them. Let the ordinary rider stick to the basic and elementary training of the horse, teaching him to go freely forward in well balanced paces and obedient to the hand and leg.

Let him first experience the joy of riding a well trained horse across a grass country, behind a pack of hounds—something that no other country in the world can offer them—or if they have not the opportunity to do this, take part in some combined training events. Then perhaps in due course there will emerge a few riders who have exceptional ability and the time to take up High School riding, if that is their ambition.

To show there is nothing new in horsemen realizing the value of dressage in the training of a hunter, let me quote from a book written by Lord Ribblesdale at the end of last century.

"Out with the Woodland Pytchley, one afternoon late in the season, I was riding with Lord Lonsdale when we put up an old dog fox in Boughton Woods. The hounds got right away on the back of the fox and we both started on the back of the hounds.

"I was riding a handy fast horse but Lord Lonsdale got right away from me in three minutes, not because he was riding a faster horse but because of his superior horsemanship and his knowledge of manege riding, which to my mind especially distinguished him from other celebrated riders to hounds."

After a time the British Riding Club was taken over by the British Horse Society and a Dressage Committee appointed of which I was Chairman, in order to carry on the work that we had started.

17 October 1969

SAFEGUARDING THE FUTURE OF HUNT SERVANTS
by the Duke of Beaufort

In 1872 a number of Masters of Hounds made the first move to help Hunt servants who were suffering from injury or ill-health, or who needed support in old age, together perhaps with lump-sum payments at death to provide for funeral expenses or to help their widows.

The modern pension scheme for retirement at age 60 or 65 was not considered necessary in those days, and indeed Masters of Hounds could hardly devise such a scheme for a series of men in kennels, many of whom moved on regularly every two or three years in order to gain experience.

In 1872 the solution was found in a Friendly Society, which any mounted Hunt servant could join. The benefits were fixed in amount, and in order to qualify for them the

Lt.-Col. Sir John Miller, Crown Equerry, driving H.M. the Queen's coach to the centenary Coaching Club dinner at Hampton Court Palace. Beside him is Anne Duchess of Westminster and behind is Col. Sir Michael Ansell.

member paid premiums varying with his age of entry. The younger he joined, the smaller premiums he paid.

Until recently, if he joined at age 25, then a premium of £3 13s a year insured him for sickness pay of 25s a week, an annuity of 35s a week at age 60, an earlier pension of 10s a week at age 55 and a lump-sum payment of £200 at death.

For nearly a century the Hunt Servants Benefit Society has been helping Hunt servants in this way, and very useful the benefits have been. Moreover, the fact that the Society's income accumulates free of tax and is heavily subsidized by benevolent foxhunters, some of whom are honorary (as opposed to benefit) members and many more of whom subscribe through caps, has meant that these benefits have been about three times as good as those which a purely commercial institution would provide. Incidentally the Society is not a recognized charity, since its distributions are confined to its members.

However, the steep rise in wages since the second war has meant that the premiums under this old scheme have become ridiculously small for a man who wants to save, and the benefits are correspondingly small. Nor, under the old scheme, could the Society, however heavily subsidized, pay pensions of more than £3 a week, owing to the restrictions in the rules of a Friendly Society.

In 1966, however, the Society took advantage of the 1956 Finance Act and put forward a new scheme, with bigger premiums but with much-improved benefits to meet modern needs. There was less emphasis on payments at death and more emphasis on pensions at age 65 or 70, lump-sum payments on retirement and widows' pensions.

All new entrants must join the new scheme, and many men insured under the old scheme have changed to the new one or are members of both.

If a man joins at age 25 now, a premium of some £17 a year will provide benefits of £4 a week for sickness, a lump sum of £100 and a pension of rather over £4 a week, both at age 65. By paying bigger premiums he can, of course, insure for higher benefits.

For a man joining at age 40, the premiums for these benefits would be about double, or say £34 a year. It is estimated that these benefits are about half as good again as those offered by an insurance company.

Hunt servants are certainly not over-paid and in general they work a seven-day week. Many Masters of Hounds and Hunt committees have decided that it is not enough to reward a man for long years of service merely with a present of some hundreds, or, very rarely, thousands of pounds. There is little security in that. One solution is for each Hunt servant to be a member of the H.S.B.S., insured under the new scheme for an adequate pension and other benefits.

Some Masters now pay the Society's premiums in addition to the normal wage and other kennel allowances. Admittedly it is expensive for a middle-aged man to join the Society, and he probably would need some help from his employers; but unless he has a pension already partly subscribed he may find it difficult to obtain a fresh place when nearing retirement.

In their own interests all (mounted) Hunt servants should join the Society—the younger the better. At the same time all supporters of foxhunting should express their thanks for all the enjoyment that the Hunt staffs provide by sending a regular subscription or making an annual donation to the Society.

16 January 1970

Miss Sheila Willcox, brilliant eventer who won Badminton in three consecutive years, and the first lady rider to win the European Championships (1957).

WHAT THE NATIONAL STUD IS ALL ABOUT
BY PETER WILLETT

THE National Stud is, and always has been, a controversial subject. The variety of opinions about its purposes and uses expressed by people within the world of racing and breeding is extraordinary.

Within recent weeks I have heard one breeder express the opinion that the original purpose of the National Stud was to stand high-class stallions at a fee that all breeders could afford, and another surmise, after a visit to the stud at Newmarket, that it was all very fine but must be costing somebody—who was not specified—a great deal of money.

The source of the uncertainties about the National Stud is that its foundation was fortuitous and was not the result of a deliberate act of policy with properly defined aims.

Like many other British institutions, it just happened, and successive generations have been left to argue what it is all about, or ought to be about.

In 1916 Col Hall Walker, later Lord Wavertree, offered to present his entire stud of Thoroughbred horses to the nation on condition that the Government purchased his breeding establishment at Tully, Co. Kildare, and his training establishment at Russley Park in Wiltshire.

The offer was accepted and a National Stud was created at Tully, while the training establishment was handed over to the War Office.

No one inside or outside the Government seems to have thought it necessary to spell out the purposes of the nation's new acquisition. Politicians and public had more urgent matters to preoccupy them at the height of the first world war.

The *Bloodstock Breeders Review* of the following year commented: "The State is now definitely committed to a practical participation in the effort to preserve and enhance the reputation these islands of ours enjoy as the fountain head of the horse breeding industry."

Comments do not come much vaguer and the Review was

silent about the methods the stud should or would adopt to fulfil its responsibilities.

Nearly 40 years and another world war later the Committee on National Stud Policy and Methods of Operation set up by the Minister of Agriculture reviewed the history of the stud and decided that the main reason for accepting Lord Wavertree's offer and establishing a National Stud had been the desire of the Government in the circumstances of the first world war to ensure the maintenance of first-class foundation stock for the breeding of high quality light horses throughout the country for the cavalry.

As the cavalry was mechanized during the inter-war period this function withered away, but successive governments retained the stud as a profitable asset producing bloodstock of the highest class.

The stud got off to a wonderful start thanks to the exceptionally high standard of the foundation stock.

Hall Walker was a somewhat unlovable eccentric whose mating plans had strong astrological overtones, but whether or not he was aided by the stars in their courses he had built up a brilliant collection of mares before 1916.

He had bred the Derby winner Minoru, the Oaks winner Cherry Lass and the St. Leger winners Prince Palatine and Night Hawk.

The 43 mares handed over to the nation included individuals due to make great names for themselves and to figure in top-class pedigrees for generations to come like Black Cherry, Blanche, Dolabella and Tillywhim.

Building on this secure foundation, the stud operated on the lines of a private commercial establishment, the produce being sold, usually as yearlings.

Only the produce thought likely to be required back at the stud for breeding after their racing careers were retained. Those earmarked as potential breeding stock were leased for racing in early days to Lord Lonsdale and later to King George VI and then Queen Elizabeth II.

Many horses of exceptional merit were bred at the National Stud. They included Blandford, one of the greatest Classic sires in the history of the Thoroughbred; the St. Leger winner Royal Lancer; the Two Thousand Guineas winner and influential sire, Big Game; Chamossaire, winner of the

St. Leger and sire of the Derby winner Santa Claus; the brilliant but non-staying Myrobella; Sun Chariot, winner of three Classic races; the Oaks winner Carrozza, and the Grand Prix de Saint-Cloud winner Hopeful Venture.

Many of the best of them, including the stallions Big Game and Hopeful Venture and the Classic fillies Sun Chariot and Carrozza, were leased for racing and then returned to the stud.

Altogether the record of the National Stud as a producer was one that could be envied by any private or commercial breeder of the same period, and the Director had been able to fulfil his directive that the stud, though not to be run primarily for profit, should be self-supporting.

In 1943 the stud was moved to Sandley, near Gillingham in Dorset, and Tully was adopted as the Irish National Stud. Six years later a further establishment, at West Grinstead in Sussex, was taken on long lease to provide additional facilities. Big Game became a successful sire at Sandley.

Nevertheless it was obvious after the second world war that the whole breeding industry was undergoing drastic changes, and the position of the National Stud within it required reassessment.

The Committee on National Stud Policy in 1955 analysed the situation as follows:

195

"For many generations the quality and the prestige of the English Thoroughbred were built up by the great privately owned studs. These studs were the property of individuals who were mostly possessed of large landed estates and considerable incomes. Most of them were self-supporting; many were profitable undertakings.

"Their owners were, for the most part, in a financial position which enabled them to put into training most of the animals they bred; they could afford not to sell their yearlings.

"Moreover a well-run and well-stocked stud farm was a valuable inheritance, a circumstance which in those days went far to ensure continuity. None of these conditions obtains today."

This was a succinct summary of the situation. The Committee concluded that the continuity of development of the breeding industry on which the reputation of the British Thoroughbred depended could no longer be assured by the private studs, and that the National Stud could perform an invaluable service in this respect.

They recommended that, for the first time, a clear definition of the purpose of the National Stud should be given and that this should be:

"To give the maximum help in order to ensure that the breeding of the English Thoroughbred horse is maintained at the same level of excellence that has gained for it a world-wide reputation."

This purpose should be achieved, they added, by standing at the National Stud one or more stallions of the highest class and by maintaining there about 15 mares representing a number of the best bloodlines to ensure that there was one establishment in this country where continuity in the breeding of the highest quality of bloodstock could be assured.

In the long run the recommendation about stallions was adopted and that regarding mares was rejected.

At this point I shall leap ahead of the narrative to draw attention to the irony that Hopeful Venture, one of the last of the produce of the National Stud to be leased to the Queen for racing, struck a powerful blow for the prestige of British bloodstock by winning the Grand Prix de Saint-Cloud in 1968 and then returning to the National Stud as a stallion.

In the meantime, in 1963, the stud was transferred from

The Middleton Hunt at Howsham: left to right, Ken Ford (First Whip), Dennis Sturgeon (Huntsman), Kenneth Mansfield (Joint Master).

the Ministry of Agriculture to the Levy Board and a decision was made to change the policy from producing horses for the market to keeping top class stallions, which might otherwise be exported.

Accordingly all the mares and fillies were sold and the stud at Sandley, being inadequate for standing several stallions, was sold and a new stud was built at Newmarket, the hub of the breeding industry.

The layout of the new stud, which is regarded as a masterpiece, incorporated many novel ideas of the Director, Mr. Peter Burrell, and placed special emphasis on economy of manpower and hygiene.

On taking over, the Levy Board stipulated that, although profits were a secondary consideration, the National Stud should be self-supporting and should not be a drain on the resources of the Board.

The policy was that the stud should stand from four to six high class stallions, in each of whom it should have a substantial interest, and also acquire shares in top class stallions for the benefit of British breeders whenever these might be available.

In accordance with this policy three shares in Ragusa were

purchased when that winner of the St. Leger and the Irish Derby went to stud. Never Say Die, Tudor Melody, the home-bred Hopeful Venture and the American-bred Stupendous are the National Stud stallions for the 1970 season.

Whatever the doubts and imprecisions of National Stud policy may have been in the past, it is clear that there have been two constant factors: the first is that the concern has always been to promote and foster the production of Thoroughbreds of the highest class; the second is that the stud should be financially self-sufficient and not be a charge on public funds for the purpose of subsidizing breeders.

6 March 1970

OVERWHELMING VICTORY FOR BRITAIN IN IRELAND

BY LT.-COL. FRANK WELDON

At Punchestown the British team overcame every adversity to achieve an overwhelming victory in the World Horse Trials Championships, which concluded on Sept. 14, while, by taking the individual title, Mary Gordon-Watson on Cornishman V made history by becoming the first ever to win two successive top-class international three-day events.

Cornishman V with the only bonus score finished 64 points ahead of Richard Meade on The Poacher, who was second, closely followed by Jim Wofford from USA on Kilkenny.

With the help of Mark Phillips on Chicago III, officially placed 11th, the team won by over 400 points from France, the only other nation to get three of its team round.

The results on paper seem so decisive as to make it look like a bloodless victory, but apart from the riders themselves, who know it best of all, only those who anxiously watched the carnage on cross-country day can really appreciate what "a desperate close-run thing" it was.

To start with, Stewart Stevens's Benson pulled up slightly lame after the steeplechase and had to be withdrawn, which was a pity as the course would have suited this athletic little horse.

So almost from the start, for he was running second, we

H.R.H. the Duke of Edinburgh at the Dorchester Hotel with Col. Sir Michael Ansell in whose honour Walter Case (left), editor of *Horse and Hound,* gave a dinner on the occasion of Sir Michael's knighthood.

were back to the old days at the Olympic Games when the team was three and all three had to get round.

The effect may be more psychological than factual, but it is sobering none the less, for there is clearly no room for error.

The fact that it rained almost incessantly made life no easier for anyone, although except in a few places where the trampling of spectators' boots round the fences made the ground slippery, the old turf stood up to it wonderfully well.

That there were obviously more spectators than had been anticipated certainly did not help the riders' task. No impenetrable barriers, like chestnut palings had been erected to keep back the crowds, and mounted stewards were conspicuously absent.

The most critical factor of all was that falls were the most frequent source of penalty. There were refusals too, but only six out of the 36 that started on the cross-country escaped without at least one fall, and of these, the Argentine horse Jefazo had already fallen at the open ditch on the steeplechase.

Richard Meade took a proper stinker on The Poacher which shook him up badly, and Chicago III was almost as sore after his tumble.

If either of these had been a little more serious, neither Peter Scott-Dunn's veterinary skill nor the osteopath Richard Meade visited in Dublin could have redressed the balance. The British team would have been eliminated.

What the results do show unmistakeably is that when conditions are tough, as they are bound to be one way or another at any championship, how marked is the superiority of British and Irish horses.

Of the 21 that completed the course seven were bred in Ireland and six in England.

At Haras du Pin, Cornishman V on looks stood out head and shoulders above all his rivals, but at Punchestown there was little to choose between him, San Carlos and Kilkenny, with The Poacher not far behind.

They were all big, strong well bred horses and at the vetting they looked as if they could carry most of the foreign horses as well. What's more, they went just as well as they looked.

Being the host nation, Ireland was allowed to have twice as many individual competitors as any other country. The Irish selection would have needed to be pretty psychic to have included Brian Mullins's Killeen Bridge and Mrs. Wilson's Broken Promise in their team. If they had, the result would have been quite close but almost any other permutation would have assured second place.

However the World Championships were a triumph for West Country horses, for Cornishman V, The Poacher and Chicago III were all bred in Cornwall, while Benson was reared on his owner's farm in Devonshire, and together they beat all comers.

Still, a horse cannot go any better than he is ridden. In Cornishman V, Mary Gordon-Watson may have something that most people would give their eye-teeth for the chance to ride; but make no mistake, this is not just a question of a brilliant horse carrying a girl around and doing it all himself.

It was a real pleasure to watch the way Mary Gordon-Watson tackled the several obstacles I saw her over. She has obviously benefited from the point-to-point experience she

Ploughman and his Shires taking part in the Horse Ploughing Match at Windsor Great Park in 1972.

got this spring on her brother's almost equally famous Barty, and she does not ride a bad race either.

Richard Meade and Mark Phillips likewise got the very best out of The Poacher and Chicago III. It was no reflection on their ability that they both suffered unlucky falls.

The dressage was unremarkable except, perhaps, for the divergence of opinion between the judges, Count Rothkirch from Germany, Gen. Wing from USA and Capt. Hall from Ireland, who were of course acting independently.

In theory, judging dressage is an exact science, but in practice it would be unusual for three judges to come up each time with exactly the same marks. Being human they are bound to interpret values differently, and the less perfect the performance, the greater the discrepancy is likely to be.

But the differences ought at least to swing each time in the same direction.

As it happened the pattern changed dramatically. First one

judge was the most severe and then another, but eventually it probably evened itself out in the wash.

From the ringside there certainly seemed little to choose between Bernd Messmann for Germany on Windspiel, Richard Meade on The Poacher and the then World Champion Major Carlos Moratorio from Argentina on Chispero. They all performed exemplary tests to lead the field within a mark of one another.

It was more difficult to compare the extremely accurate transitions by Lorna Sutherland's Popadom with the better cadence of Chicago III ridden by Mark Phillips, but they were probably about correctly marked with almost the same score in fourth and fifth places.

At the very bottom of the scale came Mrs. Wilson's Broken Promise and Brian Mullins's Killeen Bridge with cricket scores. Yet they had the satisfaction of finishing sixth and seventh, whereas it may be no more than coincidence that all those who were eliminated did passable tests.

At least the relative influence of the first, second and third days' tests was just about what it ought to be at 3:12:2.

As befits a World Championship, the distances on the speed, endurance and cross-country test were longer than usual, and this was one of the most influential factors of the whole competition.

For the first time the steeplechase was 4,200 m. instead of the usual 3,600 m., with a maximum bonus of 44 points.

The soft birch fences were easy enough, but, knowing what was to come, most riders wisely did not go too fast. Only The Poacher, Richelieu and Cornishman V earned the maximum, and the last-named rather overdid it by finishing 20 sec. under the optimum time.

Even so, quite a number of horses arrived still sweating and blowing at the start of the cross-country.

The trouble with the cross-country at any championship like this—and it applies even more at the Olympic Games—is that a course that will provide a proper test for the best horses and riders is always far too severe for the less proficient.

It was inevitable, and no fault of anyone's, that a number of competitors would be eliminated, for the spread was pretty wide.

All the same, it must be said that it was a pity so many of

the obstacles were singularly uninviting to jump, quite the opposite of the European Championships here three years ago.

There was rather a high proportion of square sawn timber, which is liable to hurt horses, especially when two or more obstacles close together are constructed of it. I believe horses find it difficult to focus their eye on thin rails, and I know quite well I do.

Some of the island fences would have been more attractive if they had been wider. This not only makes them look smaller but helps to concentrate the horse's attention, instead of wondering whether it would not be better to bypass them.

Most of the obstacles could obviously have been more strongly constructed because any number were broken, causing long delays and throwing an impossible strain on the time-keeping organization.

It is not difficult for a fence judge to take the time that one horse is held up in front of a broken fence but when another or even a third arrives on his heels, chaos is inevitable.

The main criticism centred on two obstacles long before the first horse ever jumped. Both were towards the end, Nos.

20 and 29, both incorporated wide parallel rails in front of a steep drop, and both had an awkward approach.

The Ground Jury took the unusual step of acceding to a protest by the Argentine team in the case of No. 20. They had the farther of the two rails lowered 6ins, but as this then made them a true parallel it finished up more difficult than before.

A lot of nonsense is talked about drops. Straightforward drop fences never hurt any horse, although they can be worrying to the rider, but when jumping down, the sensible horse always lowers his undercarriage pretty smartly.

Especially when he could only see what he had to do at the very last minute, it was difficult for a horse to appreciate that he had to jump up to clear the spread. Many horses tried to touch down too soon, and that is why there were so many unpleasant falls at these two fences.

However, the way the rider tackled the problem, particularly at No. 20, had a lot to do with the result. He had to throttle right down to nothing and then get the horse going again almost from rest.

To their eternal credit, Mary Gordon-Watson, Richard Meade, Mark Phillips and Lorna Sutherland were all unscathed there while it was no great fault of Tom Durston-Smith that Henry The Navigator fell.

He and Cornishman V were the only British horses to get away with it at No. 29, where Mark Phillips on Chicago III first of all dived into it, earning 80 for a stop and a fall. When eventually the obstacle had been rebuilt, they jumped it perfectly, only to slip up trying to make the sharp right-angled turn amongst the spectators who had crowded into the penalty zone to get a better view. This added a very unlucky extra 60 points.

As they had previously been twice held up amongst a knot of three competitors waiting to jump broken fences, their recorded penalty of 14 points for time was certainly incorrect. They should have finished several places higher.

Mary Gordon-Watson's most uncomfortable moment occurred when Cornishman V miraculously disentangled his legs from a more straightforward drop fence, No. 27. This was where Ronnie MacMahon on San Carlos unluckily slipped up in the overlapping penalty zones between this and the next, having jumped all the fences perfectly.

Lorna Sutherland's Popadom found the big spreads a little too wide, but no one jumped more stylishly through the difficult combination of fences at the Sheep Wash, where several met their Waterloo.

Jim Wofford went a tremendous gallop on Kilkenny to score the only maximum bonus across country, in spite of a crashing fall at No. 20.

The Russian Yuri Solos on Rok defied all the rules by tackling this fence absolutely flat-out. There is no justice in this world, for he got away with it to complete a clear round.

The most remarkable effort of the whole day was the family performance by Lt.-Col. Bill Mullins on Kilcash and his son Brian on Killeen Bridge. Both horses are novices but although father Mullins, who is over 50, hacked steadily round, Brian went one of the fastest and both jumped clear.

All the 21 survivors trotted up gaily on the last morning looking, as usual, much better than before it all started.

Provided no one went the wrong way, the third day's jumping was a formality but the British riders hammered home their superiority by jumping three of the eight clear rounds over an admirable course.

In spite of a strapped up shoulder, Richard Meade got The Poacher going as well as he has ever jumped. Mark Phillips looked supremely confident on Chicago III, while Lorna Sutherland's Popadom who also moved up a few places, was the most obedient and certain of them all.

25 September 1970

A GREAT YEAR FOR BRITISH SHOW JUMPING

WHEN members of the British Show Jumping Association gathered for their annual general meeting at the Cafe Royal, London, W.1, on Wednesday, Dec. 2, the chairman, Col. Sir Michael Ansell, described the season as "perhaps one of our greatest, if not *the* greatest. Certainly I cannot remember a better one."

The association had to strike the happy mean of providing as much service as possible for members, in order that they got the most fun from their sport, and at the same time remember that it must remain financially sound.

Costs were continually rising, and therefore, after a very long period, certain subscriptions had had to be raised.

It was unfortunate that affiliation fees for shows also had to be raised, but these fees included insurance and consequently the association gained little if anything from them.

On the other hand, the B.S.J.A. provided a service to shows, which enabled them to provide better jumping for members.

Col. Ansell continued: "I have always regarded membership as the barometer of any association, and as you will have seen this has risen slowly; but a slow-rising barometer means a good scent."

In the case of affiliated shows, for some years there had

H.R.H. Prince Philip driving the team of part-bred Cleveland Bays to a Balmoral Dog Cart, entered by H.M. the Queen in the European Driving Championships in Windsor Great Park in 1973.

been a slow decrease, but this had been halted. Nevertheless, the B.S.J.A. should be prepared for the number of shows falling, due to rising costs causing a number of smaller one-day shows to amalgamate.

The total number of horses and ponies now registered as jumpers was 7,000, but a very great proportion of these were novices, and with the possible falling away of shows it would be the duty of the association to ensure that there was an opportunity for them to be given experience. From the 4,000 young Grade C horses we would find our future international winners.

What might be termed "Equestrian Sports Clubs" were being formed, and what the chairman hoped members would encourage was the type being formed at Windsor, where the club members would have the opportunity of competing on Smith's Lawn at monthly meetings.

This was to be tied up with the polo, and it was hoped that there would be facilities for combined training, dressage and driving in addition to show jumping. The object was to provide an opportunity for bringing on young horses and for inexperienced riders to have fun. Big prize-money was not visualized—probably it would mean only competing for sweepstakes.

Col. Ansell said he believed the association should do all in its power to encourage these equestrian clubs.

He was glad to learn that some agricultural show societies with permanent sites were forming such clubs, including the Great Yorkshire and the Bath and West, the latter interspersing the activities between agricultural fixtures and pop festivals.

Shows were at times finding it difficult to continue, but were it not for the hundreds of judges, stewards and other officials, guided and encouraged by B.S.J.A. area representatives, who gave up many long hours in a completely honorary capacity, the association would be in difficulty.

Show jumping was an expensive sport; the keep of a horse was very different from that of a bicycle or a set of golf clubs. Much nonsense was talked about prize-money, and although this was now large it in no way covered costs.

This year some £180,000 was offered in jumping competitions. Much of it was provided by generous sponsors, and there were others who gave help in "kind," for example Ford of Britain, who had given two horse boxes, a luggage van and a smart bus. They also provided cars during the international shows and presented three of the new Cortinas at the Horse of the Year Show.

Col. Ansell hoped that all these sponsors found satisfaction in the success of our international riders. There was nothing more gratifying than being a supporter of the winning side.

He remarked that he had always believed that the stimulus of our sport was provided by the success of British riders. This year had been perhaps one of our greatest, if not the greatest.

In the World Championships, out of the six medals we had won four—a gold, a silver and two bronze—and above all we had won the President's Cup for the third time in six years.

The outstanding part of this success had been the fact that the four Nations Cups and the 42 individual competitions had been won by no fewer than 47 horses and 20 riders.

David Broome, the World champion; Harvey Smith, the winner of two classics in Britain; and Marion Coakes and Anneli Drummond-Hay—all were supreme.

208

At Hickstead C.S.I.O., Lt.-Col. Harry Llewellyn (left), chairman of the selection committee, and Col. Sir Michael Ansell, president of the British Equestrian Federation.

The year had produced superb promise for the future, too, for among those who had come right to the fore were five riders under 23 years old. There was no nation in the world with such a reserve, and no one should forget that we had won the European Junior Championship against 18 nations.

These successes would not have been achieved without the help of generous owners who had loaned their horses.

The cost of sending teams abroad rose annually, and each year the funds became more scarce. This year the B.S.J.A. ceased to receive a donation from the Betting Levy Board because it was not considered eligible for a grant, but thanks to the hard work and enthusiasm of Mrs. Harries, who organized the Horse of the Year Ball, the place of Lord Wigg and the Levy Board had been taken by Mrs. Harries and her committee.

The chairman then spoke of the possibility of tax problems looming. He hoped the tax authorities would treat the association as generously as possible within the law, for it did two great jobs for the country.

Firstly, Britain's jumpers beat the foreigner and so raised national prestige. Secondly, the association organized what is termed a "risk sport."

Formerly, for those wanting excitement there were opportunities in almost permanent active military service; today a substitute had to be provided in something involving risk, such as mountaineering, canoeing or riding. Show jumping provided the opportunity to get excitement and take a risk.

An alternative was to march to some embassy and sling bricks. It would seem better for the tax authorities to be generous to the show jumper.

In conclusion, Col. Ansell recorded the B.S.J.A.'s congratulations to Mr. Robert Hanson on the recognition of all he had done for show jumping when he received a C.B.E. in the New Year's Honours List, and at the same time he congratulated the president-elect, the Earl of Westmorland, for his recognition in the Birthday Honours with the K.C.V.O., and David Broome for his well deserved O.B.E.

4 December 1970

ELEGANCE AND COLOUR AT COACHING CLUB CENTENARY

THE real sporting spirit that engendered the formation of the Coaching Club just 100 years ago is still, fortunately very much alive today. Twenty-one coaches turned out for that first meet at Marble Arch, Hyde Park, on June 27, 1871.

On Tuesday last week no fewer than 14 coaches, all with their full complement of members' guests, assembled in the forecourt of historic Hampton Court Palace for the 176th Official meet, and celebration of the Club's centenary.

In the evening sunshine, and amid a crowd of several hundred admiring spectators, none of the previous meets could have provided a more elegant and colourful scene.

Then, led by the President, Mr. Sanders Watney, with the Club's guest of honour H.R.H. Prince Philip beside him on the box seat, the teams departed for an hour's drive, by permission of H.M. the Queen, through Bushy Park, the Royal Paddocks and the Home Park, returning to the Palace for cocktails and dinner in King Henry VIII's Great Hall.

After dinner and the toast to the guests proposed by the President, to which Prince Philip replied, His Royal Highness, on behalf of the Club, presented a delightful coaching clock to Mr. Reg Brown for his service of 40 years as secretary of the Coaching Club, during which he had had the distinction of serving under nine of the Club's 12 Presidents.

2 July 1971

Lucinda Prior-Palmer, who won the Badminton Horse Trials in 1973 on Be Fair, a combination that helped win bronze medals in Kiev in that year. Two years later, on the same horse, Lucinda won the European individual championship.

A FRIENDLY PARTY FOR "MASTER AND MARY"

Horse and Hound *joins with Royal Windsor Horse Show to honour the Duke and Duchess of Beaufort.*

"I SHALL never forget this evening; it will be one of the evenings I shall always treasure very much indeed." This was how His Grace, the Duke of Beaufort summed up his feelings at the end of a unique and memorable gathering, graced by the presence of their Royal Highnesses Princess Anne and Princess Alice Countess of Athlone and many leading members of the sporting and equestrian world.

Warm tributes were paid to the Duke and Duchess of Beaufort, honouring their golden wedding anniversary this year, after a most convivial dinner in the Jockey Club Rooms, Royal Ascot, on Wednesday last week. The hosts were Mr. Geoffrey Cross, Chairman of the Royal Windsor Horse Show Club, and Mr. Walter Case, Editor of *Horse and Hound*.

The company was greatly entertained by an amusingly reminiscent speech by the Duke of Beaufort, giving a vivid flavour of the hunting field, and some of his many other activities.

But first there were eloquent tributes voiced by the Marquess of Exeter and by Mr. Dorian Williams, both of long experience as Masters of Foxhounds, and associated with so many other aspects of public life.

Lord Exeter said the dinner was a great occasion, a friendly party celebrating the 50th wedding anniversary of "Master and Mary."

He recalled that the Duke of Beaufort has been a Master of Foxhounds for nearly 50 years, and as a superb amateur huntsman had for so long produced remarkable sport for large mounted fields enjoying his hospitality in his wonderful country centred on Badminton.

"But it doesn't stop there," said Lord Exeter. "He has got the most famous pack of hounds in the country, bred to work and to show." He referred to the constant crop of Badminton successes at Peterborough and elsewhere.

The Duke had played an important role as head of the governing bodies of foxhunting and field sports in general.

Unlike some huntsmen, and others who were keen on following hounds, "Master" also had the distinction of being an excellent horseman, said Lord Exeter, pointing out that the Duke excelled not only as a rider but as a judge of horses.

There were many reasons why the Duke of Beaufort was so liked and admired by all who knew him, but one important cause was his constant fulfilment of the proposition that if you were born to great possessions then you should give something in return, "put something back into the pot"; that was exactly what he had always done.

Lord Exeter went on to refer to some of the Duke's many offices and duties, including being Lord Lieutenant of Gloucester since 1931, Chancellor of Bristol University, High Steward of Bristol, Gloucester and Tewkesbury, President of the Royal Show, and the Bath and West, and a host of other duties.

Yet, Lord Exeter pointed out, it was not possible to achieve such success in so many spheres of public life alone, and the Duke of Beaufort had been fortunate in marrying in 1923 a wife who had entered so wholeheartedly into his life's work and recreations.

Play for the *Horse and Hound* Cup on Smith's Lawn in Windsor Great Park.

There was warm applause as Lord Exeter thanked the couple for their immense contribution to so many aspects of English life, and wished them well for the future, looking forward to congratulating them again on their diamond wedding anniversary.

Mr. Dorian Williams, Joint Master of the Whaddon Chase spoke of the great debt which so many Masters owed the Duke of Beaufort for his ever ready loans or gifts of hounds. When establishing the Whaddon Chase pack, he had been privileged to receive the immortal hound Ringbolt from Badminton.

He stressed the tremendous value of the Duke of Beaufort's presidency for 30 years of the Royal Windsor Horse Show and the Royal International Horse Show. Describing the wider contributions of "Master" to the horse world, Mr. Williams referred especially to the establishment of the great Badminton Three-day Event.

Not only was this an immense help in encouraging and producing Britain's world beating three-day event teams, but every year the Duke and Duchess were hosts to many thousands of people who so much enjoyed the famous Trials in Badminton Park. It was a wonderful example of their hospitality, given at Badminton in so many different ways, especially to those who had had the pleasure of staying as personal guests.

The sense of humour and fun of the Duke and Duchess of Beaufort played a great part in the enjoyment of their hospitality.

213

Mr. Geoffrey Cross expressed the pleasure of himself, and his joint host Mr. Walter Case, that such a gathering had been possible, and expressed thanks to their Royal Highnesses, and to the Duke and Duchess of Beaufort for attending.

In his reply, the Duke of Beaufort touched on many matters with a wit and humour which delighted his listeners. He spoke with warmth of his long association with Royal Windsor Show.

Arthur Portman, the former owner and editor of *Horse and Hound*, had been a friend of his said the Duke. Mr. Portman and his family had been killed in a direct hit during an early wartime air raid on London. Many people were worried about the future of *Horse and Hound* which was an important part of their lives.

His Grace said that since the appointment of Mr. Walter Case as Editor 30 years ago, "I never stopped writing him a letter every year for doing some good deed for one of the societies in which I am interested.

"Walter, on behalf of every horseman in this country I would like to thank you for all you have done for the best sport of all, foxhunting, the next best, racing, and for the horse world in general." The Duke recalled with warmth and colour some fascinating memories of his childhood and later life. He revealed that when he first entered the hunting field as a boy to hunt his own pack of harriers, he did not immediately enjoy himself. "My father gave me ponies which jumped me off; they were much too strong," he explained.

Then he was given mounts which suited him better and he was fired with an enthusiasm and love for hunting which had never left. His Grace recalled the days before 1914 with particular pleasure.

He told his listeners: "I have had luck in every way—the luck to have lived at Badminton; very few people have lived in their own homes all their lives as I have. I adore the place; I know every tree."

His Grace made special reference to the pleasure which his office as Master of the Queen's Horse had always brought him. Finally, he paid special tribute to the Duchess of Beaufort, and her constant support for him.

M.C. 5 October 1973

EPILOGUE

BY MICHAEL CLAYTON

Editor of *Horse and Hound* since December 1973

Mrs Frank Haydon, who with her husband is a leading breeder and exhibitor of the hackney horse, seen driving Brook Acres Light Mist, a winning hackney at the South of England Show.

WHEN I was fortunate enough to succeed to the Editor's chair of *Horse and Hound* the paper was already an immense success. It had captured an audience in Edwardian England, and continued to gain new readers between the two World Wars, and its progress had matched the explosion of interest in the equestrian world in post-war England to an amazing degree.

This was due to the perception and editorial flair of my predecessor, Mr Walter Case. It would have been very easy to lose one's nerve, to concentrate simply on the obvious growth and interest in riding in suburban areas, and to neglect the basic roots of the horse world in Britain which lie in the world of the Turf and hunting field. Walter Case performed the feat of providing a weekly magazine which catered for new aspirations in growing areas of the horse world, whilst continuing to satisfy its basic activities. This proved to be wise for sound editorial reasons, as well as being in line with the fervent wishes of those who were still firmly embedded in hunting and the world of racing.

Both these areas also saw a considerable post-war increase

in interest, in the case of hunting a very difficult success story to predict in the years immediately after the second World War. Yet as we near the end of the 1970s, we see more people hunting than ever before. And despite its current difficulties, British bloodstock had enormous growth in the post-war period which played a great part in the modern success story of international racing.

My own first love has always been the hunting field, and my inclination was to ensure that the place of hunting in *Horse and Hound* should be made even stronger if possible. To this end I instituted a weekly hunting column—Foxford's Hunting Diary—which I could not resist writing myself. This involved visiting Hunts all over the United Kingdom and Ireland, a fairly arduous task when the demands of *Horse and Hound* in London and the start of a new editorship were themselves considerable.

Fortunately, the rewards have been immense in terms of fresh contacts with people all over the hunting world and in many other branches of equestrian sports.

The response of the hunting world was gratifying, and it was clear that we were answering a real need. Despite the enormous changes in the rural areas which the growth of modern society has wrought, there still remains an immense interest and participation in field sports. Probably this has been induced to a large extent by the deterioration in urban life. More people than ever before wish to escape to the countryside, and to enjoy the rural sports which produce a freedom from anxiety and care which our forefathers discovered long ago.

From a practical point of view, those who ride to hounds are consumers, not merely spectators. They need to buy horses, riding kit, and all the many ancillary pieces of equipment which go with the purchase and maintenance of working horses. In 1973, just before Walter Case retired, *Horse and Hound* achieved a 70,000 circulation for the first time in its history, and I am glad to report that the circulation has held up since then despite cover price increases and the worst economic crisis since the end of the second World War. We enter 1977 with a weekly circulation of about 73,000, our 1976 Christmas Number having achieved a circulation of about 78,000.

216

Mr Michael Clayton, Editor of *Horse and Hound*, presents a silver salver to Capt. C. Price who won the *Horse and Hound* Grand Military Gold Cup on Double Bridal.

The way in which the equestrian world has withstood the vicissitudes of the economic climate in the last three years has been truly amazing. Despite inflation and rising costs of all kinds, I am sure that owners of horses and ponies have in the main decided to hang on, to ensure that wherever they may have to make personal economies it will not be to the detriment of the equestrian interests which they hold so dear.

Entries in the horse shows throughout the Spring, Summer and Autumn season, have remained remarkably buoyant. Some 2,500 shows are now listed in our annual Shows Number each March. The Royal Windsor Horse Show, for example, found it necessary to extend from a four-day show to five days in 1977, owing to the enormous pressure of entries in the Show classes.

Show jumping continues to attract enormous national television audiences, and we see show jumping classes at novice and top levels wonderfully well supported throughout the United Kingdom.

Eventing has been in a boom condition for some years, and shows no signs yet of slowing down. The driving world has expanded enormously in recent years, and the comparatively new sport of Combined Driving in particular displays every sign of vitality. Undoubtedly one important factor in the popularity of equestrian sports in recent years has been the remarkable lead given in a wide variety of these activities by members of the Royal Family.

The Queen is the leading patron of horse racing in Britain, and an enthusiastic and knowledgeable owner of classic race-horses. Queen Elizabeth the Queen Mother is of course more identified with the National Hunt scene, and the Queen Mother's presence and participation as an owner is much appreciated in this great winter sport.

Mr Marcus Kimball, M.P., Chairman of the British Field Sports Society.

The Duke of Edinburgh has long been an enthusiastic and successful Polo player, and on retiring from this game he turned immediately to the new sport of Combined Driving. Prince Philip's role as a competitor in this sport has helped to accelerate its growth, but it obviously fills a genuine need, and there are more people taking a practical interest than for many years in all branches of driving. At an international level, Prince Philip has performed a signal service as President of the F.E.I. (International Equestrian Federation), at a time when the growth of the equestrian sports has posed some of the most difficult and testing questions for its administrators. The use of drugs in competition horses and the ambivalent role of the professional have yet to be resolved satisfactorily at an international level.

Catching the public eye most of all in the equestrian world, of course, has been Princess Anne, as a distinguished rider in the major three-day events in this country, and as the first Royal representative in the British Three-day Event Olympic team, taking part at Montreal on her brilliant horse, Goodwill, in 1976.

Princess Anne's skill and courage in this extremely demanding area of equestrianism has rightly earned her the respect and admiration of the public at large. This is a sport where it is all too easy to fall off in full view of television cameras, to suffer disappointments and set-backs with new horses, to have to face challenges of courage and skill in front of mass audiences—an ordeal which never faced those whose equestrian exploits were performed less publicly before the days of television. Princess Anne has met all these tests with remarkable ability and resource, and her marriage to Captain Mark Phillips—himself one of the greatest Event riders in the world—has produced a partnership in the equestrian world which is an inspiration to many a young rider.

The Prince of Wales, like his father principally associated with the Polo field, has recently shown that he also is a dedicated and enthusiastic rider to hounds. Prince Charles's keenness for the Chase in recent years has been most welcome in a sport which all too often suffers from misguided and prejudiced opposition. It was no doubt salutory for the national press to discover that reports of Prince Charles hunting with packs of foxhounds did not evoke a storm of protest from the general public. Only a tiny minority of shrill protesters made the usual "Pavlov's dog" responses when it was learned that the Prince of Wales enjoyed riding to hounds. Nowadays Prince Charles hunts regularly and thoroughly enjoys himself, and his obvious enjoyment of hunting and his friendly manner with all those he meets in the hunting field are much appreciated.

Whilst *Horse and Hound* has a duty to report competitive sports at the top level it has also endeavoured to continue its tradition of reflecting the entire horse world. We are not solely a sporting magazine: we are a trade paper and have a duty to supply the facts and figures associated with the Bloodstock Industry and with horse and pony breeding at all levels. The results of the Hunter Sales at Leicester are as much our concern as the reporting of a Classic flat-race at the height of the racing season.

As the sale and breeding of horses have boomed in the post-war years, so have the ancillary trades concerned with riding clothes, saddlery, vehicles, stable buildings and equipment. All these feature regularly in our advertising pages which in themselves make fascinating reading for anyone at all interested in the horse world.

I welcomed the advent in 1976 of a regular monthly business column which seeks to report some of the new trends in the equestrian trades, and the response has been excellent from the start. In February 1977 we were breaking new ground in this area by the introduction of a Trade Review issue. This is a supplement containing articles reflecting new trends in all aspects of the ancillary trades, ranging from saddlery to veterinary products, and at its inception it was particularly associated with the German Equestrian Fair, the Essen Equitana.

This seemed to me appropriate in view of the growing international trade in all branches associated with equestrianism, and I am sure that in the years ahead one of our big challenges will be to meet the new opportunities available in Europe, North America and elsewhere in the world, whilst at the same time continuing to serve, and to satisfy wholly, the booming equestrian market at home.

Another innovation which has proved popular, and which I think has immense scope for the future, has been a regular weekly column specifically devoted to Junior activities, especially show jumping in the summer months. It is vital that *Horse and Hound* keeps touch with new generation of riders as well as serving the adults. Here again, the response has been most satisfying and there is ample room for growth in reflecting the many activities which young riders nowadays have before them.

One of the more sobering aspects of 1976 was Britain's failure to achieve any sort of medal in show jumping, combined training or dressage in the Olympic Games at Bromont, in Canada. We have the resources and we certainly have the riding talent to do far better than this in future, but standards are rising all over the world, and it will not be easy for Britain to re-establish the sort of supremacy which she used to enjoy. The current rate of V.A.T. on horses in Britain is in itself most unhelpful to the Bloodstock Industry and the horse dealing trade at large, and it is to be hoped that when future governments make taxation decisions they will appreciate the enormous contribution which the horse and the pony make to our economy at a domestic level and in exports, but more important still, in enhancing the quality of life in these islands.

Horse and Hound has always succeeded in chronicling the sheer fun of the horse world, and it will continue to strive to do so. I have been very fortunate in the loyalty and dedication

Queen Elizabeth the Queen Mother presents The *Horse and Hound* Grand Military Gold Cup to Maj. Gen. Sir James d'Avigdor-Goldsmid, owner of the winning horse, Double Bridal, 11 March 1977.

of the permanent staff of *Horse and Hound* and of the contributors who grace our pages regularly.

The paper was indeed lucky when I.P.C. Magazines appointed Mr Francis King as Publisher, who immediately appreciated its unique character and the importance of safeguarding its authoritative position in the horseworld.

For 25 years the commercial success of the paper owed an enormous amount to the dedication and acumen of the Advertising Manager Mr Geoff Aubrey, who retired in 1976 to be succeeded by Mr Anthony Wakeham.

The authorship of the Loriner column must remain a secret, but this is a weekly journalistic feat without equal in contemporary journalism. The freshness and expertise inherent in this column, which touches on all aspects of the hunting and equestrian world, are well known and appreciated by our readers. Sometimes Loriner provokes intense irritation, but always this column is constructive and of never failing interest.

John Oaksey, under the famous pen-name of Audax, originally used by the founder and first Editor of *Horse and Hound*, sets a standard of weekly racing journalism unmatched anywhere else in the world. His deep knowledge of racing is reinforced by his former brilliant career as an amateur rider, and I am sure his particular appeal to *Horse and Hound* readers is enhanced by the knowledge that they are reading the words, not merely of a racing scribe, but a true horseman.

Peter Willett's immensely authoritative judgements in his weekly bloodstock column also command a devoted following, and he is one of the main props of our important racing section. Reading Peter Willett regularly is an education and an entertainment, and a weekly date not to be missed by anyone with a love of the Thoroughbred horse.

Jimmy Snow from the North, F. E. Fetherstonehaugh from Ireland, and our French racing correspondent Michel Chapelon add invaluable dimensions to our racing coverage, and our Bloodstock correspondent Astra (Alan Yuill Walker) completes a formidable team indeed.

Pamela Macgregor-Morris, one of our longest serving correspondents, fills an authoritative role each season, in writing of the major showing classes at shows all over Britain. She has never shirked controversy, as our Letters to the Editor column often bears witness!

Andy Wyndham-Brown, a great veteran of the Driving world, also writes of hunters and continues to fill an important place in the paper with his reports of Hackney and heavy horse classes.

Elizabeth Polling contributes popular articles on our Native pony breeds. The introduction of a regular weekly show jumping column has proved a great success, thanks to the flair and energy of its writer, Peter Churchill, who has carved himself a well defined niche in equestrian journalism.

Cynthia Muir and Genevieve Murphy certainly capture the younger generation's attention with their weekly Junior show jumping column, which increasingly roams further afield into so many other Junior areas.

Frank Weldon's reports on three-day eventing are in a class of their own, both as an authoritative guide to the sport, and as sheer entertainment. There are many other brilliant contributors, but Ivor Herbert's series of personality profiles have been particularly popular in recent years, and we are always pleased to receive contributions from such authorities in the pony world as Glenda Spooner and Jennifer Williams. Stella Walker's fascinating articles on sporting art are a tremendous asset.

Anthony Crossley, our dressage correspondent, braved a storm of protest after some of his strictures on the standard of British dressage, but he endeavours to be as constructive as possible, and it is greatly to be hoped that Britain will make fresh progress in this area of equestrian competition which is so dominated by West Germany.

Artist John King has made a wonderful contribution to the appearance of the paper with his superb line illustrations of hunting and other sporting subjects. It has been a particular pleasure to me that one of the contributors I read as a boy continues still to provide sparkling articles to *Horse and Hound* with a wit and humour which is entirely and unmistakably his own brand. I refer of course to Dalesman (Bay de Courcy-Parry), the great hunting man whose writing has helped to enliven the pages of *Horse and Hound* for well over 50 years.

Now in his eighties, he still fills the description of being "hale and hearty", and I have enjoyed recent energetic expeditions with him in Southern Ireland. In the 1976/7 winter he returned to his native Cumberland, and from Caldbeck sent a most eloquent and effective letter to *Horse and Hound* when vandals so senselessly desecrated the grave of John Peel in a repulsive anti-hunting protest in January 1977. Dalesman had written a brilliant article celebrating the 200th anniversary of John Peel's birth in one of our Christmas issues, and no one is better fitted to convey the true spirit of hunting and field sports in general in the countryside.

There are many others who cannot be named here, and the story of *Horse and Hound* is one of continuous development and innovation. The horse world shows every sign of a great deal of progress yet in the 20th century. Despite current national and international economic problems, there seems little doubt that man's use of leisure, the conservation of wild life and the fabric of country life are matters of growing importance to society.

Horse and Hound is vitally concerned with all these areas, and its future would seem to be an exciting prospect indeed.

Our centenary year is 1984—by coincidence the title of George Orwell's grimly prophetic book. It will be one more affirmation of the survival of Britain's tradition of personal freedom and tolerance if a substantial proportion of her people, readers of this magazine, can still say with confidence and pride in 1984:

"The best of my fun, I owe it to horse and hound . . .".

Acknowledgments

The Publishers wish to thank the following for the use of photographs: Associated Newspapers Limited p. 83, Associated Press Limited pp. 131, 137, Bespix pp. 156, 169, 221, Central Press Photos Limited pp. 9, 201, Findlay Davidson p. 209, Financial Public Relations Limited p. 188, Fox Photos Limited pp. 96, 121, George Godden p. 15, David Guiver pp. 181, 203, 207, 215, Peter Harding pp. 173, 175, Stanley Hurwitz p. 182, Imperial War Museum p. 81, Keystone Press Agency Limited p. 13, Mrs Edith LaFrancis p. 35, Leslie Lane pp. 84, 153, 211, Montague Lewis p. 143, London Fire Brigade p. 89, Frank Meads pp. 60, 147, 151, 195, 218, Museum of British Transport p. 27, Desmond O'Neill pp. 28, 38, 148, 164, 170, 178, 185, 187, 191, 199, 205, 213, 217, The Press Association p. 66, Photonews p. 119, Popperfoto p. 192, The Post Office p. 41, W. W. Rouch & Co. Limited pp. 25, 43, 53, 69, 71, 73, 79, 87, 103, 109, 111, 115, 117, 127, 135, Rex Russell p. 128, Selwyn Photos p. 167, Sport & General Press Agency Limited pp. 11, 141, Swaine p. 138, Times Newspapers Limited p. 99, 'Topical' Press Agency Limited p. 95, M. Tyrer pp. 106, 112, Universal Pictorial Press and Agency Limited p. 54, Michael Wheeler p. 197.